Neoliberal Thought and Thatcherism

T0313306

The premiership of Margaret Thatcher has been portrayed as uniquely ideo-logical in its pursuit of a more market-based economy. A body of literature has been built on how a sharp turn to the right by the Conservative Party during the 1980s – inspired by the likes of Milton Friedman and Friedrich Hayek – acted as one of the key stepping stones to the turbo-charged capit-alism and globalization of our modern world. But how 'neoliberal' was Thatcherism? The link between ideas and the Thatcher government has fre-quently been over-generalized and under-specified. Existing accounts tend to characterize neoliberalism as a homogeneous, and often ill-defined, group of thinkers that exerted a broad influence over the Thatcher government. In particular, this study explores how Margaret Thatcher approached special interest groups, a core neoliberal concern. The results demonstrate a willing-ness to utilize the state, often in contradictory ways, to pursue apparently more market orientated policies. This book – through a combination of archival research, interviews and examination of neoliberal thought itself – defines the dominant strains of neoliberalism more clearly and explores their relationship with Thatcherism.

Robert Ledger has a PhD in political science from Queen Mary University of London. He has worked for a think-tank in Brussels, lectured at various universities in London and currently lives and works in Frankfurt.

Routledge Studies in Modern British History

www.routledge.com/history/series/RSMBH

Neoliberal Thought and Thatcherism

'A Transition from Here to There?'

Robert Ledger

Routledge
Taylor & Francis Group

LONDON AND NEW YORK

First published 2018 by Routledge

2 Park Square, Milton Park, Abingdon, Oxon OX14 4RN
605 Third Avenue, New York, NY 10017

Routledge is an imprint of the Taylor & Francis Group, an informa business

First issued in paperback 2021

Publisher's Note

The publisher has gone to great lengths to ensure the quality of this reprint but
points out that some imperfections in the original copies may be apparent.

British Library Cataloguing in Publication Data
A catalogue record for this book is available from the British Library

Library of Congress Cataloging in Publication Data
A catalog record for this book has been requested

ISBN: 978-1-138-28026-7 (hbk)
ISBN: 978-0-367-34941-7 (pbk)

Typeset in Bembo
by Wearset Ltd, Boldon, Tyne and Wear

Contents

Acknowledgements

This book started off life as a PhD thesis which I completed at Queen Mary University in London in 2014. I would like to express my thanks to Professor Tim Bale, whose advice helped to focus my thinking when this project was looking rather unwieldy. The clarity of his feedback, as well as his encouragement, was invaluable. I would also like to thank him for taking on my PhD supervision when he came to Queen Mary in 2012, when I had already been working on this project for four years.

A special thanks also to Dr Peter Catterall, who enthusiastically supported me and helped shape my research and the initial chapters of this book. A number of people have commented on earlier versions of this project, in particular Lord Hennessy, who acted as a mentor in my early years at Queen Mary, as well as assisting me with primary sources and interviews. I would like to thank my examiners Professor Richard Vinen and Dr Ben Jackson for their constructive feedback. I would also like to thank Richard Morris, Martin Longstaff and Peter Finn for their comments on various parts of this project.

I am grateful to the librarians and archivists who have assisted me in my research, particularly Andrew Riley at the Churchill Centre in Cambridge. I would also like to thank Dr David Craik for encouraging me in taking my interest in history further. I am grateful for the support of my family, who have helped me both financially and emotionally during my almost unending years in education.

Finally, I would like to thank my wife Rebecca, for her unwavering support.

Introduction

The policies associated with Margaret Thatcher's government, as well as the contested and often opaque term Thatcherism, have been closely linked with liberal economic ideology. Many books on the subject simply state this as a fact while others question either the assumption itself or at the very least wonder to what extent it is true.[1] The events of 1979 to 1990 have proved fascinating and controversial with much literature being generated about the formation of the policies that came to define Thatcherism, the government's time in power and, of course, its legacy.

Why, then, revisit the subject? Mainly because the link between ideas and the Thatcher government has frequently been overgeneralized and under-specified. The connection between individual thinkers and schools of thought has been to present them as a bloc, in some ways encouraged by economic liberals, in particular 'the Mont Pelerin collective'.[2] The result has often been to blur significant distinctions. For instance Eric J. Evans, in *Thatcher and Thatcherism* (2004), describes Keith Joseph's conversion to monetarism in the 1970s.

> Above all, following the theories of the so-called Chicago school of anti-Keynesian economists, F.A. Hayek and Milton Friedman, Joseph called for strict control of the money supply.[3]

Last, the application of liberal ideas to specific policies has not been explored as extensively as the overall picture of Thatcherism, political events like the Cold War and Falklands conflict or individual personalities. The intricacy of policy formulation and ideology has informed later events and trends. These points, and an attempt to differentiate the components and impact of free market ideas, form the core of this book. The strands of modern liberal economic thought, sometimes dubbed neoliberalism, will be brought into sharper focus and compared with policies of the Thatcher government. The question of how and to what extent these ideas were implemented in particular policies is the second objective of this project.

'The Thatcher government was influenced by Hayek and Friedman'; or internationally 'Thatcher and Reagan brought about free-market revolutions in the 1980s' typifies the kind of statements found in many texts.[4] The

Thatcher government has also been seen as being at the vanguard of a neoliberal project or a shift towards 'market fundamentalism'.[5] In the very broadest sense all these assumptions are true but it is rather like saying the Soviet Union was influenced by Karl Marx or, to use a more obscure example, that New Labour was influenced by Anthony Giddens. The reality is far more complex. This study adds to the growing interest in how neoliberalism has developed since the early to mid-twentieth century and its different positions. Apart from the analysis of ideological models and actual policy, this project attempts to link ideas with policymakers and politicians, if indeed any existed.

The eleven and a half years that the Thatcher government was in power is clearly of great historical significance. Contentious, polarizing and controversial, these years did much to change the political landscape of Britain. Lower taxes, for the most part low inflation, mass consumerism, homeownership, 'choice' in public services, trades unions as an 'outsider' group and privately owned utilities are all now the norm. This list would have seemed unlikely to mainstream public and establishment opinion from the Second World War until the late 1970s but to reverse the new orthodoxy now would require huge upheaval. Two unique aspects of the government between 1979 and 1990 mark it out – first, the personality, character and leadership style of Margaret Thatcher; second, the ideas, dogma or philosophy that the government's policies embodied. The former has been the subject of reams of material, biographies, films – and clichés. With almost 40 years since Margaret Thatcher came to power, and with an increasing number of government and personal papers now being declassified, there is space for further investigation of the relationship between liberal economic ideas and Thatcherism.

Aims of this study

This book has a number of objectives. At its core are a number of key questions: (a) To what extent was the Thatcher government influenced by liberal economic thought? (b) Which strands of thought and which thinkers exerted most influence and in which areas? (c) How did economic liberals view the policies of the Thatcher government? One of the slightly unusual approaches this study uses is to ask (d) to what extent did the Thatcher government reduce the power of vested interests? The significance of the latter question will be made clear when we examine the initial objectives of neoliberals during the interwar period.

Methodology

This study uses a variety of qualitative research methods. Primary sources were obtained from archives, such as the Thatcher Papers at the Churchill Library in Cambridge, the prime minister and Cabinet files at the National Archives in Kew, the Margaret Thatcher Foundation and papers of other politicians and government advisors. Interviews were conducted with some key political figures as well as thinkers and civil servants. Memoirs were a key source as well as Hansard and witness seminars. Last, ideological texts were studied in an attempt to frame neoliberal policy models. These were then compared with the actual policies formulated by the Thatcher government, some of them traced through secondary literature. Ideas are transmitted in a number of different ways, from the 'primary' thinkers themselves, for instance Friedrich Hayek's *The Road to Serfdom*, through the work of think-tanks such as the Institute of Economic Affairs (IEA), as well as periodicals and newspapers. All of these have been used to frame ideological viewpoints. The mechanisms by which ideas eventually manifest themselves in policies are also explored in this book.

A caveat regarding the primary source material is in order, however: up until the time of writing, confidential papers from the Thatcher government were only available between 1979 and 1987 due to the 30 year rule. Therefore evidence of this type is skewed towards the first and second governments. Second, many other protagonists of the period were invited for interview but declined. Third, not all the key players have left papers or written memoirs. Keith Joseph was the most important example.

Parameters of this project

This is a study that examines the influence of liberal economic thought on British government policymakers. Therefore other strands of thinking will not be examined in detail. This is not a character study. There are already several books on the various facets of Margaret Thatcher's personality, and it is not the purpose of this book to explore these any further. The emphasis is on how closely neoliberal models were applied empirically, how the government was influenced, why they departed from 'pure' ideology and what economic liberals thought of the reforms once they were put in place. Other intrigues of the period, such as the Exchange Rate Mechanism (ERM), Poll Tax and the downfall of the Thatcher government, are not discussed. Last, the breadth of this study is large because of the amount of time the Thatcher government was in power. Therefore only select case studies have been chosen, albeit those which represent a cross section of the government's programme. Each of these has some association with liberal ideas. This unsurprisingly includes economic policy, deregulation and liberalization. It also takes into account social policies such as housing. Only one privatization, electricity, is explored in detail because it conveniently allows comparison with the others that preceded it such as British Gas and British Telecom (BT).

Literature review

There is a wealth of literature that looks at Margaret Thatcher, her government and the wider politics of the time. There are also several books that examine neoliberal ideology and some that integrate these ideas with the politics of Thatcherism. The best of these, perhaps, is now over 20 years old – *Thinking the Unthinkable* by Richard Cockett (1995), which identifies the work and development of the Mont Pelerin Society and IEA with their inspiration, the Fabian Society. The book puts a particular emphasis on the think-tanks that proliferated in the post-war period. Cockett does compare neoliberal ideas with the direction of the first Thatcher government, ending on a note of disappointment. Andrew Gamble has written on Thatcherism from the left, for instance in *Marxism Today* in the 1970s and later in works like *Thatcher's Law* (1989, with Celia Wells) and *Britain in Decline* (1994a). Gamble was the first to characterize the government's programme as 'the free economy and the strong state' and later wrote a book of the same title. Martin Holmes wrote an early and authoritative account of Thatcherism in his 1985 book *The First Thatcher Government, 1979–1983*. Holmes identified what he thought was the major success of that government, the defeat of inflation, but suggested that other policies were too cautious. A subsequent book, *Thatcherism: Scope and Limits* (1989) drew a similar conclusion, this time with privatization and trade union reform as second term successes.

Think-tanks have been considered a major part of the battle of ideas, particularly in the years before the Conservatives came to power in 1979. Andrew Denham covered four of these (the IEA, Centre for Policy Studies (CPS), Adam Smith Institute (ASI) and Social Affairs Unit (SAU)) as well as their impact on policies like health and education in *Think-Tanks of the New Right* (1996). Michael Kandiah and Anthony Seldon's collection *Ideas and Think Tanks in Contemporary Britain* (1996) again concentrates on think-tanks but across the political spectrum. An organization on which less writing exists, the Bow Group, is catalogued in James Barr's *Bow Group: A History* (2001). The book revealed how the group sought to have an effect similar to the Fabians but quickly became part of the Conservative Party apparatus, before aligning more explicitly with economic liberalism in the 1970s. Finally, Norman Barry has written several excellent works, including *The New Right* (1987) and *On Classical Liberalism and Libertarianism* (1986), which act as comprehensive introductions to both neoliberalism and liberal economic ideology in general.

Neoliberalism

A much-maligned term, neoliberalism has, by a growing body of literature, been set in both its historical context and its different strains. Several recent books explore the origin of neoliberalism and its variants. Rachel S. Turner's *Neoliberal Ideology. History, Concepts and Policies* (2008) defines the three broad schools of neoliberalism: German *Ordoliberalism*, the Austrian School associated with Friedrich Hayek and Ludwig von Mises and the Chicago School of Milton Friedman, George Stigler and Gary Becker.[6] This differentiation provides the emphasis for this study. Mark Skousen, in *Vienna & Chicago. Friends or Foes? A Tale of Two Schools of Free-Market Economics* (2005) explores the key differences between two of these approaches to neoliberalism. This includes how Austrians and Chicagoans have held separate views on monopoly, competition, monetary control and the business cycle.[7] Philip Mirowski and Dieter Plehwe's collection *The Road from Mont Pelerin. The Making of the Neoliberal Thought Collective* (2009) examines these separate positions in more detail, from the German thinkers of the 1930s to the more familiar Chicago School. There is a particular focus on how neoliberals view state power and democratic processes, as well as a focus on the deliberately collective nature of the Mont Pelerin Society.[8] *Masters of the Universe. Hayek, Friedman, and the Birth of Neoliberal Politics* (2012) by Daniel Stedman-Jones again dissects the early variant of neoliberalism in Europe and its transformation once it had crossed the Atlantic. Stedman-Jones identifies two Chicago Schools, an earlier one led by Henry Simons more in the 'social' Ordoliberal tradition, and the increasingly radical and economics-driven Friedmanite School from 1946.[9] There is some analysis of how ideology was applied in housing policy and enterprise zones in the UK and US in the 1980s. The book also examines Hayek's relationship with the Ordoliberals, and provides some emphasis on the welfare sentiments contained in *The Road to Serfdom*, which slowly eroded within the neoliberal collective as the Chicago School gained in influence.[10] This study will modify this last point by arguing that Austrian thinking has remained closest to classical liberalism by focusing on microeconomics and maintaining even more of a distaste for the state than its austere Chicagoan counterparts.

Boas and Gans-Morse's 2009 article 'Neoliberalism: From New Liberal Philosophy to Anti-Liberal Slogan' illustrates how the term has become increasingly opaque, and achieved negative connotations, over the past 20 years.[11] They also explore the development from German neoliberalism to the catch-all term of the 2000s. There are many examples that prove these points. For instance, Richard Falk, in *The Iraq War and Democratic Politics* (2005), wrote 'globally, neo-conservatism amounts to the adoption of a more militarist version of neoliberalism, which includes a renewed avowal of the security role of the United States as global hegemon'.[12] Similarly in Anthony Held and David McGrew's *Globalization/Anti-Globalization* (2002) neoliberalism is used interchangeably with neoconservatism.[13] The term is sometimes even used in the mainstream British press, for example when the *Guardian* journalist Polly Toynbee described Conservative politician Chris Grayling in 2012 as having found inspiration 'from all the neoliberal small statism wafting across the Atlantic, imbued with the Ayn Rand and Fox News meanness of spirit'.[14] In the same newspaper in July 2017 'Thatcherite Conservatism' was framed as venerating Ayn Rand, Friedrich Hayek and Milton Friedman.[15] A much more detailed critique of neoliberalism from the left is David Harvey's *A Brief History of Neoliberalism* (2005). Harvey expands the 'free economy–strong state' argument to include Deng Xiaoping's China.[16] The book also identifies the contradictions between neoliberal theory and practice, setting out that the reality has not necessarily been a smaller state.[17] Nevertheless, Harvey sees neoliberalism in conspiratorial tones, as the 'new imperialism'. Jamie Peck, in *Constructions of Neoliberal Reason* (2010) follows several of these arguments but highlights the manner in which neoliberalism has adapted or tried to 'fix markets' since its inception.[18] Peck sees neoliberalism as 'regulation-in-denial'.[19] Along with Harvey he views neoliberals as trying to 'retask' the state, and similarly to Boas and Gans-Morse, and Stedman-Jones, that Ordoliberalism was a moderate version of the movement compared to its successors.[20] William Davies's *The Limits of Neoliberalism: Authority, Sovereignty and the Logic of Competition* (2014) articulates how neoliberalism has led to a subordination of politics to economic principles, while Matthew Eagleton-Pierce evaluates the main ideological tenets in *Neoliberalism: The Key Concepts* (2016).

The Austrian School

There are several key ideological texts that stand as the cornerstone of neoliberal thought. The most noted one is Friedrich Hayek's *The Road to Serfdom* (1944), which set out his all-important critique of the state. Hayek's analysis, based on the totalitarian regimes of the period warned of the insidious and incremental nature of the state apparatus. This inspired the politics of the Chicago School, the work of Public Choice theory and the rhetoric of Ronald Reagan and Margaret Thatcher. This line of thinking would also inform Keith Joseph's analysis of post-war Britain as moving like a 'ratchet-effect' to the left. Hayek's tome *The Constitution of Liberty* (1960) was broader ranging and libertarian while the content of his speeches, pamphlets and letters suggest his thinking became more radical in his later years. *Choice in Currency. A Way to Stop Inflation* (1977) advocated the end of the state's monopoly on issuing currency while *Social Justice, Socialism and Democracy* (1979) sets out his well-known antipathy towards socialism as well as scepticism towards concepts of social justice and 'unlimited' democracy. Hayek's early work concentrated more on economics rather than his better-known philosophical work. During his intellectual battles with Keynes in the 1930s Hayek challenged views on attempting to control the business cycle in 'Prices and Production' (1931) and 'Monetary Theory and the Trade Cycle' (1933). This would clash with Friedman's later work on monetarism. One of the aims of this book is to make these kinds of distinctions clearer. Eminent historians of Thatcherism have even recently talked of 'monetary economists like Hayek and Friedman'.[21] Although he did have much to say on monetary issues it is somewhat misleading to use this label because of Hayek's distinctly laissez-faire instincts on the topic. As Andrew Gamble has written: 'It was often assumed at that time that Hayek and Friedman were the two leading monetarists. But Hayek never accepted monetarism.'[22] Gamble explored Hayek's core philosophical positions, and how they explain his embrace of liberalism and antipathy towards socialism in *Hayek. The Iron Cage of Liberty* (1996).

Friedrich Hayek is the most prominent Austrian thinker studied in this book. Ludwig von Mises was Hayek's mentor and produced work, such as

Socialism (1922) and *Bureaucracy* (1944), which took possibly the closest position to classical liberalism of the early neoliberals. Others in the Austrian tradition, such as Joseph Schumpeter and Murray Rothbard, are also briefly mentioned in later chapters. The Austrian School will be shown to take a qualitative and normative approach that focuses on ideal, but dynamic, market processes.

The Chicago School

If the Austrians had a more philosophical element to their work, then the other renowned neoliberal school took a more empirical and quantitative – or positivist – approach. The development of the Chicago School is discussed at length in Van Horn *et al.*'s 2011 collection *Building Chicago Economics: New Perspectives on the History of America's Most Powerful Economics Program*. Early Chicagoans like Henry Simons and Frank Knight are shown – as well as by others such as Stedman-Jones – to have taken more moderate or 'social' positions on many issues. After 1946 a new wave of thinkers coalesced at the school, such as George Stigler, Gary Becker, Aaron Director and most notably Milton Friedman. The latter's *A Monetary History of the United States, 1867–1960*, written with Anna Schwartz in 1963, was to set out one of the key arguments to challenge Keynesianism, the quantity of money theory or monetarism, as a guide to macroeconomic policy. This analysis was based on how the Federal Reserve acted during the Great Depression, the book concluding that a stable money supply would have attenuated the worst impact of the slump. Friedman's most important book was probably *Capitalism and Freedom* (1962) and is the other widely known text of neoliberalism along with *The Road to Serfdom*. Friedman's central tenets of economic liberalism and libertarianism were crucial in the conservative movements in Britain and the US, although there were few who subscribed, as Friedman did, to both. Friedman was very active in the political debates of the 1970s, effectively bringing into the public sphere his ideas, such as economic 'shock therapy', for example in 'The Road to Economic Freedom: The Steps from Here to There' (1977), monetarism in 'Money and Economic Development' (1972) and challenging conventional wisdom such as the Phillips Curve in *Price Theory* (1976). Friedman wrote (with Rose Friedman) a popular and more general summary of his thought in *Free to Choose* (1980), which also included his long-running ideas on education vouchers.

George Stigler's work on competition and monopoly became a vital part of the modern Chicago School, exploring regulatory 'capture' and a reduced role for 'anti-trust' legislation. This is outlined in the *Theory of Price* (1966) and its genesis explored in Hammond and Hammond's *Making Chicago Price Theory. Friedman-Stigler Correspondence 1945–57*. This work was to have some overlap with Public Choice theory. Gary Becker was another Nobel laureate from the Chicago School who expanded an economic analysis to include social issues and human behaviour in general.[23] Becker's work, however, is generally not explored in this book.

Public Choice theory

Public Choice theory extended Hayek's critique of the state and was called by the thinkers themselves the 'economics of politics'. The work of James Buchanan, once of the Chicago School, is central: for instance *The Calculus of Consent: Logical Foundations of a Constitutional Democracy* (1962), co-written with Gordon Tullock, as well as *The Demand and Supply of Public Goods* (1968) and *Toward a Theory of Rent-Seeking Society* (1980). Tullock is the other key figure and his work includes *The Politics of Bureaucracy* (1965) and *The Vote Motive* (1976). Buchanan and Tullock developed Public Choice at the University of Virginia in the 1960s around a number of key insights. For them, those in government acted in just as much of a self-interested manner as those in the private sector, claiming that bureaucracy tends to unchecked expansion, and last that individuals in government are prone to 'rent-seeking behaviour', essentially greater reward for the same tasks. The impact of Public Choice theory will be touched upon in this book. Its influence was probably most clearly seen in Ronald Reagan's 1981 inaugural address: 'government is not the *solution* to our problem; government *is* the problem'.[24]

Ordoliberalism

The neoliberal thinking that originated from interwar Germany, called Ordo-liberalism for clarity, has until recently been often omitted from many books on both economic liberalism and Thatcherism. Ordoliberalism centres on a number of thinkers in 1930s and 1940s Germany: Wilhelm Röpke, Alfred Müller-Armack, Walter Eucken, Franz Böhm and Alexander Rüstow. The majority of their work is hardly known in the English-speaking world and therefore translations are few and far between. Exceptions include Röpke's *A Humane Economy: The Social Framework of the Free Market* (1958) and Andrew Nicholls's authoritative history, *Freedom with Responsibility. The Social Market Economy in Germany, 1918–1963* (1994). Samuel Gregg has also written a biography, *Wilhelm Röpke's Political Economy* (2010). It is left to more recent studies on neoliberalism, such as those by Stedman-Jones, Boas and Gans-Morse, Turner, and Mirowski and Plehwe, to determine the main principles of Ordoliberalism. These include an emphasis on price, as well as wanting to prevent monopoly formation, and therefore maintaining competition. Ordo-liberal thinking most notably manifested itself in the post-war West German economic model: the 'social market economy', borrowing Müller-Armack's term. *The Theory of Capitalism in the German Economic Tradition* (2000), edited by Peter Koslowski, provides more detail on Ordoliberal thinkers while articles such as 'Adam Smith and Ordoliberalism: On the political form of market liberty' (2012) by Werner Bonefeld and 'At the Origins of Neo-liberalism: The Free Economy and the Strong State' (2010) by Ben Jackson give further context. The movement's journal, the 'Ordo yearbook', also has short translations that provide some insight into how Ordoliberal thinking has developed. The idea 'free economy–strong state' was first framed by Rüstow in 1932. It was this that Andrew Gamble assigned to the Thatcher govern-ment, making the link between the early Ordoliberals and Thatcherism.[25]

Political histories of Thatcherism and biographies

There are several political histories of the Thatcher government, often focus-ing on the personality and battles of the prime minister herself. A detailed single volume is John Campbell's, *Margaret Thatcher: Iron Lady* (2003), which covers every minutia of her premiership. This has been more recently joined by two authoritative official biographies, *Margaret Thatcher. The Authorized Biography. Volume One: Not for Turning* (2013) and *Margaret Thatcher Volume Two: Everything She Wants* (2015) by Charles Moore, as well as the more thematic *Not for Turning. The Life of Margaret Thatcher* (2013) by Robin Harris. Both reveal insights into the former prime minister's politics as well the role played by ideas. In keeping with other biographies, however, there is a tend-ency to group neoliberal thinking into a homogeneous set of ideas. For instance Moore talks about Hayek's economic 'shock treatment' while, as we have already seen, Harris puts Hayek and Friedman in the same bracket as 'monetary economists'.[26] Although neither is incorrect, this creates ambiguity. This study attempts to provide more clarity on how different neoliberals influenced the Thatcher government.

Richard Vinen's *Thatcher's Britain: The Politics and Social Upheaval of the 1980s* (2009) puts Thatcherism in a historical context of reaction against the policies of the 1960s and 1970s. Vinen sees Thatcher's politics as a desire to return to the conservative Britain of the 1950s as well as framing Thatcherism to a certain extent as a defender of a 'post-war consensus' of the 1940s and 1950s variety, rather than the progressive version of the 1960s.[27] The book also rejects a post-1990 orthodoxy of the 'Thatcher and sons' type due to the specific considerations that existed during the period.[28] Vinen identifies Thatcherism as a combination of ideology and Tory 'Statecraft'.[29] The latter was set out by Jim Bulpitt in 'The Discipline of the New Democracy: Mrs Thatcher's Domestic Statecraft' (1985), as the use of neoliberalism as a tool to pursue the more traditional Conservative objective of achieving and holding onto power. A historical approach is also taken by Farrall and Hay in the 2014 collection *The Legacy of Thatcherism. Assessing and Exploring Thatcherite Social and Economic Policies.*

The Anatomy of Thatcherism (1992) by Shirley Robin Letwin explored the various aspects of the government's ideology, including the values and ethics implicit in the politics of Margaret Thatcher herself. Letwin also sets out a hierarchy of ideas, that nationalism (or patriotism) and anti-socialism were more important than liberal economics.[30] John Ranelagh described the unusual collection of personalities that he believed most influenced the prime minister, in *Thatcher's People* (1991). These included British neoliberals like John Hoskyns, Norman Strauss and Alan Walters, as well as Hayek and Friedman and advisors like Bernard Ingham and Charles Powell. *Making Thatcher's Britain* (2012), edited by Ben Jackson and Robert Saunders, examines some of the considered wisdom of the period and puts these events into a broader historical context. Jackson's chapter, 'The think-tank archipelago: Thatcherism and neoliberalism' sheds light on the IEA 'outsider' reputation as well as the think-tanks' subtle, but significant, shift in focus from anti-competitive business practices in the 1950s and 1960s to the problems of government in the 1970s and 1980s.[31] Saunders's chapter, 'Thatcherism and the seventies', frames Thatcherism as initially diagnostic rather than prescriptive and rooted in its particular narrative of the events of the 1970s.[32] Saunders identifies this as one reason the Conservatives under Thatcher, and later John Major, lost momentum as the targets and memories of the 1970s faded.[33] *The Conservatives since 1945* (2012) by Tim Bale sets the policies of the Thatcher government into the broader history of the party, such as council house sales, and questions the impact of think-tanks in particular on the party's strategy.[34] A more market orientated set of policies is also traced back to the start of Edward Heath's leadership in 1965.[35] Adrian Williamson's *Conservative Economic Policymaking and the Birth of Thatcherism, 1964–1979* breaks the ideological underpinnings of the Conservative Party in the 1960s and 1970s into several strands, emphasizing the influence of Enoch Powell as well as pro-European, pro-competition, Tories.

Memoirs

The majority of the influential politicians of the time have written memoirs. The two that most significantly mention ideas are those of Geoffrey Howe and Nigel Lawson. Margaret Thatcher's three books, *The Downing Street Years*, *The Path to Power* and *Statecraft* are also of use. Some accounts by Cabinet members of the Thatcher government, like Willie Whitelaw, Lord Carrington and Michael Heseltine, rarely mention ideas, while James Prior and Ian Gilmour both criticize the policies of Thatcherism. Cecil Parkinson and Kenneth Baker provide useful insights for their involvement in, respectively, privatization and deregulation, and education reform. Likewise Norman Tebbit's *Upwardly Mobile* includes detail on his time implementing trade union reform and financial deregulation. Ken Clarke's *Kind of Blue* provides insights into the government's approach towards vested interests. The notable omission is Keith Joseph, who did not write a memoir. It is left to other archives, his speeches and the biography written by Andrew Denham and Mark Garnett, *Keith Joseph* (2001), to construct his thought. Other influential figures that have written books on the period, although not elected politicians, include *Just in Time. Inside the Thatcher Revolution* (2000) by John

Hoskyns and *Paradoxes of Power, Reflections on the Thatcher Interlude* (2007) by Alfred Sherman.

Chapter summary

Chapter 1 examines the development of neoliberalism, from the early twentieth century to the foundation of the Mont Pelerin Society until the election of the Conservatives in 1979. It looks at key thinkers, such as Friedrich Hayek, Milton Friedman and Ludwig von Mises; as well as the main neoliberal schools of thought. These are outlined as the Austrian, Chicagoan, Ordoliberal and Public Choice schools. The important think-tanks of the period, the IEA, CPS and Bow Group, are also examined. Chapter 2 looks at the influence of economic liberal ideas in the post-war period. The ideological debates of the 1970s are explored, with specific reference to monetarism and the trade union movement. These two chapters will show how neoliberalism developed as a set of ideas and how several strains of thought became seen as a homogeneous collective.

Chapter 3 explores the 'monetarist' phase of economic policy. This is shown to be particularly ideological and perhaps the 'purest' application of neoliberal policy recommendations by the Thatcher government. Nevertheless, the different approaches of neoliberals towards monetary control will be highlighted. Chapter 4 looks at two lesser-known liberalization policies of early Thatcherism: exchange control removal and enterprise zones. Although the former proved to be a straightforward act of liberal faith it nevertheless almost forced the government into a U-turn. Enterprise zones provide a fascinating insight into the forces implicit in the Thatcher government's policy-making: deregulation with a heavy dose of state action.

How the Thatcher government sought to reduce the power of vested interests is examined in greater detail in Chapters 5, 6, 7 and 8. These chapters focus on trade union reform, privatization (with particular reference to electricity), broadcasting policy and financial deregulation. Although there was no coordinated attempt to tame special interest groups this objective was implicitly a long-term one for both economic liberals and some Conservative politicians. These chapters will set out why vested interests are disliked by the various neoliberal schools and how they were confronted by the Thatcher government. Trade union reform will be shown to be the most effective reform in reducing the power of a vested interest while privatization, broadcasting and deregulation fell short of this aim or attenuated one group only to allow another to emerge.

Social reforms domestically presented more of a challenge in implementing policies rooted in economic liberalism. Housing is looked at in Chapter 9. The manner in which the Thatcher government approached this area owed something to neoliberalism, again with consistent state intervention.

The conclusion brings these various case studies together. The proximity of the Thatcher government to neoliberal ideas was graduated. In each example broad neoliberal thinking existed, with varying degrees of clarity. Friedmanite neoliberalism will be shown to be closest to Thatcherism because of its attempt to use the state to move in steps towards a more liberal economy and society. Ordoliberalism as well as the Austrian School had a much more limited impact. The Thatcher government will be shown to have attempted to 're-task' the state, often for political reasons, that fell short of liberal ideals.

The Thatcher government was influenced by neoliberalism, although mainly through conduits. Its policies were also influenced by traditional Conservative thinking as well as political pragmatism. Ideas of 'statecraft' loom large in Thatcherism as well as the 'supporting wind' of neoliberal ideas during the period. This book broadly identifies three main strains of neo-liberalism – the Austrian School, Chicago School and Ordoliberal School. There is some evidence to suggest Hayek had a philosophical impact on some British politicians, mainly through advisors and commentators. There was also some very limited lineage between Freiburg and the 'free economy–strong state' ideas attributed to the Thatcher government. The main influence however, directly or not, was from the Chicago School because it engaged with the world as it was and used the machinery of the state: for example, monetary control, which fed into government policy through those influ-enced by Milton Friedman, such as Alan Walters, Peter Jay, Tim Congdon and Terry Burns. The Chicago School was less focused on social outcomes than the Ordoliberals but less idealistic than the Austrians. These differences were made more opaque when the ascendency of the Chicago School under Friedman as well as Hayek wanted to unify and maintain the collective integ-rity of his Mont Pelerin Society. The military dictatorship of Augusto Pino-chet in Chile was then important in linking neoliberalism with authoritarianism. This sullied the reputation of the neoliberal project, thinkers associated with Chile like Friedman, and by association the governments of Margaret Thatcher and Ronald Reagan.[36] For all these reasons neoliberalism has come to denote a number of positions that have rarely been clearly defined. Several writers have juxtaposed the moderate and progressive con-notations of early Ordoliberalism with the harsh interpretations and vilifica-tions of neoliberalism that proliferated after Pinochet.

Neoliberal ideas, unsurprisingly, were most closely linked with economic policy and deregulation. Their impact on social policy was more diluted and more fiercely resisted. Many of these policies did not satisfy neoliberals. Some advocated Ordoliberal ideas, such as competition promotion in privatization, but most thought that markets were not 'free' enough and overly comprom-ised by politics and special interests. Thatcherism was initially focused on macroeconomic stability while supply-side reforms increased during the course of the government. The shift of the former under Nigel Lawson dis-pleased monetarists, while the compromised fashion of the latter led to much criticism from Hayekians at the IEA. Finally, the case studies examined in this book appear to confirm that the Thatcher government 're-tasked' the state, which has been identified as an inherent feature of neoliberalism. That is to say that reforms were broadly liberal, but with political objectives, and led to outcomes that as well as being criticized from the left, did not satisfy the separate strains of neoliberal thought.

Notes

1 One example of the explicit link between Hayek and Thatcherism is found in Anthony Seldon and Daniel Collings, *Britain under Thatcher* (London: Longman, 2000), 68.
2 Margaret Thatcher Foundation (hereafter MTF), MTF 117203, 'Friedrich Hayek letter to Arthur Seldon', 13 May 1985.
3 Eric J. Evans, *Thatcher and Thatcherism* (Abingdon: Routledge, 2004), 7.
4 Joseph Stiglitz, *Freefall. Free Markets and the Sinking of the Global Economy* (London: Penguin, 2010), 17–18.
5 Taylor Boas and Jordan Gans-Morse, 'Neoliberalism: From New Liberal Philosophy to Anti-Liberal Slogan', *Studies in Comparative International Development* 44:2 (June 2009), 138.
6 Rachel S. Turner, *Neoliberal Ideology. History, Concepts and Policies* (Edinburgh: Edinburgh University Press, 2008), 4, 219.
7 Mark Skousen, *Vienna & Chicago. Friends or Foes? A Tale of Two Schools of Free-Market Economics* (Washington, DC: Capital Press, 2005), 6–7.
8 Hayek admitted he would prefer to temporarily lose democracy rather than freedom. Philip Mirowski, 'Postface: Defining Neoliberalism', in *The Road from Mont Pelerin. The Making of the Neoliberal Thought Collective*, ed. P. Mirowski and D. Plehwe (Harvard: Harvard University Press, 2009), 446; Dieter Plehwe, 'Introduction', in *The Road from Mont Pelerin. The Making of the Neoliberal Thought Collective*, ed. P. Mirowski and D. Plehwe (Harvard: Harvard University Press, 2009), 8.
9 Daniel Stedman-Jones, *Masters of the Universe. Hayek, Friedman, and the Birth of Neoliberal Politics* (Oxford: Princeton University Press, 2012), 122.
10 Stedman-Jones, *Masters*, 335.
11 Boas and Gans-Morse, 'Neoliberalism', 137.
12 Richard Falk, 'The global setting', in *The Iraq War and Democratic Politics*, ed. Alex Danchev and John MacMillan (London: Routledge, 2005), 27.
13 David Held and Anthony McGrew, *Globalization/Anti-Globalization* (Cambridge: Polity Press, 2003), 100.
14 Polly Toynbee, 'To condemn those who pay so little is not job snobbery', *Guardian*, 20 April 2012, 35.
15 Matthew D'Ancona, 'What do the Tories do now? One question, three solutions', *Guardian*, 3 July 2017, accessed 3 July 2017. www.theguardian.com/commentisfree/2017/jul/03/tories-dup-deal-thatcherites-philip-hammond-ruth-davidson.
16 David Harvey, *A Brief History of Neoliberalism* (Oxford: Oxford University Press, 2005), 1.
17 Harvey, *Brief*, 21.
18 Jamie Peck, *Constructions of Neoliberal Reason* (Oxford: Oxford University Press, 2010), xiii, 8.
19 Peck, *Constructions*, xiii.
20 Peck, *Constructions*, 4, 17.
21 Robin Harris, *Not For Turning. The Life of Margaret Thatcher* (London: Bantam Press, 2013), 179.

22 Andrew Gamble, *Hayek. The Iron Cage of Liberty* (Cambridge: Polity Press, 1996), 168.
23 Gary Becker, *The Economic Approach to Human Behavior* (London: University of Chicago Press, 1990 [1976], 5–14.
24 Ronald Reagan, Inaugural Address, 20 January 1981, accessed 13 October 2010. www.reaganfoundation.org/reagan/speeches/.
25 Werner Bonefeld, 'Adam Smith and Ordoliberalism: On the Political Form of Market Liberty', *Review of International Studies* 39:2 (July 2012), 235.
26 Charles Moore, *Margaret Thatcher. The Authorized Biography. Volume One: Not for Turning* (London: Allen Lane, 2013), 624; Harris, *Not For Turning*. 179.
27 Richard Vinen, *Thatcher's Britain. The Politics and Social Upheaval of the 1980s* (London: Simon and Schuster, 2009), 7, 31, 292, 306.
28 Vinen, *Thatcher's Britain*, 8, 306.
29 Vinen, *Thatcher's Britain*, 274.
30 Shirley Robin Letwin, *The Anatomy of Thatcherism* (London: HarperCollins, 1992), 325.
31 Ben Jackson, 'The Think-Tank Archipelago: Thatcherism and Neoliberalism', in *Making Thatcher's Britain*, ed. Ben Jackson and Robert Saunders (Cambridge: Cambridge University Press, 2012), 49, 54–55.
32 Robert Saunders, 'Thatcherism and the Seventies', in *Making Thatcher's Britain*, ed. Ben Jackson and Robert Saunders (Cambridge: Cambridge University Press, 2012), 25–26.
33 Saunders, 'Thatcherism', 40–42.
34 Tim Bale, *The Conservatives since 1945* (Oxford: Oxford University Press, 2012), 137, 200.
35 Bale, *Conservatives*, 130–135.
36 Boas and Gans-Morse, 'Neoliberalism', 137.

1   Neoliberal thought

There are a number of principles to keep in mind when attempting to define a term such as neoliberalism. The concept contains a number of threads, which in and of themselves can be fairly diverse. In addition, the historical moment in which these developed is very much key to understanding their significance. Nevertheless, it is the historian's job to bring these divergent ideas together, in a way that aids the reader's understanding. As mentioned in the introduction, the term neoliberalism has increasingly been used as a catch-all label, often as a pejorative. For our purposes it has been very easily attached to the policies of the Thatcher government. This chapter will break down the term into a series of 'schools', building on the recent literature articulating a 'family' of 'neoliberalisms'.[1] These include some that may be familiar, such as Milton Friedman's Chicago School, and others that are lesser known, such as the Ordoliberal – or Freiburg – School. How these influenced British politicians is the subject of Chapter 2.

Defending classical economics: the Austrian School

Joseph Schumpeter feared that embedded within the success of capitalism lay the forces that could eventually destroy it. Many intellectuals in the first half of the twentieth century were typically antagonistic to the market, barely tolerant of capitalism and critical of the attitudes, extremes and insecurity it appeared to precipitate. This ranged from Marxists, the critique of 'finance capital' by Austrian Rudolf Hilferding and the later, more accommodating, followers of Keynes. All wanted to overturn or at least attenuate the effects of laissez-faire. It was unsurprising that in the aftermath of the catastrophic financial problems of the 1930s and subsequent war to which these conditions had seemingly led, thinkers advocated the taming and regulation of unfettered capitalism. The idea of market failure also encouraged growing state intervention in the economy, that is to say the belief that the market system can cause externalities (adverse and unintended effects) that damage wider society and require government intervention. Yet if Schumpeter's point seemed to be relevant, he himself belonged to a group of intellectuals that would have profound effects in the latter half of the twentieth century. Schumpeter was a classical liberal and belonged to the 'Austrian School' of economists.

With socialist thought in the ascendency in the late nineteenth century, Carl Menger founded the Austrian School, studying classical economic thought, in 1870s Vienna. Menger, whose work included *The General Theory of the Good*, wanted to create a new theoretical framework that would more clearly define Adam Smith's system of 'universal opulence'.[2] Menger's work concentrated on individual behaviour as well as price.[3] Eugen von Böhm-Bawerk was also a noted Austrian thinker at the turn of the century. It was the third generation though, led by Ludwig von Mises and inspired by Menger and Böhm-Bawerk, which began to make significant contributions to what we might now consider neoliberalism. Mises included social science and political philosophy, as well as economics in his work and became mentor to the young Friedrich Hayek in the 1920s.[4] Mises and Hayek developed thinking on the business cycle during this period. They identified government monetary policy as the primary cause for cycles of boom and bust, believing that interest rates and the supply of money were being manipulated away from their 'natural levels'.[5] In an era, particularly following the stock market crash of 1929, when most economists advocated more government intervention, Austrians like Mises and Hayek had a drastically different view. For them, state interference was at the core of the problems experienced in Western countries.

Hayek taught at the London School of Economics in London in the 1930s and entered into a series of public and private debates with John Maynard Keynes over the course of the decade. The full effect of Hayek and the Austrians was not to be felt until much later but his 1944 book, *The Road to Serfdom*, became a liberal classic. Hayek, at the height of British reverence towards Keynes and the Beveridge Report, made an unfashionable argument: the state was not necessarily a benevolent force. Hayek based his analysis on both the Nazi and Soviet regimes, supposedly at either ends of the ideological spectrum. Fascists and communists had assembled huge state bureaucracies, and were oppressive, autocratic and violent towards their own citizens.[6] As well as the potential malignancy of an expanding state, Hayek saw socialist utopias as ultimately leading to collective misery. According to Andrew Gamble, Hayek thought socialism similar to the 'archaic religions' of traditional society but that liberalism was the natural order of things, based on experience, in modern societies.[7] *The Road to Serfdom* advocated renewed trust in the power of the market and that individual liberty could only be obtained under capitalism. There has been some debate over the 'social' aspects found at this stage of Hayek's thinking. For instance, he stated that 'there can be no doubt that some minimum of food, shelter, and clothing, sufficient to preserve health and the capacity to work, can be assured to everybody'.[8] This will be explored in more detail in Chapter 9 (Social policy). Andrew Gamble identified the other key claims of Hayek's critique of socialism – it destroyed the basis of morals, personal freedom and responsibility;

impeded the production of wealth and may cause impoverishment; and sooner or later leads to totalitarian government.[9] *The Road to Serfdom* most notably outlined the latter and proved an unlikely success. This led to a speaking tour of the United States for its author and subsequently a teaching position at the University of Chicago, although not in the economics department, in 1950. It also attracted the attention of Conservative Party Chairman Ralph Assheton as well as Winston Churchill during the general election campaign of 1945.[10]

Hayek later claimed that of his generation there were only a handful of economists, apart from himself, that believed in classical liberalism: 'there were just perhaps (Wilhelm) Röpke, Bill Hutt, and two or three others.'[11] They were part of a broader movement that began as an obscure club for intellectual supporters of capitalism. The Paris Conference of 1938 was the first convention of this group of (26) economists and philosophers, including Hayek, Mises, Röpke and Walter Lippman (an American journalist who had influenced Hayek). Those present discussed the defence of market economics and individual liberty but were not to convene again until after the war, when the Mont Pelerin Society was born.[12]

The Austrian School, however, was about more than just Hayek. Ludwig von Mises was a vocal critic of many of his neoliberal contemporaries. Austrian thinking led more easily – in later years – to a more libertarian or market fundamentalist strain of neoliberalism. During the first half of the twentieth century, however, the Austrians developed their thinking alongside another set of academics, in interwar Germany.

The Freiburg School of the 1930s and 1940s

Earlier in the 1930s another group of liberals coalesced in the German university city of Freiburg, near the border with France. It was here that 'neoliberalism' was literally born. What made neoliberalism worthy of a prefix? The basic difference with what we might think of as nineteenth-century free trade liberalism or laissez-faire is that neoliberals accepted – even desired – some role for the state. This was to be a reference point for the neoliberals of the 1930s – from Hayek to the Freiburg and Chicago Schools – they all conceded something more than laissez-faire was needed.[13] Although the Austrian School – less convinced that laissez-faire had failed even in the 1930s – would subsequently become associated with neoliberalism, the concept was initially developed in Freiburg.[14] The group's ideas acted as a liberal response to the crisis of capitalism in the late 1920s and throughout the following decade.[15] Neoliberalism was first defined by Freiburg thinker Alexander Rüstow – originally used to denote a moderated revival of classical liberalism – in his 1932 essay *Free Economy – Strong State*.[16] The Freiburg School was committed to a market economy but also held that the state had a role to play in providing the conditions necessary for it to operate. This was rooted in the events of the time. The Weimar Republic was seen as prey to special interest groups.[17] The 1929 Wall Street Crash and subsequent Great Depression were viewed by some as the death knell for laissez-faire, while individual liberty was trampled on in Nazi Germany. The Freiburg School sought to reconcile these problems. This early version of neoliberalism wanted the state to ensure competition and to act against the forming of monopolies They also sought social cohesion as a way to make market forces more effective. The key thinkers at Freiburg were Walter Eucken and Franz Böhm. Other intellectuals in Germany at this time – such as Rüstow but also Wilhelm Röpke and Alfred Müller-Armack – were economic liberals who recognized the destructive implications of the market.[18] These German thinkers, however, put humanistic and social values on a par with economic ones and in the 1940s Eucken and Röpke became concerned with ideas like social security and social justice.[19]

Ordoliberalism

For reasons of clarity these early German neoliberals will be called 'Ordoliberals'. From the early 1950s, this subsequently became a more recognizable term associated with the West German journal *ORDO*, founded in 1948 by Eucken and Böhm. It provides emphasis because during this period the Mont Pelerin Society was formed, made up of a nucleus of notable thinkers that urged pro-market strategies. Mont Pelerin members took a variety of positions, however, some that were closer to classical liberalism than others. This notwithstanding, in the space of a few years the different views in the collective became interchangeable to some observers. The two major strands were to become the more classically liberal Hayekians, or Austrians, and the more 'neoliberal' Friedmanites, or Chicagoans, who took a more expedient position on many issues. Mont Pelerin meetings were said to always split into two camps: the Austrians and the Chicagoans.[20] In fact Ordoliberals recognized the difference with other members of Mont Pelerin and the Austrian School. Ordoliberals dubbed more classical liberal thinkers such as Ludwig von Mises 'paleoliberals'.[21] In one correspondence between Rüstow and Röpke the former wrote that Hayek 'and his master Mises deserved to be put in spirits and placed in a museum as one of the last surviving specimen[s] of the extinct species of liberals which caused the current catastrophe'.[22] Nevertheless, the early thinking of the Ordoliberals would be lost as the work of Hayek, and in particular Milton Friedman, came to define economic liberalism.

What then, is Ordoliberalism? Ordoliberalism was the first comprehensive market response to the challenges of socialism. Despite accepting the primacy of a market economy and its associated price mechanism, Ordoliberals advocated capitalism in conjunction with a firm legal framework, social and ethical considerations. Ordoliberals demanded a strong state as the means of restoring and sustaining the free economy.[23] An 'Ordo Manifesto' was set out as early as 1936 by Eucken, Böhm and Hans Grossmann-Doerth, outlining Germany's need for an 'economic constitution'.[24] Eucken elaborated upon this in the first edition of *ORDO* in 1948. He set out his belief that a written constitution and controlled economic activity were crucial in achieving his ultimate objective: freedom.[25] Both Eucken and Böhm were interested in the confluence of economics with the law.

Early Ordoliberal thought can be crystallized by the much-used term 'social market economy'. Alfred Müller-Armack first defined social market economy in the 1940s and it became the central plank of the West German post-war economic 'miracle'.[26] Müller-Armack was determined that political interventions should not destroy the price mechanism while Rüstow even proposed 'market police'.[27] Röpke classified interventions as 'market compatible' (those that did not affect price mechanisms) and 'market incompatible' (those that did).[28] Exchange controls and quotas, for instance, were market incompatible.[29] Ordoliberals rejected the Austrian laissez-faire tradition, because they believed this system was bound to create socially destructive outcomes, especially in the form of 'proletarianized' workers who would demand welfare to the detriment of liberty and the security of private property.[30] The preservation of competition and prevention of monopoly were core themes of Ordoliberals such as Röpke.[31] Ordoliberals therefore viewed their model as a way of maintaining order and markets as an 'instrument' in securing preferable social outcomes.[32] Ordoliberals viewed individuals as ends in themselves.[33] This is fundamentally different from subsequent neoliberals, who saw economic liberty as the precursor to political freedoms and social goods, almost viewing markets themselves as the desired outcome.[34]

West German Finance Minister and later Chancellor Ludwig Erhard was linked to both the Ordoliberals and Friedrich Hayek.[35] After the war Eucken, Böhm, Rüstow and Müller-Armack exerted considerable influence upon West German economic policy. Böhm was a prominent member of the Bundestag, while Müller-Armack served as State Secretary in the Ministry of Economics, close to Erhard.[36] In his role after the war Erhard responded to shortages by ending price controls. This step, a show of faith in market forces, began the remarkable resurgence of the West German economy.[37] Erhard also put together a committee – featuring Franz Böhm – to draft a competition law in 1949.[38] Echoing the Ordoliberal approach during the period Erhard wrote (in 1957) 'the principle of competition must be established. If economic monopolies are formed, they must be removed, and, until this can be done, State control must be exercised'.[39]

The Ordoliberal inspired mantra came to look like 'markets where possible, state where necessary'. The role of the state was one of the key themes that cut through all these ideas of neoliberalism and is one reason why it is important to define the difference between them. Critics of Ordoliberalism believe they had a limited idea of freedom and that when democracy and the market collided, the latter prevailed.[40] In fact Ordoliberals did see majority decisions in democracy as capable of reducing the civic rights which they considered crucial in economic affairs.[41] The idea that the state knew best can be on one side seen as a variation on conservative patriarchy, on the other as a drift to authoritarianism. In addition, Röpke highlighted society's need of strong Christian moral values.[42] A criticism of Ordoliberalism was that its ideas were borne out of Nazi Germany meaning that these thinkers accepted that only an anti-libertarian state apparatus could ensure market mechanisms. This was clearly at odds with a classical thesis, such as the one found in *The Road to Serfdom*. Hayek, however, was soon branded a neoliberal. He also fiercely defended Ordoliberals against any Nazi connection.[43]

The criticism itself, that Ordoliberalism had anti-democratic and anti-libertarian undertones was contentious. If the first Ordoliberal model was post-war West Germany then the state was conservative but relatively open, particularly in comparison with its Eastern neighbours. The social cohesion achieved and rapid economic growth became the envy of Europe, not least Britain. Ordoliberalism has had a profound impact on the economic policy-making of Germany, before and after unification.[44] Ordoliberal principles, such as those concerning competition policies, may have also influenced post-war European treatics and as a result indirectly affected British politics.[45] Angela Merkel has also openly expressed her admiration for Ordoliberal thinkers such as Walter Eucken.[46] Rachel Turner has written that countries that have adopted neoliberal measures did so as a response to a group or events. If British neoliberalism in the 1970s was a reaction to organized labour then Turner believes post-war West Germany, the first neoliberal influenced state, was a response to Nazism.[47] Ordoliberals sought to maintain order, limit the influence of special interest groups and utilize a strong state that was limited by rules and the force of law. Seen from a twenty-first century per-spective this model is less remarkable.

Why is Ordoliberalism important and what significance does it have regarding the Thatcher government? First, it is the foremost manifestation of neoliberal ideas in a cohesive set of policy recommendations and has fea-tured only intermittently in much of the literature on the subject. Second, writers like Andrew Gamble have made a direct linkage between Ordo-liberalism and Thatcherism by evoking the idea of 'free economy–strong state'.[48] Third, Ordoliberalism is thought by some to have consistently influenced German policymaking from the 1940s until the present. British politicians consistently eyed the rapid growth of post-war Germany with envy. The West German economic 'miracle' was a primary concern for the initial research of the CPS when Keith Joseph and Margaret Thatcher estab-lished the think-tank in 1974. Indeed the institute invoked a number of Ordoliberal ideas in its 1975 pamphlet 'Why Britain Needs a Social Market Economy'.[49] Keith Joseph initially considered naming the CPS the 'Erhard Foundation' and 'Institute for a Social Market Economy', and he also sought out Röpke's *Humane Economy*.[50] Despite his often ideological pro-nouncements Joseph accepted that it might be 'necessary for the state to stimulate enterprise'.[51] Adrian Williamson has outlined how Europe became a potent influence on many Conservative politicians in the 1960s and 1970s, not just economic liberals and nationalists like Enoch Powell, but mainstream Tories who favoured a Christian Democratic approach, the party most closely aligned with Ordoliberalism in Germany.[52]

The relationship between free markets and the role of the state is a key theme when examining the connection between neoliberal ideas and Thatcherism. The potential Ordoliberal elements in some Thatcherite reforms are explored in later chapters. It is also of historical interest that Ordoliberalism has been both largely ignored in the English-speaking world as well as engulfed by other interpretations of neoliberalism. Ordoliberals believed that 'Anglo-Saxon' theory predominated after the war.[53] In particular the term became sullied from the mid-1970s because of its association with the military dictatorship of Augusto Pinochet in Chile.[54] Neoliberalism has subsequently been consistently framed as being opposed to democracy and social goods, privileging economic over political freedom. This can be shown to be generally in contradiction to the original version of neoliberalism, Ordoliberalism. This book uses Ordoliberalism as a moderate, rules-based and socially orientated counterpoint to the utopian thinking of the Austrian School. Chicagoan neoliberalism will be shown to position itself somewhere between the two.

The Mont Pelerin Society

Friedrich Hayek convened a meeting of like-minded liberals at the 'Colloque Walter Lippmann' in Paris in 1938. Interrupted by the war, it was not until 1947 that Hayek managed to secure a more formal organization, the Mont Pelerin Society, named after its initial Swiss venue. For some, like David Harvey, thus began the 'long march' of neoliberalism.[55] Certainly Hayek had the long term in mind. Using the Fabian Society as his historical model, Hayek sought to change attitudes over a period of years. He persuaded Anthony Fisher, a chicken farmer who had been taken by liberal ideas, to found a think-tank as a vehicle for shifting the ideological climate back towards economic liberalism. This Fisher did, with some success, establishing the IEA in 1955 and then attempting to replicate this overseas. Hayek recognized that the results of fundamentally altering opinion might take some time and that the great social movements were led not by politicians but by men of ideas.[56] While attempting to break the perceived hold on the establishment that ideas like Keynesianism had, Hayek somewhat perversely promoted anti-collectivist sentiments by maintaining a degree of ideological homogeneity within his own collective. He later admitted that he avoided criticism of what he considered Milton Friedman's macroeconomic 'nonsense' for the sake of Mont Pelerin unity.[57] Articulating his position vis-à-vis the use of the state compared to Friedman, Hayek once commented 'Milton's monetarism and Keynesianism have more in common with each other than I have with either'.[58] The Austrian, however, was conscious not to allow the group to splinter into Hayekian and Friedmanite wings. In addition Hayek also noted that 'the Ordo circle ... was, shall we say, a restraining liberalism'.[59] Mises derided the Freiburg School as 'ordo-interventionism' and not much better than 'totalitarian socialists'.[60]

Nevertheless, some writers have made comparisons between the work of early neoliberals in the 1930s and 1940s.[61] Ben Jackson and Daniel Stedman-Jones draw attention to the sections endorsing some degree of a social safety net in *The Road to Serfdom*, making some correlation with the work of the Ordoliberals.[62] Andrew Gamble has also noted even in later works like *The Constitution of Liberty* that Hayek appeared to sanction surprising amounts of state intervention.[63] Henry Simons too, at the 'first' Chicago School, held views in the 1930s on monopoly, social welfare and regulation that were closer to Ordoliberalism than his Friedmanite successors.[64] The historical context of this early moderate neoliberalism was important. The Great Depression, the Second World War and a widespread disillusionment with laissez-faire informed this accommodation between classical liberalism and state action. Ludwig von Mises was identified as being closest to classical liberal thinking, or as Jackson puts it, 1970s neoliberalism.[65]

Mises's uncompromising positions were even deemed by Hayek to be naive and extreme.[66] Yet Mises's work *Bureaucracy* (1944), as well as Karl Popper's *The Open Society and Its Enemies* (1945) and *The Road to Serfdom* are considered by Stedman-Jones as the three key neoliberal texts of the 1940s.[67] If Hayek had any 'social' inclinations during the 1930s and 1940s it was only a minor part of his thinking. The majority of *The Road to Serfdom* railed against socialism and central planning. His work as a whole saw little room for social provision or any role for the state be it providing stable monetary conditions or regulating monopoly. Nevertheless, later generations of Austrian thinkers saw Hayek as only on the fringes of their movement as a result of this acceptance, albeit limited, of a role for the state. For instance Walter Block lambasted *The Road to Serfdom* and its allusions to state action. Block did not believe Hayek was a 'complete liberal' or an unambiguous advocate of the marketplace, but rather relatively more liberal than his contemporaries in the 1930s and 1940s.[68] Others saw the thought of Mises, then Murray Rothbard – who believed the state should be abolished – as the true manifestations of the Austrian School.[69] Rothbard, an American 'Austrian' economist was later described as a libertarian and used the term 'neoliberal' to criticize thinkers such as Hayek and Milton Friedman.[70] These sentiments probably demonstrate the hard-line positions taken by most Austrian School thinkers, rather than that Hayek was actually a statist.

Hayek could be strategic. The Mont Pelerin Society was a significant organization that shifted opinion to some extent over the post-war period. During its first 15 years the influence in the Society of Chicago School thinkers grew, mainly at the expense of the Ordoliberals. This culminated in 1961 with the resignation of Wilhelm Röpke, then the Mont Pelerin Society's president.[71] Accounts of this internecine neoliberal warfare suggest Hayek sided with the Society's rising stars, Milton Friedman and George Stigler, in purging the old-fashioned Europeans.[72] By the 1970s founder Mont Pelerin Society member Friedman had become a prominent voice in the political debates of Britain and the United States. One of its offshoots, the IEA, has been cited by numerous politicians as altering the economic and political debate in Britain.[73] Margaret Thatcher famously (or at least supposedly) wielded Hayek's later work, *The Constitution of Liberty*, in a meeting in 1975.[74] Whether Hayek, and economic liberalism, could have exerted so much influence in the longer term if the Mont Pelerin Society had fractured is debatable, if moot. Yet his own thinking could be quite different from the best-known proponents of neoliberalism, the Chicago School.

The Chicago School

The Chicago School of economics was established in the 1920s and 1930s by, among others, Frank Knight, Henry Simons, Jacob Viner and Lloyd Mints.[75] As we have seen, this 'first' Chicago School held some positions closer to those of the Freiburg neoliberals. Henry Simons had stated that monopoly was 'the great enemy of democracy ... in all its forms' and that 'political and economic power must be widely dispersed and decentralised in a world that would be free'.[76] Nevertheless, Simons was a mentor to Milton Friedman on issues such as monetary theory and the causes of the Great Depression.[77] Friedman was to become the leader of the department from 1946, which Stedman-Jones has dubbed the 'second' Chicago School, and also included George Stigler, Aaron Director and Gary Becker.[78] During the 1950s the positions of the school underwent a metamorphosis, in part due to long-running projects, such as the 'Free Market Study Group' and the 'Anti-Trust Project'.[79] First, this altered the Chicagoan perception of monopoly and competition. With George Stigler at the forefront, Chicagoans came to believe that monopolies were sustained by government but that also large companies could replicate the competition function.[80] Stigler – sceptical of government action[81] – nevertheless sought to influence public policy.[82] Friedman, who in 1951 appeared to still be Simons's protégé, later relaxed his attitude towards any imposition of competition, stating that in most markets there existed 'giants and pygmies side by side' and that there was a tendency to 'over-emphasise monopoly'.[83] Second, the kind of 'social' proposals made by the early neoliberals were slowly eroded.[84] This may have been because of the changing realities of Western societies as the memory of the desperation of the 1930s and 1940s began to fade. Stedman-Jones believes business activism against the New Deal, as well as the Cold War, were important in 'radicalizing' neoliberalism.[85] Friedman explained the shift by saying Simons was willing to entertain a relatively active role for the state because he wrote 'at a time when government was small by today's (1962's) standards'.[86]

Milton Friedman produced the first of several influential works in 1962 with *Capitalism and Freedom*, soon followed by *A Monetary History of the United States*, co-written with Anna Schwartz. Friedman had opinions on a wide variety of topics, such as education vouchers, rent control and even legalizing recreational drugs, but these books crucially outlined his ideas on 'monetarism', that the quantity of money in an economy was the key driver of inflation. American economist Irving Fisher's 1911 work set out the simple quantity theory of money, showing that an increase in the volume of money decreased its value. Although abhorring inflation, Keynes rejected this thesis in his critique of Weimar Germany. Fisher's theory was later adopted by Friedman.[87]

Importantly, after *Capitalism and Freedom*, Friedman argued that economic freedom was the precursor to political freedom.[88] Friedman viewed markets as a means to disperse power and therefore freedom, whereas he thought these tended to be concentrated by the political process.[89] This was a departure in the development of neoliberalism and also provided some justification for Friedman's later assistance to the Pinochet regime in Chile.[90] David Graeber, in *Debt: The First 5000 Years* (2011) gives another perspective – not incompatible with neoliberalism – on the relationship between the state and the market: 'the State and the Market tower above all else as diametrically opposed principles. Historical reality reveals, however, that they were born together and have always been intertwined.'[91]

In general, however, the Chicago approach was a positivist one based on evidence, data and proof.[92] It also received a higher profile due to Friedman's political activism – he advised a number of US presidents and candidates, from Barry Goldwater to Ronald Reagan – and the clarity of his rhetoric. He managed to condense a little understood and complex theory, monetarism, into a memorable sound bite: 'inflation is always and everywhere a monetary phenomenon'.[93] The strength of Friedman's ideas and personality, backed up by the prolific academics at Chicago, were some of the reasons the school became the most prominent in the neoliberal movement after 1950. To suggest, as some contemporary writers on neoliberalism have done, that this was part of the historical development of a homogeneous collective that coalesced around Chicagoan thinking from this point is again a simplification. It was true that the 'social' and anti-monopoly elements of neoliberalism faded in the 1950s but these sentiments can only be significantly attached to the Ordoliberals or first Chicago School. Neither the schools of thought nor the individuals retained rigid positions. Nevertheless there remained consistent distinctions between the Austrians and Chicagoans that are worth setting out.

First, Austrians focused on microeconomic processes: Friedman of course made his name writing about macroeconomics. Monetary control required a government to restrict or expand the supply of money to limit inflation. Hayek's work on the business cycle in the 1930s advocated a laissez-faire approach to monetary policy that would, according to Hayek, allow an economy to more quickly move to equilibrium. In essence, Austrians rejected the concept of macroeconomics.[94] The two positions also differed on the need for a gold standard and fixed exchange rates, as Hayek supported, and Friedman's preferred floating rates. Chicagoans also believed empirical research was a necessity to prove their positions. This was never a priority for the Austrians, particularly Mises, and although Hayek did concede some empirical testing was relevant he also thought 'statistical studies don't get us anywhere'.[95]

Last, the two differ on competition, monopoly and regulation. The Austrian view on 'antitrust' laws was that they were unnecessary, counterproductive and a violation of liberty.[96] Chicagoans moved some way to that but were never as 'hardline' as the Austrians. Skousen believed this was because many Chicagoans aided government in formulating antitrust laws in the United States.[97] That is not to say there was not a great deal on which the two schools did agree but fundamentally there was a difference. Whereas the Austrians took a more puritanical view of market processes, Chicagoans accepted that the state could be used to further their objectives. That is to say thinkers like Milton Friedman believed they could propose practical stepping stones to a more liberal society, or as he himself remarked much later, 'you have to have some mechanism of going from here to there'.[98] The Ordoliberals, however, reconciled themselves to a clearly defined role for the state from the 1930s.

Public Choice theory

The main strands of neoliberal thinking have so far been identified as the Austrian and Chicago Schools led by Hayek and Friedman respectively, and the lesser-known earlier variant Ordoliberalism. The last significant grouping is Public Choice theory based at the University of Virginia. Gordon Tullock and James Buchanan were the thinkers most closely associated with Public Choice theory. Sometimes known as the economics of politics, Public Choice followed themes examined in *The Road to Serfdom*, which outlined what Hayek believed was the dangerous growth of the state. There is a link with several of the schools of thought studied here. Hayek's work warned of the dangers of an expanding state, Buchanan was once of the Chicago School while Razeen Sally believes an Ordoliberal view of state power also influenced Public Choice.[99]

The Calculus of Consent (Tullock and Buchanan, 1962) and *The Politics of Bureaucracy* (Tullock, 1965) presented examples of the concerns of Public Choice theorists. The core features were that bureaucrats were characterized as operating in just as self-interested a manner as those in the private sector. Government, for Public Choice theorists, was too 'large and basically inefficient'.[100] They argued that bureaucracy was prone to expansion, inefficiency and waste, and that government was associated with processes that hamper market forces, such as perfect monopolies.[101] Tullock and Buchanan invoked the idea of 'rent seeking' in bureaucracy, that is to say a payment 'over and above that which resources could command in any alternative use'.[102] Rent seeking was said to be endemic in government and reflected a 'diversion of value from consumers generally to the favoured rent seeker, with a net loss of value in the process'.[103]

Public Choice writers advocated a reduction in central government and more emphasis on local responsibility. Last, Buchanan and Tullock introduced the concept, similar to market failure, of government failure. Margaret

Thatcher capitalized on the belief that government failure was just as if not more likely than market failure.[104] Public Choice theory looked at bureaucracy from a different perspective during this period and became influential. Not all neoliberals, however, agreed with the ideas of Public Choice, thinking they made too much of an accommodation with the state.[105] Admired by the Austrians for her libertarianism, novelist and writer Ayn Rand may also have had an indirect impact. Her ideas of 'objectivism' rejected any kind of state interference, encapsulated by her books *The Fountainhead* (1943) and *Atlas Shrugged* (1957). Rand's thinking has also been described as anarcho-capitalism. She influenced philosophers like Robert Nozick, was admired by Milton Friedman and also acted as a mentor to Alan Greenspan, subsequently the long serving chairman of the US Federal Reserve.[106]

A number of British thinkers took up the ideas of Public Choice. Madsen Pirie, of the ASI (formed in 1977) later wrote that governments found it very difficult to cut their size and cost, while the incentive for the bureaucrat was to increase rather than diminish the work done in their department.[107] The IEA's Arthur Seldon also popularized public choice ideas in the 1960s and 1970s, characterizing many employees of the state – from teachers to miners – as 'rent-seekers'.[108] The idea of inefficiency in government sat neatly with other neoliberal themes such as reduced intervention in the economy and increased personal choice and liberty. The anti-state or smaller state movement, though, probably had greater influence on the politics of the United States. Despite running huge budget deficits these ideas were perhaps most closely linked with Ronald Reagan's presidency: 'Government is not the *solution* to our problem. Government *is* the problem.'[109] Nevertheless reducing the size of the state has been consistently aligned with neoliberalism and by association the Thatcher government. Donald Savoie, in *Thatcher Reagan Mulroney. In Search of a New Bureaucracy* (1994), wrote that Thatcher publicly endorsed Public Choice as well as recommending literature on the subject to senior civil servants.[110] The prime minister urged reform of bureaucracy in Cabinet meetings, to reduce 'unnecessary duplication, coordination and inefficiency' as well as setting up the Rayner and later Ibbs's task forces to investigate ways of achieving these aims.[111] Public Choice also chimed with Keith Joseph's idea of the 'ratchet effect' of socialism.

Slimming down the size of the state has been a notable neoliberal theme. It was implicit in the work of the Chicago, Austrian and Public Choice schools, if not necessarily in Ordoliberalism. It closely followed the message of Hayek's *The Road to Serfdom*. In addition, the emphasis of neoliberal think-tanks, according to Ben Jackson, shifted subtly during the 1970s from its previous focus on anti-competitive business practices to the problems of government. This may have reflected the funding of organizations like the IEA, who received donations from large companies like IBM, BP and Marks and Spencer.[112] Whether Public Choice theory exerted significant influence on the Thatcher government, however, is debatable. Conservatives had proposed greater professionalism and business methods in the civil service since the

1960s.[113] In addition, whether government actually shrank during Thatcherism has also been contested. Contemporary critics on the left believe that neoliberals sought to 're-task' the state or simply use government in a different way, as opposed to doctrinaire reduction.[114]

Conclusion

This chapter has outlined the main strands of neoliberal thinking, from the early twentieth century into the post-1945 period. They range from the interventionist Ordoliberals to the libertarian Austrian School and the later Friedmanite Chicago School. The various groupings differ in their approach to money, regulating markets, competition and much else besides. It has been demonstrated that neoliberalism is not a homogeneous set of ideas and these will be outlined in more detail over the following chapters. It should also be clear that British politicians and policymakers were not presented with a discrete set of neoliberal options in the 1970s and 1980s. Even the best-known principles, such as monetarism, were keenly debated by economic liberals. The Thatcher government, therefore, had a number of policy options, even within a neoliberal paradigm.

Neoliberals such as Friedrich Hayek and Milton Friedman provided the intellectual foundations of a response to what they saw as the rise of collectivism in the early to mid-twentieth century. They represented thinking from the Austrian and Chicago Schools respectively and although agreeing on much, also took distinctive positions on several issues. The Freiburg School of thinkers also called Ordoliberals in 1930s and 1940s Germany was in fact the first recognizable version of neoliberalism. Influencing post-war West Germany this movement put more emphasis on social outcomes and measures such as enforcing competition than their Austrian and Chicagoan counterparts. The Ordoliberal heritage was later aligned with Thatcherism by academics such as Andrew Gamble by invoking the 'free economy–strong state' theme. Nevertheless, although Hayek and the Austrian School were seemingly at the forefront of the revival of economic liberalism, it was the Chicago School and its accommodation with the state that would most closely influence the Thatcher government.

Notes

1 Dieter Plehwe, Bernhard J. A. Walpen and Gisela Neunhöffer, 'Introduction: Reconsidering Neoliberal Hegemony', in *Neoliberal Hegemony: A Global Critique*, ed. Dieter Plehwe Bernhard J. A. Walpen and Gisela Neunhöffer (Abingdon: Routledge, 2007), 2.
2 Mark Skousen, *Vienna & Chicago. Friends or Foes? A Tale of Two Schools of Free-Market Economics* (Washington, DC: Capital Press, 2005) 25.
3 Skousen, *Vienna and Chicago*, 25.
4 Norman Barry, 'Austrian Challenge to Orthodoxy', *Economic Affairs* 4:3 (April–June 1984), 57.
5 Skousen, *Vienna and Chicago*, 33.

6 F. A. Hayek, *The Road to Serfdom* (Chicago, IL: University of Chicago Press, 2007 [1944]), 81.

7 Andrew Gamble, *Hayek. The Iron Cage of Liberty* (Cambridge: Polity Press, 1996), 8–9, 180.

8 Hayek, *Road to Serfdom*, 148.

9 Gamble, *Hayek*, 24.

10 Tim Bale, *The Conservatives since 1945* (Oxford: Oxford University Press, 2012), 29.

11 Friedrich Hayek speech to the Mont Pelerin Society ('Professor Hayek's Closing Speech'), 9 March 1984, Margaret Thatcher Foundation (hereafter MTF), accessed 13 September 2012. www.margaretthatcher.org/document/117193.

12 Richard Cockett, *Thinking the Unthinkable. Think-Tanks and the Economic Counter-Revolution, 1931–83* (London: Harper Collins, 1995), 9.

13 Bruce Caldwell, 'The Chicago School, Hayek, and Neoliberalism', in *Building Chicago Economics. New Perspectives on the History of America's Most Powerful Economics Program*, ed. R. Van Horn, P. Mirowski and T. A. Stapleford (Cambridge: Cambridge University Press, 2011), 316.

14 Oliver Marc Hartwich, *Neoliberalism: The Genesis of a Political Swearword* (St Leonards: CIS occasional papers, 114, July 2009), 22.

15 Ralf Ptak, 'Neoliberalism in Germany. Revisiting the Ordoliberal Foundations of the Social Market Economy', in *The Road from Mont Pelerin. The Making of the Neoliberal Thought Collective*, ed. P. Mirowski and D. Plehwe (Harvard: Harvard University Press, 2009), 110.

16 Taylor C. Boas and Jordan Gans-Morse, 'Neoliberalism: From New Liberal Philosophy to Anti-Liberal Slogan', *Studies in Comparative International Development* 44:2 (2009), 137, 146.

17 Ptak, 'Neoliberalism in Germany', 110.

18 Ptak, 'Neoliberalism in Germany', 102–103.

19 Boas and Gans-Morse, 'Neoliberalism', 147.

20 Skousen, *Vienna and Chicago*, 1.

21 Boas and Gans-Morse, 'Neoliberalism', 147.

22 Hartwich, *Genesis*, 24. See also Philip Plickert, *Wandlungen des Neoliberalismus – Eine Studie zur Entwicklung und Ausstrahlung der 'Mont Pelerin Society'* (Stuttgart: De Gruyter Oldenbourg, 2008), 105.

23 Werner Bonefeld, 'Adam Smith and Ordoliberalism: On the Political Form of Market Liberty', *Review of International Studies* 39:2 (July 2012), 234.

24 Franz Böhm, Walter Eucken and Hans Grossmann-Doerth, 'The Ordo Manifesto of 1936' (first published in Ordnung der Wirtshaft, no. 2, 1936), in *Germany's Social Market Economy: Origins and Evolution*, ed. Alan Peacock and Hans Willgerodt (Basingstoke: Macmillan, 1989), 15–26.

25 Walter Eucken, 'What Kind of Economic and Social System?' (first published in Ordo, vol. 1, 1948), in *Germany's Social Market Economy: Origins and Evolution*, ed. Alan Peacock and Hans Willgerodt (Basingstoke: Macmillan, 1989), 31, 34, 37.

26 Boas and Gans-Morse, 'Neoliberalism'. 146.

27 Hartwich, *Genesis*, 19.

28 Christian Watrin, 'Alfred Müller-Armack – Economic Policy Maker and Sociologist of Religion', in *The Theory of Capitalism in the German Economic Tradition*, ed. P. Koslowski (London: Springer, 2000), 209; Samuel Gregg, *Wilhelm Röpke's Political Economy* (Cheltenham: Edward Elgar, 2010), 89.

29 Gregg, *Wilhelm*, 89.

30 Bonefeld, 'Adam Smith', 238.

31 Gregg, *Wilhelm*, 77; Manfried E. Streit and Michael Wohlgemuth, 'The Market Economy and the State. Hayekian and Ordoliberal Conceptions', in *The Theory*

of Capitalism in the German Economic Tradition, ed. P. Koslowski (London: Springer, 2000), 231.

32 Bonefeld, 'Adam Smith', 244.

33 Wernhard Möschel, 'The Proper Scope of Government Viewed from an Ordo-liberal Perspective: The Example of Competition Policy', *Journal of Institutional and Theoretical Economics (JITE)/Zeitschrift für die gesamte Staatswissenschaft* 157:1 (2001), 7.

34 Norman Barry, *The New Right* (Beckenham: Croom Helm, 1987), 33.

35 MTF 117173, Letter to *The Times* by Friedrich Hayek, 17 July 1981, accessed 13 September 2012, www.margaretthatcher.org/document/117173.

36 Gregg, *Wilhelm*, 42.

37 'The Commanding Heights. The Battle for the World Economy', PBS Documentary (2002), accessed 10 May 2012. www.pbs.org/wgbh/commanding heights/hi/story/index.html.

38 Ludwig Erhard, *Prosperity Through Competition* (New York: Frederick A. Praeger, translated by Edith Temple Roberts and John B. Wood, 1958, first published as *Wohlstand für Alle* in 1957), 118.

39 Erhard, *Prosperity*, 118.

40 Philip Mirowski, 'Postface: Defining Neoliberalism', in *The Road from Mont Pelerin. The Making of the Neoliberal Thought Collective*, ed. P. Mirowski and D. Plehwe (Harvard: Harvard University Press, 2009), 443.

41 Bruno Molitor, 'Schwäche der Demokratie' [The Weakness of Democracy], *ORDO. Jahrbuch für die Ordnung von Wirtschaft und Gesellschaft* [Ordo Yearbook of Economic and Social Order] (Stuttgart: Gustav Fischer Verlag, Band 34, 1983), 38.

42 Ptak, 'Neoliberalism in Germany', 116.

43 MTF 117173, Hayek letter to *The Times*.

44 S. Dullien and U. Guérot, 'The Long Shadow of Ordoliberalism,' *IP Journal* 17 July 2012, accessed 20 January 2013. https://ip-journal.dgap.org/en/ip-journal/topics/long-shadow-Ordoliberalism. Dullien and Guérot explain the long-standing impact of Ordoliberalism on German economic policy, up to the Euro-zone debt crisis.

45 Möschel, 'Ordoliberal Perspective', 3.

46 Peter Coy, 'Will Merkel Act, or Won't She?' Bloomberg Businessweek, 30 November 2011, accessed 7 February 2014. www.businessweek.com/magazine/will-angela-merkel-act-or-wont-she-11302011.html#p2.

47 Rachel S. Turner, *Neoliberal Ideology. History, Concepts and Policies* (Edinburgh: Edinburgh University Press, 2008), 219.

48 Andrew Gamble, *The Free Economy and the Strong State. The Politics of Thatcherism* (Basingstoke: Palgrave Macmillan, 1994), 38–45.

49 Centre for Policy Studies, *Why Britain Needs a Social Market Economy* (Chichester: Barry Rose, 1975), accessed 26 May 2017. www.cps.org.uk/files/reports/original/111028103106-WhyBritainneedsaSocialMarketEconomy.pdf.

50 MTF114757, 'Ralph Harris record of conversation (visit from Keith Joseph)', 14 March 1974; MTF114760, 'Sir Keith Joseph note ("The Erhard Foundation")', 21 March 1974; Andrew Denham and Mark Garnett, *Keith Joseph* (Chesham: Acumen, 2001), 241.

51 Richard Vinen, *Thatcher's Britain. The Politics and Social Upheaval of the 1980s* (London: Simon and Schuster), 64.

52 Adrian Williamson, *Conservative Economic Policymaking and the Birth of Thatcherism, 1964–1979* (Basingstoke: Palgrave Macmillan, 2015), 200.

53 Ernst Heuss, ' "Die Grundlagen der *Nationalökonomie*" vor 50 Jahren und heute' ['Die Grunglagen der *Nationalökonomie*': Fifty Years Ago and Today], *ORDO. Jahrbuch für die Ordnung von Wirtschaft und Gesellschaft* [Ordo Yearbook of Economic and Social Order] (Stuttgart: Gustav Fischer Verlag, Band 40, 1989), 30.

54 Boas and Gans-Morse, 'Neoliberalism', 150.
55 Ben Jackson, 'At the Origins of Neoliberalism: The Free Economy and the Strong State, 1930–1947', *The Historical Journal* 53:1 (March 2010), 130.
56 Eamonn Butler, *Hayek* (New York: Universe, 1985a), 1.
57 MTF 117203, Letter from Friedrich Hayek to Arthur Seldon, 13 May 1985, accessed 1 August 2017. www.margaretthatcher.org/document/117203.
58 'The Road from Serfdom. Foreseeing the Fall', Friedrich Hayek interviewed by Thomas W. Hazlitt, 1977, published in *Reason*, July 1992, accessed 29 December 2013. http://reason.com/archives/1992/07/01/the-road-from-serfdom.
59 Streit and Wohlgemuth 'The Market Economy', 229.
60 Hartwich, *Genesis*, 24.
61 Caldwell, 'The Chicago School', 316.
62 Jackson, 'Origins', 132–139; Daniel Stedman-Jones, *Masters of the Universe. Hayek, Friedman, and the Birth of Neoliberal Politics* (Oxford: Princeton University Press, 2012), 335.
63 Gamble, *Hayek*, 175.
64 Stedman-Jones, *Masters*, 335.
65 Jackson, 'Origins', 140.
66 Jackson, 'Origins', 141.
67 Stedman-Jones, *Masters*, 31; Cockett, *Thinking*, 83. Karl Popper's 1945 work *The Open Society and its Enemies* rallied against what he thought was the Aristotelian philosophical tendency towards totalitarianism.
68 Walter Block, 'Hayek's Road to Serfdom', *Journal of Libertarian Studies* 12:2 (Fall 1996), 342, 365.
69 Jeffrey M. Herbener, 'Ludwig von Mises and the Austrian School of Economics', *Review of Austrian Economics* 5:2 (1991), 37.
70 Caldwell, 'The Chicago School', 329.
71 R. M. Hartwell, *A History of the Mont Pelerin Society* (Indianapolis, IN: Liberty Fund, 1995), 124.
72 Angus Burgin, *The Great Persuasion, Reinventing Free Markets since the Depression* (London: Harvard University Press, 2012), 150.
73 Interview with Lord Ryder, 23 February 2011; Sir Adam Ridley, personal correspondence with the author, 15 May 2013.
74 John Ranelagh, *Thatcher's People. An Insider's Account of the Politics, the Power and the Personalities* (London: Harper Collins, 1991), ix.
75 Stedman-Jones, *Masters*, 90.
76 Jackson, 'Origins', 142; Stedman-Jones, *Masters*, 99.
77 Stedman-Jones, *Masters*, 93.
78 Stedman-Jones, *Masters*, 91, 335.
79 Daniel Stedman-Jones, 'The Influence of Transatlantic Neoliberal Politics,' seminar at Queen Mary University London, 22 October 2013.
80 Stedman-Jones, 'Influence'.
81 Jamie Peck, 'Orientation: In Search of the Chicago School', in *Building Chicago Economics: New Perspectives on the History of America's Most Powerful Economics Program*, ed. Robert Van Horn, Philip Mirowski and Thomas A. Stapleford (Cambridge: Cambridge University Press, 2011), xlvi.
82 Edward Nik-Khah, 'George Stigler, the Graduate School of Business, and the Pillars of the Chicago School', in *Building Chicago Economics: New Perspectives on the History of America's Most Powerful Economics Program*, ed. Robert Van Horn, Philip Mirowski and Thomas A. Stapleford (Cambridge: Cambridge University Press, 2011), 137.
83 Milton Friedman, *Capitalism and Freedom* (Chicago, IL: University of Chicago Press, 1962), 121–123; Stedman-Jones, *Masters*, 96–98. Friedman's 1951 essay 'Neoliberalism and its Prospects' stated that government should preserve competition.

84 Stedman-Jones, *Masters*, 335.
85 Stedman-Jones, 'Influence'; Stedman-Jones, *Masters*, 329.
86 Friedman, *Capitalism*, 32.
87 Eamonn Butler, *Milton Friedman* (Aldershot: Gower, 1985b), 26.
88 Stedman-Jones, 'Influence'.
89 Matthias Matthijs, *Ideas and Economic Crises in Britain from Attlee to Blair 1945–2005* (Abingdon: Routledge, 2011), 110.
90 Friedman, 'Commanding Heights'.
91 David Graeber, *Debt, The First 5,000 Years* (New York: Melville, 2011), 18.
92 Skousen, *Vienna and Chicago*, 62.
93 Stedman-Jones, *Masters*, 210.
94 Skousen, *Vienna and Chicago*, 7–8.
95 Gamble, *Hayek*, 12; Hayek, 'Road' interview.
96 Gamble, *Hayek*, 72–73.
97 Skousen, *Vienna and Chicago*, 199, 218.
98 Skousen, *Vienna and Chicago*, 246; Milton Friedman, 'Say "No" to Intolerance', *Liberty* 4:6 (July 1991) 20.
99 Razeen Sally, *Classical Liberalism and International Economic Order. Studies in Theory and Intellectual History* (London: Routledge, 1998), 124–125.
100 Gordon Tullock, *The Politics of Bureaucracy* (London: University Press of America, 1987 [1965]), 221.
101 Gordon Tullock. *The Vote Motive. An Essay in the Economics of Politics, with Applications to the British Economy* (Hobart Paperback No. 9) London: IEA, 1976)), 36.
102 James M. Buchanan, 'Rent Seeking and Profit Seeking', in *Toward a Theory of the Rent-Seeking Society*, ed. J. M. Buchanan, R. D. Tollison and G. Tullock (College Station, TX: Texas A&M University Press, 1980), 3.
103 Buchanan, 'Rent Seeking', 7.
104 Peter Clarke, *A Question of Leadership* (London: Hamish Hamilton, 1991), 316.
105 Alexander Shand, *The Capitalist Alternative: An Introduction to Neo-Austrian Economics* (Frome: Wheatsheaf, 1984), 182–183.
106 E. Hadas in conversation with Samuel Brittan, 'Is Capitalism Morally Bankrupt?' *Standpoint* (November 2008), accessed 6 May 2012. www.standpointmag.co.uk/node/573/full. Friedman, 'Intolerance,' 17–18.
107 Madsen Pirie, *The Logic of Economics* (London: Adam Smith Institute, 1982), 28–29.
108 Noel Thompson, 'Hollowing Out of the State: Public Choice Theory and the Critique of Keynesian Social Democracy', *Contemporary British History* 22:3 (September 2008), 366.
109 Ronald Reagan, Inaugural Address, 20 January 1981, accessed 13 October 2010. www.reaganfoundation.org/reagan/speeches/.
110 Donald J. Savoie, *Thatcher Reagan Mulroney. In Search of a New Bureaucracy* (London: University of Pittsburgh Press, 1994), 27, 106.
111 Records of the Cabinet Office (hereafter CAB) CAB 128/66/22, 'minutes from the Cabinet Meeting 22/11/1979'; Bale, *Conservatives*, 276.
112 Ben Jackson, 'The Think-Tank Archipelago: Thatcherism and Neoliberalism', in *Making Thatcher's Britain*, ed. Ben Jackson and Robert Saunders (Cambridge: Cambridge University Press, 2012), 47–49.
113 Bale, *Conservatives*, 138.
114 Jamie Peck, *Constructions of Neoliberal Reason* (Oxford: Oxford University Press, 2010), 4; David Harvey, *A Brief History of Neoliberalism* (Oxford: Oxford University Press, 2005) 21.

2   Neoliberal ideas in Britain after 1945

The political decision-making process is guided, or at least influenced, by ideas; as Keynes put it, 'practical men, who believe themselves to be quite exempt from any intellectual influence, are usually the slaves of some defunct economist'.[1] In Britain, certain goals have tended to be attached to different prime ministers and their governments. Edward Heath was intent on entry into the European Community, Neville Chamberlain wanted to avoid war, while Tony Blair offered a reconstructed New Labour or 'Third Way' vision for Britain. Partly as a result, each era of British politics is synonymous with certain legacies but rarely is it known for a particular ideological intensity. There are, however, exceptions. Clement Attlee's post-war Labour government has a reputation, due to its programme of nationalization and the assembly of the welfare state, as having being more radical than other administrations. This is matched or even eclipsed by the scope of the changes introduced by Margaret Thatcher's Conservative government. Were the policies that began in 1979 reactionary or as Richard Cockett put it, a counter-revolution? If they were genuinely new, then from where did they originate? An accepted view has formed that the Thatcher government implemented several free market-inspired recommendations and that important policy-makers became converts to these at various points before 1979 – in the case of Geoffrey Howe, during the 1950s, Keith Joseph in the 1960s and Margaret Thatcher during the 1970s.[2] This chapter will set the scene in the years before Thatcher came to power, examining how neoliberal ideas began to gain traction in political discourse during the post-war period. The main focus will be the 1970s and the years the Conservatives spent in opposition.

Background

Liberal thinkers – including Adam Smith, John Locke, David Hume, Jeremy Bentham and John Stuart Mill – had a profound impact on British politicians during the industrial revolution and the country's period of imperial expansion. They made the case for trade, private property, the rule of law, utilitarianism and individual liberty. The intellectual opposition to liberalism during the 1800s formed the basis for the left-right positions taken up by British politicians into the twentieth century: social democracy and capitalism. Adam Smith, in particular, was later reclaimed by neoliberals and Conservative politicians in selective ways. Smith's idea of the 'invisible hand' was embraced while his promotion of social goods like education was downplayed.[3] The apparently seamless link between classical liberals of the Enlightenment and twentieth-century neoliberals may have allowed important ideological distinctions to be blurred.[4]

Ideas can take decades to filter down into the domain of mainstream politics and often the point in time where certain principles are introduced is very different from the environment in which they were originally written.[5] The Fabian Society was founded in 1884. Led by writers and thinkers like George Bernard Shaw, Sidney and Beatrice Webb, the Fabians brought socialism into mainstream political arguments. One study cited by Andrew Gamble suggested that from around 1860 collectivist doctrines began to supplant individualist ones in their hold on public opinion.[6] Richard Cockett, in *Thinking the Unthinkable* (1995), described the period from 1880 to the 1930s as a battle of ideas between liberals and collectivists that was ultimately won by the latter.[7] Cockett also stressed the importance of the Fabian Society in giving intellectual weight to 'collectivism'.[8] The Fabians were the first 'think-tank' in Britain and were the most prominent organization of their kind during this period. The example of how the Fabians exerted influence over public policy in Britain acted as a model for neoliberals such as Friedrich Hayek.

The impact of the Fabian Society manifested itself most famously in the 1942 Beveridge Report. The report's recommendations became widely accepted during the war and gave the Attlee government the impetus it needed to introduce many of them. Industries were nationalized, the National Health Service (NHS) was founded and the welfare state would look after the British people from the 'cradle to the grave'. If socialism had finally gained some respectability in the UK, another thinker was to prove just as significant for the post-war era: John Maynard Keynes. A classical economist, a member of the Liberal Party and certainly not a socialist, Keynes was to be crucial in ending laissez-faire policies in Britain. The Depression and unemployment of the 1920s and 1930s had a considerable impact on Keynes and his core aim became the achievement of full employment.[9] Like many thinkers who exerted mass appeal, Keynes's work was simplified and extrapolated.[10] His most influential book, *The General Theory of Employment, Interest and Money* (1936), was dense and difficult to interpret but the term 'Keynesianism' came to mean demand management and counter-cyclical government spending and monetary policy designed to combat unemployment and avert recession.[11] In summary, the thought of Keynes, the influence of the Fabian Society and Beveridge Report were all interpreted as justification for expansive state intervention in the economy.

The Conservative Party after the Second World War

British political historians have tended to become animated over the suggestion that after 1945 a consensus or 'settlement' existed between the two major
parties.[12] It is not the purpose of this study to revisit these arguments. What is
more important for our purposes is to appreciate that the notion of a post-
war settlement existed in British political discourse, and that this became a
potent rhetorical device for some Conservatives in the 1970s. As well as a
consensus among Britain's political classes, writers articulated the country's
'post-war decline'. In this telling, Britain was – by the 1970s – in hock to
overbearing trades unions and special interests, its economy in sclerotic
decline and overseas clout in retreat.

Contemporary historians reject the consensus thesis, the extent of crises in
the 1970s and cast doubt on the idea trades unions wielded as much power as
many claimed.[13] Vinen has written that in some respects Margaret Thatcher
was a defender of consensus, particularly in foreign policy, albeit more specifically of a 1940s, rather than a 1960s 'progressive' variety.[14] Nevertheless
Conservative politicians were able to capitalize on both the consensus, and
'declinist', narratives that neoliberals began to build. Matthijs has described
the party, along with the right wing press, as portraying the British state as
under siege in the 1970s by the trades unions.[15] Neoliberals were openly
questioning Keynesian answers to economic problems before and during this
period. Opposition to Keynesian counter-cyclical spending was one issue that
united the different strains of neoliberalism examined here.[16] Bernard Donoughue, an advisor to Harold Wilson and James Callaghan during the 1970s,
described how the Keynesian approach was undermined by the 'critical
debate taking place in the universities and the media and by the great public-
ity given to advocates of monetarism'.[17]

The Institute of Economic Affairs (IEA)

How did economic liberalism gain influence in Britain after the war? Much
has been made of the impact of think-tanks, foremost of which is the IEA. As
we saw in Chapter 1, as a result of Hayek's advice, the wealthy Anthony
Fisher founded the IEA in 1955. It has been considered the most important
British think-tank in the post-war period and had a distinctive strategy. Ralph
Harris and Arthur Seldon, in charge of the IEA during its formative years,
produced pamphlets and papers that promoted free market ideas but were
'pure' in their approach. The IEA was not aligned to a political party and did
not present specific policy recommendations. This work was not a question
of what was possible, rather exercises that returned to liberal economic principles. A normative approach, framing the world as it could be as opposed to
how it was, represented the influence of Hayek's Austrian lineage. As a result
the institute was initially considered outside mainstream political debate and
somewhat eccentric.[18] This image, however, may have suited the group and

they did in fact receive sizeable donations from high profile businesses and seek to court influence.[19] In addition, neoliberal influence exerted itself in the FBI (Federation of British Industries) and later the CBI (Confederation of British Industry) from the late 1950s until the early 1970s under the leadership of Arthur Shenfield and J. B. Bracewell-Milnes.[20] Both attended Mont Pelerin meetings and under their leadership the organization called for pro-business neoliberal measures such as a reduction in excessive government spending, confronting the trades unions, tax reform, cutting subsidies for the nationalized industries, opting out of the NHS, removing subsidies on housing rents and less bureaucracy.[21] These details have often been omitted from historical accounts of the period and indicate the role business leaders had in the post-war battle of ideas as well as weakening the notion that the FBI/CBI were part of a social democratic or Keynesian 'consensus'. Keith Joseph was introduced to the IEA in 1964 and Margaret Thatcher began to visit their offices around the same time. The think-tank had at that time recently published a book of essays called *The Rebirth of Britain*.[22]

The Bow Group

The IEA, however, was not the only think-tank that became linked with neoliberalism. The Bow Group was founded in 1951 by members of the Conservative Party and although not free of political influence like the IEA, it became an important proponent of the free market. Geoffrey Howe, one of the key contributors to the Bow Group and editor (between 1960 and 1962) of its publication *Crossbow*, said that the organization was originally set up to promote a classless Conservative Party, a multiracial Commonwealth, liberal economics and One Nation conservatism.[23] Howe said the idea for the group was primarily political seeking to provide a rival to the Fabian Society.[24] There was some contact between the IEA and the Bow Group, however, with members of the latter attending meetings of the former and IEA members writing articles for *Crossbow*.[25] From its inception the Bow Group contributed numerous pro-market articles that were to have some subsequent influence on the Thatcher government. Geoffrey Howe, for one, believes the group has not been given the credit they deserved for this work.[26] The Bow Group though, was a different kind of organization from the IEA. Former members Julian Critchley and Simon Jenkins both noted by the mid-1960s the group was being used by ambitious young politicians as a platform for Conservative candidate selection and became an important component in the party's structure.[27] According to Barr's history of the Bow Group, it was only under Peter Lilley's chairmanship from 1973 to 1975 that the organization became explicitly aligned with economic liberalism and that it came into competition with the CPS when that was formed in 1974.

An example of the primacy of the IEA in promoting liberal economics can be seen when Geoffrey Howe decided to ask their advice on pension arrangements, as 'the Bow Group could not provide the level of expertise on the semi-professional basis which the IEA's founders, Arthur Seldon and Ralph Harris, could'.[28] Howe's links with the IEA and the Bow Group along with his quiet determination subsequently made him perhaps the most committed economic liberal in the first Thatcher government. John Hoskyns later wrote of Howe in office that he 'repeatedly did the things that few of his predecessors would have dared to do. He seemed to me to be all action and very little talk'.[29] Howe's long-standing zeal for free market ideas was matched in government as chancellor. Others, such as Keith Joseph and even Margaret Thatcher, were more cautious.

The rise of 'declinist' literature in the 1970s helped augment interest in neoliberalism.[30] The ongoing economic difficulties Britain experienced during the decade led intellectuals, politicians and the public to investigate alternative strategies. The IEA continued to publish pamphlets and papers in the 1970s but they were joined by other pro-market think-tanks. As we have seen, the CPS was founded in 1974 and although technically independent, clearly had close affiliation with the liberal economic wing of the Conservative Party. The Bow Group aligned itself with economic liberalism at this time and another group, the ASI was also set up. The ASI, founded by Madsen Pirie and Eamonn Butler, was not connected to a political party and unlike the IEA, actively sought to influence government policies.

The impact of think-tanks on British politicians during this period has been contested, contemporary writers increasingly doubting they had significant effect.[31] Conversely, the historical role of Enoch Powell – himself a regular visitor to, and sympathizer with, the IEA – as a key figure in the rise of neoliberal thought in post-war Britain continues to grow. Powell resigned as Chief Secretary to the Treasury over the Macmillan government's economic policies in 1958, which he believed to be inflationary. Powell, also a member of the Mont Pelerin Society, had strong links with the IEA in the 1960s and allegedly attributed almost biblical significance to Hayek's *The Constitution of Liberty*.[32] Ralph Harris (as well as Hayek and Friedman) thought Powell the best hope of implementing their ideas in Britain but his hugely controversial 'Rivers of Blood' speech in 1968 ended his career on the front bench and meant the task of pursuing reforms sought by the IEA was left to others.[33] Nevertheless, most historical narratives pinpoint Powell as the British politician keeping the liberal economic flame alive in the Conservative Party after the war. Indeed, according to Camilla Schofield, Powell's combination of anti-Keynesianism and nationalism readied Britain for 'Thatcher's crusade'.[34] Vinen too highlights the importance of Powell on Thatcherism, saying his influence was 'vastly more important' than 'Austrian philosophers' or 'American economists'.[35] Adrian Williamson has written how 'Powellism' – market orientated nationalism – became an important – although initially a fringe – component of Conservative thinking, as well as Thatcherism.[36] This thesis is supported by Tory politicians such as John Nott, who later described how the 1970s-era 'Economic Dining Club' he attended with the likes of Nicholas Ridley and John Biffen wanted to 'anchor Enoch Powell in the Conservative Party'.[37]

Liberalism beyond the Conservative Party

The road from 1945 to 1979 has been portrayed as one where economic liberalism struggled to exert influence in Britain, except for a few marginal think-tanks and eccentric Tory politicians. When neoliberalism surfaced in the discourse of the 1970s, it was via Friedman's monetarism and Hayek's more overarching influence. This narrative, however, excludes a number of other – albeit less documented – voices. At the peak of the two-party duopoly in the 1950s the Liberal Party reached an electoral nadir of just six seats. Under the leadership of Jo Grimond, however, the Liberals slowly revived in the 1960s. The party was the UK representative of the Liberal International, or World Liberal Union. Prominent Ordoliberal Wilhelm Röpke was a patron of the Liberal International during the 1950s, along with other Mont Pelerin members.[38] In one article, and a letter to the Liberal International in London, the German set out how 'Neo' liberalism was a separate entity from the 'Palaio' variety he had previously criticized.[39]

Röpke's work – which appealed to Conservatives as well as Liberals – was also translated into English in the UK, for instance in *The Free Trader* in the late 1940s. Elliott Dodds's 1944 book *Let's Try Liberalism* also made several admiring references to Röpke's ideas.[40] The 1957 collection *The Unservile State* – which included contributions by Grimond, Dodds and Alan Peacock – saw an early accommodation in Britain with a number of neoliberal positions.[41] A more enigmatic publication, *Time and Tide*, also sought Röpke's articles in the late 1940s and early 1950s. Its deputy editor attended Mont Pelerin meetings and even published Röpke's 1949 presentation at Seelisberg, 'The Proletanised Society'.[42] None of these points demonstrates that economic liberalism had more than a fringe appeal in post-war Britain. Nevertheless it adds some context, showing that a linear narrative from *The Road to Serfdom* to Thatcherism via neoliberal think-tanks and Conservative politicians did not exist.

A consistent theme of this study is to examine the roots of British neoliberalism. Continental and transatlantic, as well home-grown, neoliberalism played its part. The most prominent connection, politically and ideologically, for British neoliberals was the United States. Neoliberals had a transatlantic link long before the well-publicized ideological 'special relationship' between Margaret Thatcher and Ronald Reagan in the 1980s. Friedrich Hayek taught in London and knew Milton Friedman at Chicago. They were both founder members of the Mont Pelerin Society. Ideas were shared between Britain and the United States as free market think-tanks proliferated, including the Heritage Foundation, the American Enterprise Institute and the Hoover Institution in the US.

The 1964 Republican Presidential candidate Barry Goldwater was a controversial figure, not least because he had opposed civil rights legislation. Nevertheless Goldwater brought his version of libertarian and free market ideas to the fore in his campaign as well as his book, *Conscience of a Conservative*.[43] Goldwater was instrumental in refashioning the Republican Party, moulding together two strands of thinking. It became the party that backed a smaller federal government and championed capitalism. In this respect Goldwater combined the ideas of Hayek and Public Choice theory. Second, social conservatism grew louder in its opposition to the (socially) liberal policies of the period, particularly after 1964, towards President Lyndon Johnson's 'Great Society' programmes. The process continued under Richard Nixon and by the time of Ronald Reagan's presidential victory in 1980 the politics of fiscal and social conservatism had become hugely influential in the United States. The American writer George Nash has described this process, of the coming together of the various strands of conservatism, as 'fusionism'.[44] This followed a similar, if less pronounced path in Britain. More liberal social policies in Britain, the 'permissive society', led to a backlash. Margaret Thatcher shared the conservative political instincts of Reagan. The trend can also be seen in the thinking of Keith Joseph, who made a call in 1974 to 'remoralise our national life'.[45] He sought to roll back the economic collectivism and social permissiveness of the post-war years and like many others wanted it replaced by the individualism of capitalism and collectivism of social conservatism.[46]

The early 1970s: the ideological battle takes shape

During his period in office in the 1960s Harold Wilson had presided over a sterling crisis and eventual devaluation and been forced to shelve the *In Place of Strife* legislation that attempted to deal with growing trade union strikes. Edward Heath won the 1970 election with a manifesto, titled *A Better Tomorrow*, of free market measures promising to reform Britain's ailing economy.[47] Wilson derided this as 'Selsdon Man' (after the Selsdon Park Hotel where the manifesto was discussed and set out) and the programme was discarded in 1972 as pressure on Heath mounted. 'Selsdon' has in fact been traced back to Heath's first year as party leader, in 1965, and a pro-market agenda rooted less in academic or think-tank theory than a desire for greater 'professionalism'.[48] Williamson has described how from 1964 the Conservatives 'adopted a set of core policies on tax, union reform and competition, especially European competition. These pre-dated, but remained a part of, Thatcherism'.[49] Other policies that would come to fruition under the Thatcher government, such as council house sales and proposals to introduce business practices into the civil service, also developed under Heath.[50]

The economic picture in 1970s Britain, however, looked evermore chaotic. The explanations and analyses of these events prompted an ideological debate of growing intensity.[51] As we have seen, the crisis narrative was exploited by the right to propose a number of neoliberal influenced policies.[52]

Pro-market thinkers, many directly from or influenced by the Mont Pelerin Society, had ploughed a lonely furrow for 20 years, but were now being taken more seriously. An example of the disdain that many British politicians had held towards economic liberalism was a comment made in the House of Commons during a debate in 1968 on inflation by Labour MP for

Stoke-on-Trent Central, Robert Cant. 'If the Friedman Chicago school of monetary theory is laughed at in the United States, why should we take it seriously here?'[53] This was to change, however. Think-tanks like the IEA *were* being taken notice of in the 1970s and ideas they promoted were being debated in the political mainstream. Monetarism was a key theme in discourse during this period. Milton Friedman had worked extensively on the causes of the Great Depression. His critique concluded that a contraction of the money supply had led to depression, while post-war inflation was caused by excessive monetary expansion. Monetarism blamed inflation in the 1970s on government intervention in the economy. The monetarist prescription was to limit or control the money supply. Later monetarists in Britain split into several camps, including those who, like Friedman, believed in controlling the monetary base or others, such as those at the London Business School (LBS) and the University of Liverpool who developed the 'rational expectations' theory. This split was to become important during the first Thatcher government.[54]

Monetarism was a good example of the different approaches of neoliberals. Austrians, such as Hayek, saw little role for the state whereas Chicagoans like Friedman believed that government had a responsibility for macroeconomic management.[55] In the 1970s monetarism became *de rigueur* in some British newspapers, most notably the *Daily Telegraph, Financial Times* and *The Times*.[56] Samuel Brittan's *Financial Times* column took on a more free market tone from 1969, while Peter Jay (who wrote Jim Callaghan's 1976 Labour Party Conference speech) had taken a more neoliberal stance by 1974.[57] Future Conservative politicians like Richard Ryder have also cited Maurice Green at the *Daily Telegraph* as an influence in spreading free market ideas.[58] Alan Walters, an academic and later an advisor to Margaret Thatcher, wrote *Money in Boom and Slump* for the IEA in the late 1960s. It set out to prove that increasing the quantity of money in an economy, compared to growth in national income, caused inflation.[59] By using historical data Walters not only transmitted a Friedmanite idea, he employed the empirical style of the Chicago School. Terry Burns, then at the LBS, said that Walters more convincingly explained the monetary events between 1973 and 1975 than many others.[60]

Margaret Thatcher's official biographer Charles Moore states the future prime minister had by September 1977 certainly read Walters's *Money in Boom and Slump*. Likewise monetary economist Tim Congdon described his views being formed by, as well as theorists like Don Patinkin and Gottfried Haberler, the growing influence of Milton Friedman and his explanation of the inflation of the early to mid-1970s.[61] Future Conservative Chancellor of the Exchequer Norman Lamont said that he first learnt of Friedman's ideas by reading *Money in Boom and Slump*. [62]

Over the course of the decade politicians in Britain absorbed ideas like monetarism, even if under sufferance. Labour MP Robin Cook said in 1979 that Friedman's 'spirit has hovered over our debates'.[63] Keith Joseph, after becoming involved with the IEA in the 1960s, and announcing his conversion to liberalism prior to the 1970 election, remained strangely quiet about pro-market policies while serving as a high-spending minister in Edward Heath's government 1970–4. When returned to opposition, Joseph lambasted that government's record, embraced monetarism and went on a speaking tour of the UK preaching neoliberal ideas. He founded the 'Hayekian' CPS, along with Margaret Thatcher (although she later played down her role) in 1974 as an alternative to the Conservative Research Department (CRD) to promote the ideas of the free market.[64] One of Joseph's aims at the CPS was to investigate and emulate the West German economic model, even using the term 'social market economy' (although the word 'social', disliked by Margaret Thatcher, was allegedly added only to soothe the austere monetarist prescription). Joseph had hopes for a British 'social market economy' and produced a pamphlet based on his lecture tour called *Monetarism is Not Enough*. As we have seen, Joseph had an interest at this time in Ordoliberal West German politicians like Ludwig Erhard and thinkers like Wilhelm Röpke. The 1975 CPS pamphlet 'Why Britain Needs a Social Market Economy' reads like an Ordoliberal manifesto, namechecking Erhard and Alfred Müller-Armack and setting out a 'compassionate' programme of competitive markets – with the state as the guarantor against monopolies – to produce social outcomes.[65]

Other Conservative politicians openly became proponents of neoliberal ideas. For instance Rhodes Boyson, along with Ralph Harris and Ross McWhirter, set up the Constitutional Book Club in 1970. It published 'Right Turn' that year as well as publications that included 'Goodbye to Nationalization' (O'Sullivan and Hodgson, 1971), 'Must History Repeat Itself' (Fisher, 1974) and 'Rape of Reason' (Marks and Cox, 1975).[66] Other right-wing groups that formed during this period included the National Association for Freedom (NAFF), whose prime concern was the assertion of individual rights against those of the trades unions.[67]

Conservatives were not the only ones interested in strategies like monetarism. David Owen, then of the Labour Party, said he became convinced of the necessity of monetary discipline via Peter Jay, from 1973.[68] James Callaghan also seemed to acknowledge the new thinking in his speech to the Labour Party Conference as leader in 1976 – a speech penned by Jay, his son-in-law.[69] Labour's prime minister was under pressure from the IMF and its loan conditions of that year. Terry Burns identified the IMF in the 1970s as at the vanguard of a movement towards more market orientated economic policies.[70] Historians use these points to demonstrate that in fact the Thatcher government was not the first to employ neoliberal measures.[71] What we can say, however, is that the Thatcher government was considerably more enthusiastic in its embrace of economic liberalism than its predecessor. The acknowledgement of neoliberal ideas like monetary control by both political parties, sections of the press, and institutions like the IMF indicated the broad interest by the 1970s in more market orientated policies.

Bridging the gap between ideology and politics

There are a number of important and influential writers and advisors who played a role in transporting neoliberal ideas into the realm of mainstream politics. Think-tanks, as well as journalists and other 'conduits' played an important role in this process. Adam Ridley, who worked at the CRD and subsequently the Treasury, believed the interest of Conservative politicians 'in a monetarist approach stemmed exclusively from intermediate exponents' such as Peter Jay and Samuel Brittan, the IEA and other figures like Gordon Pepper.[72] Other pro-market advocates such as Alfred Sherman, John Hoskyns and Norman Strauss came to influence future policymakers during this period. Sherman, who during the 1970s thought Margaret Thatcher had 'beliefs, not ideas' was the first director of the CPS, after its inception in 1974.[73] Sherman was attracted to ideological absolutism. He had fought in the Spanish Civil War in the 1930s on the side of the communists before subsequently converting to economic liberalism. As an advisor to Conservative politicians he offered an uncompromising and 'pure' free market programme often focusing on Hayek's ideas.[74] Sherman proved instrumental in persuading Keith Joseph that neoliberal ideas were the answer to Britain's economic problems. Joseph and Sherman were the principal ideological influences upon Margaret Thatcher in the early 1970s.[75]

John Hoskyns was another prominent advisor during Thatcher's years as Leader of the Opposition. Similarly committed to the market as Sherman, as well as 'all-encompassing theories', Hoskyns co-authored the Stepping Stones Report in 1977 that was eventually considered too radical to publish.[76] Stepping Stones set out a political strategy, in particular towards trade union reform that the Conservatives could potentially employ to improve both Britain's economic performance, and the party's long-term fortunes. Norman Strauss was another liberal who advised the Conservative Party in opposition in the 1970s as well as the CPS. Gordon Pepper advised Geoffrey Howe and Margaret Thatcher on monetarism during their years in opposition.[77] Pepper worked in the City of London and provided a link between the business and finance sector and the Conservative Party. As well as influencing in particular Geoffrey Howe, Pepper had access to Conservative leaders when they gained power. Several documents reveal meetings and letters between Margaret Thatcher and Pepper.[78] He consistently urged a strict monetary policy and became a critic of the government after 1987 when Nigel Lawson abandoned monetary targets.[79]

Tim Congdon was another monetary economist who influenced Conservative politicians in the late 1970s and while they were in office. Margaret Thatcher wrote in her memoirs that Congdon was an 'astute' economist while Nigel Lawson also mentioned him. His opinions were sometimes sought by the Thatcher government.[80] Congdon himself, in an interview in 2012, cited Peter Jay (while working together at *The Times*) as important in helping to form his own monetarist beliefs and unique in his prediction of the boom and subsequent inflation during the Heath years and its aftermath.[81] Jay has been consistently cited by politicians and journalists as an influence during the 1970s. Sherman, Hoskyns, Pepper, Congdon and Strauss were all important because they acted as conduits between raw theory and the business of policymaking. That is not to say that Conservative politicians like Joseph and Thatcher suddenly became ideological theorists. Robin Harris wrote that Margaret Thatcher's exposure to the CPS and thinkers like Sherman allowed her to work through the connection between her political instincts and her political position, but that she was never 'converted' to neoliberals like Hayek and Friedman.[82] Rather that these ideas provided the 'instruments' to seek to achieve already determined political goals that the then available tools seemed ill-equipped to reach.[83] Bernard Donoughue thought that 'the strong campaign by the Friedmanite monetarists definitely added force and conviction to the Thatcherite critique of Labour and also began to capture the intellectual power centres of decision-making'.[84]

Alfred Sherman said in 1990 that 'people like Keith and Margaret turned to Hayek and Friedman to justify what they already thought' while Enoch Powell expanded this to the party as a whole in 1989: 'comprehensive theories are antipathetic to the Conservative mentality. It is suspicious of theory.'[85] These opinions give credence to the 'statecraft' thesis or a more general climate of ideas.[86] For historians like Richard Vinen, 'Thatcherism was always about power, and it is the nature of power to adjust to circumstances'.[87] Conservative politician Peter Lilley has said that rather than exerting direct influence on Margaret Thatcher, the think-tanks of the 1970s provided a 'supporting wind'.[88]

When Edward Heath was challenged for the leadership of the Conservative Party in 1975 some in the party hoped Keith Joseph would stand. A number of controversial speeches, invoking among other things eugenics, meant he did not seek the post. Tory MPs from the economic liberal wing of the party still wanted a representative, however, allowing Margaret Thatcher to stand and surprisingly, win. The year before Friedrich Hayek had been awarded the Nobel Prize in Economics with Milton Friedman emulating this in 1976. The tide was turning for neoliberals. At the same time the movement began to see a longer decline in its reputation. This has been attributed by writers like Taylor Boas and Jordan Gans-Morse to Milton Friedman's connections with the Pinochet regime in Chile from 1975.[89] The link was made that neoliberalism had authoritarian and anti-democratic tendencies, which could also feed into ideas of a 'strong-state'. The accusation that neoliberalism required curbs on democratic processes has been levelled at not only Friedman, but also the Austrian and Freiburg Schools.[90]

Margaret Thatcher as leader of the opposition

The years in opposition from 1974–79 saw a flurry of research and policy initiatives by groups close to the Conservative Party. New leader Margaret

Thatcher was sympathetic to the principles of economic liberalism but was not, in public, zealously pro-market at this time. She, like her mentor Keith Joseph, had loyally served Edward Heath's government without dissenting over the U-turns or abandonment of the 1970 Selsdon programme. Thatcher was not as vocal about the virtues of the market compared to others like Geoffrey Howe, Nigel Lawson or Joseph himself. It was this period in the mid- to late 1970s when high inflation and trade union strikes provided a space for the Tories to propose a different strategy, or at least one that pursued more of the neoliberalism that the Callaghan government had already embarked upon. The difficulties Labour had in accommodating the unions and running the economy meant the Conservatives could allow Callaghan to govern himself out of office. The IMF loan of 1976 was an apparent symbol of Britain's post-war decline, from major world power to debtor; the 'sick man of Europe'. The IMF attached structural conditions to the loan, which in part explained Callaghan's change in policy towards inflation. In their work, *Goodbye Great Britain*, Kathleen Burk and Alec Cairncross argue that 1976 was a year of crisis in particular and the turning point in ideas of economic management.[91]

Monetarism, however, was divisive in Britain, particularly as the only practical application of the doctrine was at that time in Chile. From 1975, Chilean dictator Augusto Pinochet allowed a group of economic liberals dubbed the 'Chicago Boys' to guide economic policy. They had either attended the University of Chicago in the 1950s and 1960s, or its affiliated institution, the Catholic University of Chile.[92] The crucial link here was with Milton Friedman, both a liberal and a libertarian. Presumably he would have approved of the economic policies and the intervention to control the money supply but not the oppression of human rights. In a letter to Pinochet in 1975, Friedman argued for 'shock treatment' to cure Chile's ills, to reduce government spending by 25 per cent within six months and for 'the removal of as many obstacles as possible that now hinder the private market'.[93] Friedman also used a phrase more synonymous with Ordoliberalism: 'The key economic problems of Chile are clearly twofold: inflation, and the promotion of a healthy social market economy.'[94]

Friedman later commented that economic reform in Chile created a 'miracle' and that the adoption of pro-market policies allowed the country to make the transition to democracy in 1990. Friedman remarked in 2000 that 'the really important thing about the Chilean business is that free markets did work their way in bringing about a free society'.[95] Friedrich Hayek also praised Chile as a development model. Margaret Thatcher, although broadly sympathetic to the Pinochet regime, did challenge Hayek on this in a 1982 letter. 'The progression from Allende's Socialism to the free enterprise capitalist economy of the 1980s is a striking example of economic reform. However, some of the measures adopted in Chile are quite unacceptable.'[96]

Friedman and Hayek's attitude towards Chile signified a principle that has been attributed to contemporary understandings of neoliberalism, that when democracy and markets collide, the latter will prevail. The theme is one that applies to many interpretations of neoliberalism – that of a general disregard or disdain of democracy. Last, it presupposes another neoliberal principle, that essentially markets create conditions for the state and civil society, not the other way round. From the more benign idea of the state of thinkers like Friedman and Ordoliberals like Röpke and Rüstow, to the harsher real-world manifestations like Pinochet's Chile, the market is the most important component in society. In this respect, using the state to secure conditions propitious for market mechanisms is the defining feature of neoliberalism.

Jim Bulpitt has written that monetarism was used as a tool of Conservative 'statecraft' and argued it was an attempt to 'disentangle the central state from "interests"' as well as a way to regain power.[97] In the 1970s though, the Chilean example made it easy for British politicians to criticize monetarism and other neoliberal measures by presenting the approach as part of an extreme programme. Dr Jeremy Bray, Labour MP for Motherwell and Wishaw, said in the House of Commons in 1976, 'when Friedman took on the job of advising the Chilean dictators they made slashing cuts in money supply, whereupon the rate of inflation escalated fantastically and the level of unemployment soared'.[98] In addition, the idea of macroeconomic control of the money supply was not agreed upon within the Mont Pelerin Society and threatened to cause a split between its two most notable protagonists. In a letter to the IEA's Arthur Seldon in 1985, Friedrich Hayek wrote, 'I have long regretted my failure to take time to criticize Friedman's Positive Economics' but was worried about 'the constant danger that the Mont Pelerin society might split into a Friedmanite and a Hayekian wing'.[99] For Hayek, control of money was yet another form of government intervention that was illiberal and would distort the market economy. Hayek advocated ending government monopoly on issuing legal tender to allow currency competition.[100]

Monetary policy as a means of bringing inflation under control, however, was becoming more prominent in British politics. Even Labour ministers were abandoning Keynesianism. David Owen was 'very disillusioned with the Labour Party in the 1970s' but 'hugely encouraged by Jim Callaghan's speech in 1976' (which Keith Joseph quipped could have been written by Milton Friedman) and that 'Thatcher was helped by Callaghan and Healey's acceptance of monetarism'.[101] Critics on the left, such as Andre Gunner Frank, have criticized the 1970s governments of James Callaghan and Jimmy Carter as having introduced neoliberal measures by stealth despite being elected on social democratic programmes. For Gunner Frank, this laid the foundation for Thatcherism and Reaganomics.[102] The reality was that both Carter and Callaghan had to wrestle with the difficult conditions of rising energy prices and 'stagflation'. Both were voted out of office in favour of more neoliberal manifestos.

The Right Approach (1976), *The Right Approach to the Economy* (1977) and Stepping Stones (1977) have been viewed as key documents from the period and have been examined in much of the literature on Thatcherism. *The Right*

Approach was published as a Conservative Party pamphlet. It did not contain radical measures but did underline some of the general themes: 'Socialist policies have been a major cause of these distortions of our economy. The Socialist obsession with extending the power of the State has led to widespread nationalisation and to massive growth of government spending and bureaucracy.'[103] *The Right Approach* did make a brief allusion to monetarism when talking about collective bargaining. 'Monetary restraint, including the setting of targets for monetary expansion, is a key feature of economic policy, though by no means the only one. Excessive wage claims should clearly not be accommodated by an easy expansion in bank lending.'[104] Rising labour costs and trade union demands had exacerbated stagflation in the 1970s by causing 'wage stickiness' (the cost of wages not responding to other market signals, such as declining productivity).

The following year came *The Right Approach to the Economy*, authored by Conservative MPs Keith Joseph, Geoffrey Howe, David Howell and Jim Prior. This again emphasized the necessity of realistic and responsible collective bargaining. In this document, however, the explicit control of the money supply was outlined as well as a reduction in the Public Sector Borrowing Requirement (PSBR).[105] There was a prescription of 'strict control by the Government of the rate of growth of the money supply and of its own spending. Unless public spending is reduced, price inflation cannot be contained.'[106] Here we can see the direct application of neoliberal thinking into (albeit in opposition) a policymaking document. Margaret Thatcher later thought much of the party's politics were weak in opposition but the formulation of ideas was vital.[107] There were two main themes of *The Right Approach* and *The Right Approach to the Economy*: the urgency to tackle industrial relations and the persistent problem of inflation. From 1976 to 1978 the Callaghan government attempted to forge a 'social contract', an underlying agreement with the Trades Union Conference (TUC) to limit pay rises to (an arbitrary) 5 per cent . Over this period the fragile compromise seemed to have some effect as inflation declined and strikes were kept at bay.[108] So good, in fact, were things looking for the Labour government that Callaghan almost called an election in autumn 1978, his personal popularity constantly remaining higher than that of Margaret Thatcher.

This was to prove a pivotal moment in post-war British history. Callaghan dithered and did not go to the polls and was to rue his decision as the social contract came apart. The 'Winter of Discontent' cost him his majority and gave added legitimacy to not only the Conservative policy recommendations in opposition but also the general intellectual climate that a change in approach was needed. Margaret Thatcher also identified individual responsibility and law and order as paramount, as opposed to the permissive and collectivist culture that she thought had predominated since the 1960s.[109] She saw the turmoil of 1970s Britain as a loss of state authority that had to be reversed.[110] The crisis and declinist narrative, particularly after the Winter of Discontent, were relentlessly exploited by Thatcher.[111] The strikes of 1978 and 1979 also inadvertently acted as a 'stepping stone', of the kind described by Hoskyns in his unpublished report.[112]

Although her beliefs during this period were developing, by the time she came to power Thatcher was more explicit in extolling the potency of the market. In a speech in 1979 she said: '[T]he greatest economic successes since 1945 have come in those nations where free enterprise has been allowed to flower without impediment.'[113] One account sets out Thatcher's three object-ives upon coming to power: to significantly change the conduct of fiscal and monetary policy, a 'conscious redefinition of the role of the state in the economy with a renewed emphasis on the virtues of the free market', and a gradual rebalancing of relations between labour and capital in favour of the latter.[114] The reimposition of the authority of the state and an economy powered more by free enterprise gives broad credence to a 'free economy–strong state' thesis, although in a cruder way than envisaged by the Freiburg neoliberals of the 1930s. For them a strong state was about allowing markets to operate efficiently and providing preferable social outcomes by preventing monopoly and corruption of the political process. Nevertheless, the Conser-vative Party – and not only on the free market wing – was in favour of revi-talizing the Office of Fair Trading to promote competition by 1979.[115]

Stepping Stones, a policy project led by John Hoskyns working with Norman Strauss during 1977 and 1978, was never published. It is of some sig-nificance for the insights it provides into the ideas being tabled at the time, the internal divisions in deciding policy and the battle between neoliberal ideology and political expediency. Margaret Thatcher decided that the publication of Stepping Stones would be too much of a risk and could make the public wary of her leadership. In her memoirs, however, she claimed Stepping Stones had been the main inspiration behind policy formulation.[116] Some historians believe Stepping Stones has been mythologized by Thatcherites, while others see certain policies, such as trade union legislation, as evidence that the approach was actually employed in power.[117] Hoskyns's role was to 'produce and outline a "strategy framework" for the Tory Party to cover what we have called the *Turn-around*'. This was intended to formulate a set of policies that could provide substance for a manifesto or programme in government.[118]

Strategically Hoskyns thought that policies 'will in some cases require changes in "public consciousness" before they are politically possible'.[119] This was envisaged as 'Phase Three of a process which starts with the injection of new ideas, in order to soften up public opinion, followed by public debate, leading finally to the implementation of policy through legislation'.[120] This fitted with Hayek's views on shifting the ideological climate before the gov-erning reality could change. This process had in fact been taking place for several years before Hoskyns's 1978 comment. As we have seen, some politi-cians, journalists, commentators and academics had accepted some of the tenets of neoliberal thought over the previous decade. This shift meant that some of the policies found in Stepping Stones would indeed become 'politi-cally possible'.

One conversation between Geoffrey Howe and Hoskyns in August 1977 showed the priorities of the then shadow chancellor. Hoskyns said that Howe's key policies were curing inflation ('he agreed the real explanations of inflation are a combination of Keynes and Friedman') and to create a liberal economic climate by deregulation, switching from direct to indirect taxation and reducing the overall tax burden.[121] Howe also wanted to 'liberalize exchange control on capital outflows' and discussed his enterprise zone idea.[122] It is also clear that Hoskyns became infuriated at the reluctance of Margaret Thatcher and her Shadow Cabinet, as well as the CRD, to take a more radical position. In one note to Keith Joseph, Hoskyns wrote 'my interpretation is at present that she (and therefore her advisors) are completely lost and confused'.[123] The friction between Hoskyns and Chris Patten at the CRD was also a regular theme. Hoskyns accused Patten of being 'concerned with election results only. He therefore sees no need for the stick-on-stick process of changing attitudes and behaviour for the long haul.'[124]

The Right Approach, The Right Approach to the Economy and Stepping Stones had some impact in guiding the Conservative Party's policies. There were a number of other groups that would also be significant, such as the Economic Reconstruction Group, and Nicholas Ridley's report on the nationalized industries. Rarely were the think-tanks, journalists, academics and advisors direct disciples of one ideological viewpoint. What we can say, however, is those that made direct policy recommendations were leaning more towards Friedman's Chicago School. This is for the simple reason the positivist approach of the Chicagoans produced evidence, data analysis and therefore real-world models. The more philosophical and abstract Austrian School, based on first principles, was less suited to direct influence or the 'politically possible'. This may have also been a reason that the modern reading of neoliberalism in general took on a Chicagoan hue. These distinctions though, were probably not important to the Conservatives as the 1979 election approached. The problems of an unstable economy and trade union militancy were uppermost in voters', and the Party's, thinking. The events of the decade, and most recently the Winter of Discontent, created the opportunity for a change in approach. Margaret Thatcher won a clear majority on 3 May 1979 and wrote to Friedrich Hayek a few days later:

> I am very proud to have learnt so much from you over the past few years. I hope that some of those ideas will be put into practice by my Government in the next few months. As one of your keenest supporters, I am determined that we should succeed. If we do so, your contribution to our ultimate victory will have been immense.[125]

Whether the *Constitution of Liberty*, and Hayek's ideas in general, would in fact be 'what we believe' – as Thatcher is once reported to have insisted – is examined in the following chapters.

Conclusion

Neoliberal ideas were contextualized and condensed by think-tanks, intellectuals and journalists that, over the space of 30 years, altered the ideological climate. Eventually these principles gained traction. The model which the think-tanks and writers like Hayek wanted to emulate, in the British context, was the Fabian Society. Much has been made of the impact of neoliberalism but in the 1970s the first major policy that gained a degree of acceptance in Britain was the cross-party interest in monetary control. Journalists such as Peter Jay and Samuel Brittan provided a bridge between theory, think-tanks and public opinion. Newspapers like the *Daily Telegraph*, *Financial Times*, *The Times* and *The Economist* were important in altering perceptions in the 1970s. Last, economically liberal 'conduits' influenced politicians by promulgating the virtues of the market. Gordon Pepper, John Hoskyns and Alfred Sherman, among others, helped persuade some Conservative politicians of the credibility of neoliberal ideas. Out of these politicians it was Geoffrey Howe who had the longest standing interest in liberal economics and who most doggedly pursued neoliberal ideas during the first Thatcher government. He was determined in his policy of monetary restraint to tame inflation and was at the forefront in implementing several liberal reforms: removal of exchange controls, enterprise zones and lower rates of income tax.

Notes

1 John Maynard Keynes, *The General Theory of Employment, Interest, and Money* (Basingstoke: Palgrave Macmillan, 2007 [1936]), 383.
2 Richard Cockett, *Thinking the Unthinkable. Think-Tanks and the Economic Counter Revolution 1931–1983* (London: Harper Collins, 1995), 232–236, 261.
3 Mark Skousen, *Vienna & Chicago. Friends or Foes? A Tale of Two Schools of Free-Market Economics* (Washington, DC: Capital Press, 2005), 3–4; Daniel Stedman-Jones, *Masters of the Universe. Hayek, Friedman, and the Birth of Neoliberal Politics* (Oxford: Princeton University Press, 2012), 107.
4 Stedman-Jones, *Masters*, 100.
5 Cockett, *Thinking*, 328. Cockett expands upon an idea from Samuel Brittan in 1972 that 'every age accepts the doctrines evolved to deal with the previous one and neglects the message most relevant to its own time'.
6 Andrew Gamble, *Hayek. The Iron Cage of Liberty* (Cambridge: Polity Press, 1996), 6. Gamble cites A. V. Dicey's study *Lectures on the Relation between Law and Public Opinion in England during the Nineteenth Century* (London, 1926).
7 Cockett, *Thinking*, 6.
8 Cockett, *Thinking*, 14–15.
9 Peter Clarke, *A Question of Leadership* (London: Hamish Hamilton, 1991), 166–168.
10 Clarke, *A Question*, 170.
11 Bernard Donoughue, *Prime Minister: The Conduct of Policy under Harold Wilson and James Callaghan* (London: Jonathan Cape, 1987), 79.
12 Paul Addison's *The Road to 1945* (1975) is one classic 'post-war consensus' text. This was symbolized by *The Economist* in 1954 by the term 'Butskellism', which apparently represented the overlapping economic policies of Conservative Chancellor R. A. Butler and his Labour predecessor Hugh Gaitskell.

13 For instance, *The Myth of Consensus: New Views on British History, 1945–64 (Contemporary History in Context)*, ed. H. Jones and M. Kandiah (Basingstoke: Palgrave Macmillan, 1996).

14 Richard Vinen, *Thatcher's Britain. The Politics and Social Upheaval of the 1980s* (London: Simon and Schuster, 2009), 31.

15 Matthias Matthijs, *Ideas and Economic Crises in Britain from Attlee to Blair 1945–2005* (Abingdon: Routledge, 2011), 116–117.

16 Wernhard Möschel, 'The Proper Scope of Government Viewed from an Ordoliberal Perspective: The Example of Competition Policy', *Journal of Institutional and Theoretical Economics (JITE)*/Zeitschrift für die gesamte Staatswissenschaft 157:1 (2001), 10.

17 Donoughue, *Prime Minister*, 80.

18 Interview with Lord Owen, 17 January 2010.

19 Ben Jackson, 'The Think-Tank Archipelago: Thatcherism and Neoliberalism', in *Making Thatcher's Britain*, ed. Ben Jackson and Robert Saunders (Cambridge: Cambridge University Press, 2012), 47–49; Tim Bale, *The Conservatives since 1945* (Oxford: Oxford University Press, 2012), 49, 60.

20 Neil Rollings, 'Cracks in the Post-War Keynesian Settlement? The Role of Organized Business in Britain in the Rise of Neoliberalism before Margaret Thatcher', *Twentieth Century British History* 24:4 (2013), 640.

21 Rollings, 'Cracks', 646–652.

22 Andrew Denham and Mark Garnett, *Keith Joseph* (Chesham: Acumen, 2001), 137.

23 Interview with Lord Howe, 13 July 2009.

24 Interview with Lord Howe.

25 Interview with Lord Howe.

26 Interview with Lord Howe.

27 James Barr, *The Bow Group. A History* (London: Politicos, 2001), 93–94.

28 Barr, *Bow Group*, 111.

29 John Hoskyns, *Just in Time. Inside the Thatcher Revolution* (London: Aurum Press, 2000), 399.

30 Roger Middleton, *The British Economy since 1945. Engaging with the Debate* (Basingstoke: Macmillan, 2000), 65.

31 Adrian Williamson, *Conservative Economic Policymaking and the Birth of Thatcherism, 1964–1979* (Basingstoke: Palgrave Macmillan, 2015), 226.

32 Simon Heffer, *Like the Roman. The Life of Enoch Powell* (London: Weidenfeld and Nicolson, 1998), 266.

33 Heffer, *Like The Roman*, 367, 424.

34 Camilla Schofield, '"A nation or no nation?" Enoch Powell and Thatcherism', in *Making Thatcher's Britain*, ed. Ben Jackson and Robert Saunders (Cambridge: Cambridge University Press, 2012), 98.

35 Vinen, *Thatcher's Britain*, 6.

36 Williamson, *Conservative*, 4.

37 John Nott, *Here Today, Gone Tomorrow: Reflections of an Errant Politician* (London: Politicos, 2002), 135–137.

38 The Papers of Wilhelm Röpke, Institut für Wirtschaftspolitik, Cologne, Germany (hereafter Röpke); correspondence between Röpke and John H. MacCullum Scott (Hon Secretary of Liberal International), 1952–55.

39 Röpke, letter from Röpke to MacCallum Scott, 5 April 1954.

40 Röpke, correspondence between Röpke and Deryck Abel, Secretary of the Free Trade Union 1946–47.

41 Ben Jackson, 'Currents of Neo-Liberalism: British Political Ideologies and the New Right, *c.*1955–1979', *English Historical Review* 131 (2016), 827–830.

42 Röpke, correspondence between Röpke and Veronica Wedgwood, deputy editor of *Time and Tide*, 1946–53; letter from Röpke to Bertrand de Jouvenel, 27 September 1949.

43 Jeff Faux, *The Global Class War. How America's Bipartisan Elite Lost Our Future – and What It Will Take to Win It Back* (Hoboken, NJ: John Wiley, 2006), 82.

44 Stedman-Jones, *Masters*, 12.

45 Matthew Grimley, 'Thatcherism, Morality and Religion', in *Making Thatcher's Britain*, ed. Ben Jackson and Robert Saunders (Cambridge: Cambridge University Press, 2012), 83.

46 Andrew Denham and Mark Garnett, *Keith Joseph* (Chesham: Acumen, 2001), 263–264.

47 Conservative Party Manifesto, 1970, accessed 10 October 2010. www.conservative-party.net/manifestos/1970/1970-conservative-manifesto.shtml.

48 Bale, *Conservatives*, 130–135.

49 Williamson, *Conservative*, 21.

50 Bale, *Conservatives*, 137–138.

51 Norman Barry, *The New Right* (Beckenham: Croom Helm, 1987), 115.

52 Matthijs, *Ideas*, 116–119.

53 Robert Cant, *Parliamentary Debates* (Commons), 766, 20 June 1968, 1304–6.

54 Patrick Minford, 'Inflation, Unemployment and the Pound', in *Margaret Thatcher's Revolution. How it Happened and What it Meant*, ed. S. Roy and J. Clarke (London: Continuum, 2005), 50–66.

55 Barry, *New Right*, 23.

56 Cockett, *Thinking*, 183.

57 Jackson, 'The Think-Tank Archipelago', 54.

58 Interview with Lord Ryder 23 February 2011; Jackson, 'The Think-Tank Archipelago', 55.

59 Alan Walters, *Money in Boom and Slump. An Empirical Inquiry into British Experience since the 1880s* (Tonbridge: IEA, 1971 [1969], 16–17.

60 Interview with Lord Burns, 12 May 2011.

61 Interview with Tim Congdon, 24 February 2012. Don Patinkin was a monetary economist influenced by Keynes but one-time lecturer at the University of Chicago. Gottfried Haberler was of the Austrian School and specialized in international trade.

62 Stedman-Jones, *Masters*, 207.

63 Robin Cook, *Parliamentary Debates* (Commons), 969, 4 July 1979, 1424–502.

64 Stedman-Jones, *Masters*, 177.

65 Centre for Policy Studies (CPS), *Why Britain Needs a Social Market Economy* (Chichester: Barry Rose, 1975), 6–8.

66 Cockett, *Thinking*, 176.

67 Vinen, *Thatcher's Britain*, 83.

68 Interview with Lord Owen, 17 January 2010.

69 Kenneth O. Morgan, *Callaghan. A Life* (Oxford: Oxford University Press, 1997), 535; Donoughue, *Prime Minister*, 82.

70 Interview with Lord Burns, 12 May 2011.

71 Stedman-Jones, *Masters*, 215–272.

72 Sir Adam Ridley, personal correspondence with the author, 2 May 2013.

73 Cockett, *Thinking*, 266.

74 Interview with Lord Ryder, 23 February 2011; Gamble, *Hayek*, 167.

75 Alfred Sherman, *Paradoxes of Power. Reflections on the Thatcher Interlude*, ed. M. Garnett (Exeter: Imprint Academic, 2005), 45–50.

76 Vinen, *Thatcher's Britain*, 82.

77 Lord Howe of Aberavon, 'Can 364 Economists all be Wrong?', in *The Chancellors' Tales, Managing the British Economy*, ed. H. Davies (Cambridge: Polity, 2006), 105.

78 Records of the Prime Minister's Office: Correspondence and Papers, 1979–1997. Held at the National Archives, Kew, London. PREM19/183 (Hereafter PREM19), meeting between Thatcher and Pepper, 18 July 1979, letter from Pepper to Thatcher, 16 May 1979, PREM19/33, monetary seminar 18 July 1979.

79 M. J. Oliver, 'The Macroeconomic Policies of Mr Lawson', *Contemporary British History* 13:1 (1999), 178.

80 Interview with Tim Congdon, 24 February, 2012.When interviewed, Tim Congdon said he believed Margaret Thatcher sometimes read his work although he was not close to her personally. Nigel Lawson, in his memoirs (1993) wrote that Tim Congdon used to attend meetings of the 'Gooies', prominent economists of the day.

81 Interview with Tim Congdon, 24 February 2012.

82 Robin Harris, *Not For Turning. The Life of Margaret Thatcher* (London: Bantam Press, 2013), 100–101.

83 Harris, *Not For Turning*, 100.

84 Donoughue, *Prime Minister*, 80.

85 John Ranelagh, *Thatcher's People. An Insider's Account of the Politics, the Power and the Personalities* (London: Harper Collins, 1991), 182–183.

86 Jim Bulpitt, 'The Discipline of the New Democracy: Mrs Thatcher's Domestic Statecraft', *Political Studies* 34:1 (1986), 19–39.

87 Vinen, *Thatcher's Britain*, 4.

88 Interview with Peter Lilley, 7 February 2011.

89 Boas and Gans-Morse, 'Neoliberalism,' 150.

90 Bruno Molitor, 'Schwäche der Demokratie' [The Weakness of Democracy], *ORDO. Jahrbuch für die Ordnung von Wirtschaft und Gesellschaft* [Ordo Yearbook of Economic and Social Order] (Stuttgart: Gustav Fischer Verlag, Band 34, 1983), 38; F. A. Hayek, *Social Justice, Socialism & Democracy. Three Australian Lectures by F. A. Hayek* (Turramurra, NSW: Centre for Independent Studies, 1979), 39–45.

91 Kathleen Burk and Alec Cairncross, *'Goodbye Great Britain'* (London: Yale University Press, 1992), 215.

92 David Harvey, *A Brief History of Neoliberalism* (Oxford: Oxford University Press, 2005) 8.

93 Letter to General Pinochet from Milton Friedman, 21 April 1975, in *Two Lucky People. Memoirs*, ed. Milton Friedman and Rose Friedman (Chicago, IL: University of Chicago Press, 1998), 591–594.

94 Friedman and Friedman, *Two Lucky People*, 591.

95 'The Commanding Heights. The Battle for the World Economy', PBS Documentary (2002), accessed 10 May 2012. www.pbs.org/wgbh/commanding heights/hi/story/index.html.

96 MTF, Letter from Margaret Thatcher to Friedrich Hayek, 17 February 1982, MTF 117179.

97 Bulpitt, 'Discipline'; Jim Tomlinson, 'Thatcher, Monetarism and the Politics of Inflation', in *Making Thatcher's Britain*, ed. Ben Jackson and Robert Saunders (Cambridge: Cambridge University Press, 2012), 77.

98 Jeremy Bray, *Parliamentary Debates* (Commons), 910, 3 May 1976, 843–982.

99 MTF 117203, Letter from Friedrich Hayek to Arthur Seldon, 13 May 1985;

100 Gamble, *Hayek*, 169–170; F. A. Hayek, 'Toward a Free Market Monetary System', *Journal of Libertarian Studies* 3:1 (Spring 1979), accessed 10 February 2014. http://mises.org/journals/jls/3_1/3_1_1.pdf, 1–5.

101 Interview with Lord Owen, 17 January 2010, *Parliamentary Debates* (Commons), 953, 4 July 1978, 253–380; Keith Joseph said

We thought that the Prime Minister, in that notable speech at the 1976 Labour Party Conference – a speech that could have been drafted by Milton

Friedman – had finally established in the Labour Party's understanding that no country can spend its way out of unemployment.

102 Andre Gunner Frank, 'No End to History! History to No End?' *Social Justice* 17:4 (Winter 1990), 17.

103 MTF 109439, *The Right Approach* (London: Conservative Central Office, 1976), accessed 19 October 2010. www.margaretthatcher.org/document/109439, 21.

104 Ibid., 38.

105 Geoffrey Howe, *Conflict of Loyalty* (Basingstoke: Macmillan, 1994), 101.

106 MTF 110203, *The Right Approach to the Economy* (London: Conservative Central Office, 1977) accessed 19 October 2010. www.margaretthatcher.org/document/110203, 7.

107 Margaret Thatcher, *The Path to Power* (London: Harper Collins, 1995), 317.

108 H. Conroy, *Callaghan* (London: Haus Publishing, 2006) 106. The obvious exception to this was the fire service strike from November 1977 to January 1978 when Second World War 'green goddesses' were brought into service.

109 E. A. Reitan, *The Thatcher Revolution. Margaret Thatcher, John Major, Tony Blair, and the Transformation of Modern Britain, 1979–2001* (Oxford: Rowman and Littlefield, 2003), 18.

110 Andrew Gamble, 'Privatization, Thatcherism and the British State', in *Thatcher's Law*, ed. A. Gamble and C. Wells (Oxford: Basil Blackwell, 1989), 1.

111 Matthijs, *Ideas*, 115.

112 Matthijs, *Ideas*, 115.

113 The Papers of Margaret Thatcher (Cambridge: Churchill Archives, hereafter THCR), 2/6/2/170. Draft speech for Margaret Thatcher, written by Hugh Thomas for the European Democratic Union dinner, 12 July 1979.

114 Matthijs, *Ideas*, 122.

115 Williamson, *Conservative*, 140, 155; Conservative Party Manifesto 1979, accessed 29 May 2017. www.conservativemanifesto.com/1979/1979-conservative-manifesto. shtml.

116 Margaret Thatcher, *The Downing Street Years* (London: HarperCollins, 1993), 40.

117 Vinen, *Thatcher's Britain*, 90; Matthijs, *Ideas*, 132.

118 The Hoskyns Papers (Cambridge: Churchill Archives, hereafter HOSK), 1/21 'Second Draft of note by Hoskyns to Keith Joseph summarising the "assignment you would like me to undertake"', 14 July 1977.

119 HOSK 1/105, 'Progress report of the Policy Search Group', 10 April 1978.

120 HOSK 1/105, 'Progress report'.

121 HOSK 1/33 'Detailed notes by Hoskyns for Norman Strauss and Terry Price relating to his meeting with Geoffrey Howe', 26 August 1977.

122 Ibid.

123 HOSK 1/18, 'Handwritten notes by John Hoskyns following Keith Joseph's conversation with Margaret Thatcher on the development of Hoskyns's ideas', 10 July 1977.

124 HOSK 1/80, 'Copy of a letter by Hoskyns to Keith Joseph relating to a note by Christopher Patten, "Further thoughts on strategy"', 27 February 1978.

125 MTF 112178, 'Letter from Margaret Thatcher to Friedrich von Hayek', 18 May 1979.

3 Economic policy and the Thatcher government

Chapters 1 and 2 looked at the different schools of thought that led the resurgence in liberal economics before and after the Second World War and how they began in the 1970s to exert influence on the British political process. The ideological debate was particularly focused on the control of inflation. Neoliberal thinkers believed that markets and fiscal conservatism should be privileged over Keynesian economic instruments. This chapter will consider the early economic policy of the Thatcher government. Neoliberal models will be shown to have been implemented in a more faithful way in economic rather than other policies examined later in this book. Last, although a number of thinkers can be seen to have had an impact, it was the expedient brand of neoliberalism of Milton Friedman and the Chicago School that was more important than other strands, such as Friedrich Hayek and the Austrian School. Monetary policy will be examined first as this was central to the government's early anti-inflation strategy. Chapter 4 will look at exchange control removal and enterprise zones as pro-market signals as well as the first step towards broader deregulation.

It was during the crises of the 1970s that journalists, politicians and possibly even the general public began to entertain the possibility of challenging the status quo. The model of Keynesian economic policies, collective bargaining by powerful trades unions and heavily regulated private enterprise appeared to be faltering. Some, such as the left of the Labour Party and militant trade union leaders (as well as an increasingly vocal Trotskyist left) believed this was the opportunity to pursue a more socialist path. The inevitable crises and eventual collapse inherent in capitalism were, according to Marxist analysis, apparently close at hand.[1] What these groups proposed was higher taxes, more nationalization and state control. MPs like Tony Benn came to encapsulate this line of thinking in mainstream British politics and it was to cause the schism in the Labour Party that led to the creation of the centre-left Social Democratic Party (SDP) in 1981. On the pro-market right, however, a different viewpoint was taken. According to liberals, the problems of the 1970s were down to the 'ratchet' effect of socialism. Neoliberal thinkers proposed a shift to market orientated policies which would allow British companies and individuals to create wealth and help the economy grow. The public sector was perceived to be 'crowding out' the private sector during this period. It was this polarized ideological debate that made the change of the era so turbulent. For economic liberals though, the basic importance of free markets was not in question, but what they should look like.

The first Thatcher government's economic policy

With a majority of 43 seats and after a decade of apparently interminable problems, manifest in the Winter of Discontent, James Callaghan's 'sea-change' narrative suggested many would be receptive to a new approach in 1979.[2] Several of the themes that became most synonymous with Thatcherism: privatization, a showdown with the trades unions, Big Bang in the City of London; lay ahead. Some economic liberal writers have concluded that the first Thatcher government was too slow in bringing about reform and that the only major success was the reduction in inflation.[3] In its pursuit of this goal unemployment rocketed to three million by January 1982, up from under a million in 1975. The quest to defeat inflation and reduce public borrowing, however, was the primary goal for the Conservatives in 1979. Inflation had dogged the British economy for several years (it was 10 per cent in May 1979, down from 27 per cent in 1975).[4] By 1983 it had fallen to 4 per cent and remained low until the end of the decade and the 'Lawson Boom'. The methods used to bring this down were to exacerbate an already deep recession, the dogmatic adherence to monetary control suggesting economic policy in the Thatcher government was guided by ideology.

Neoliberals, such as those from the Chicago School or LBS, believed a key role of government was to maintain stable and benign macroeconomic conditions.[5] Although the means to achieve the objective differed, the importance of this was shared by all the strains of neoliberalism studied here. For instance, one of the architects of Ordoliberalism, Walter Eucken, outlined in 'Policy for a Competitive Order' his prime goals as monetary policy and a stable currency, isolated from political influence.[6] The most prominent 'monetarist', however, was Milton Friedman. He firmly opposed inflation, as did all neoliberals, for a number of reasons. Friedman had written extensively on the monetary conditions that he believed caused the 1930s Depression and that a contraction of the supply of money made a recession much worse.[7] According to Friedman, where inflation occurred in an attempt to prevent or ease unemployment it caused several problems. Wages and prices increased while productivity and output often did not. 'Wage stickiness' occurred, whereby wages should have (if left to the free market) decreased with declining productivity but were either maintained or increased.

Friedman's critique of the Philips Curve showed that inflation and unemployment were not mutually exclusive; one could not simply be bought at the cost of the other but could happen concurrently.[8] This challenged post-war orthodoxy. In his 1963 book *A Monetary History of the United States*, written with Anna Schwartz, Friedman's much repeated phrase was first set out: 'Inflation is always and everywhere a monetary phenomenon.'[9] Friedman rejected Keynesian demand management, asserted that the Philips Curve was a temporary phenomenon and that both unemployment and inflation had risen in the 1960s and 1970s.[10] His ideas were taken up in the 1970s by think-tanks such as the IEA, journalists such as Peter Jay and Samuel Brittan and economists like Gordon Pepper, David Laidler, Brian Griffiths, Alan Walters and Geoffrey Wood.[11] The growing interest in this theory also attracted academics like Terry Burns and Alan Budd, who examined the international dimension of monetarism at the London Business School.[12] Burns later said they had introduced monetary elements into his LBS research because the previous Keynesian models and forecasts had performed poorly during 1972 and 1973.[13] Keith Joseph was the most prominent politician interested in monetarism during this period and made several speeches that advocated the technique. It was the IMF, however, which first imposed monetary discipline on a British government, as part of the conditions of the 1976 loan.[14]

Monetarists reasoned that excess money had to be squeezed out of a system to bring inflation under control, so that prices would increase only in a slow and steady fashion. The monetarist models stated that when inflation was rising, the rate of growth of money supply should be reduced, while deflation should be met with a monetary expansion.[15] By most calculations, the first Thatcher government set about a monetarist economic strategy, reducing the growth of the quantity of money in the economy through a variety of policy instruments – raising interest rates, abandoning prices and incomes policies, reducing the PSBR, and reducing spending while altering the tax burden. In July 1979, economic advisor to the chancellor, Peter Middleton, produced a paper on different monetary approaches. This included 'A Monetary Base for the UK' by Gordon Pepper, 'Cash Base Control and Institutional Change in the UK Financial System' by Geoffrey Wood, 'Controlling the UK Money Supply' by Brian Griffiths and 'A Proposal for the Control of the UK Money Supply' by Duck and Sheppard.[16] These differing approaches were critiqued, some as being too complex and unworkable. Pepper's approach was seen as closest to the classical monetary base control (MBC) model.[17] It was this technique of attempting to influence the quantity of money in the British economy that was pursued in the first two years of the Thatcher government. The aggregate £M3 was chosen as the most appropriate method of doing this and targets were set, although consistently overshot. The choice of aggregate itself proved contentious. Nigel Lawson consistently backed the 'broad' money aggregate £M3 while for instance, Milton Friedman generally based his work on £M2, which included 'time deposits', and sometimes on 'narrow' money, £M0.[18]

The aggregates, targets and methods of monetary control were much criticized and debated by economic liberals. There was no broad neoliberal economic model and much disagreement over whether the very concept of macroeconomics was even liberal.[19] Austrians and Hayekians believed monetary control was another method of government intervention that would distort market forces. Hayek consistently proposed other monetary principles, first the gold standard, then competition of currency itself, as ways to restrain inflation.[20] Articles in the *ORDO* journal during the first Thatcher term perceived the monetary squeeze in Britain as too tough on the private sector but too 'soft' on a state sector that still received sizeable subsidies.[21] Ordoliberals believed a concerted effort to reduce the fiscal deficit would be a surer way to combat inflation, which is what in fact happened. The tight monetary control of the first two years was perhaps the most ideological policy of the first term. It was explicitly neoliberal in the Friedmanite sense. After 1981 other influences marked economic policy, particularly the LBS and 'rational expectations' on monetary strategy.

Geoffrey Howe, although declaring in 2006 that 'I think those who proclaim either monetarism or Keynesianism as 'isms' in which you have to believe are profoundly misguided' and that 'now, I do not believe in monetarism', went about fervently trying to defeat inflation as Chancellor of the Exchequer.[22] Howe's measures in his first three budgets, most notably in 1981, and his use of high interest rates eventually brought it down. Direct taxation was reduced (83 per cent to 60 per cent as a top rate in the 1979 Budget) while indirect taxation like VAT was increased. The First Thatcher government, however, was hamstrung in its attempts to reduce the PSBR by its election promise to honour the Clegg Commission. This had recommended substantial increases in public sector pay and the Conservatives, during the 1979 campaign, felt that without an assurance to keep these they would lose crucial votes. Clegg made Howe's aim of reducing public spending all the more difficult. Indeed, when Milton Friedman was asked his opinion on the government's anti-inflation strategy (upon news that spending was increasing) his response was typically iconoclastic (also invoking the Virginia School), blaming 'resistance from bureaucracy, the Civil Service and the Conservative Party' but praising the prime minister for 'sticking to her guns'.[23]

The 1980 Budget saw the introduction of the Medium Term Financial Strategy (MTFS), devised by Financial Secretary to the Treasury Nigel Lawson. A theme that Lawson believed in (and was to return to when he was chancellor with the European Exchange Rate Mechanism) was that market credibility required a stabilizing force and the certainty of rules. Back in 1976 Lawson said

> parliamentary control over monetary policy means in practice that the policy would be expected to follow certain rules, whether they be rules of the gold standard or rules for a certain increase in the money supply as propounded by Professor Friedman or in the ideas of Professor Hayek.[24]

Lawson, working under Howe at the Treasury, set out a plan for a medium term strategy of setting declining targets for both the PSBR and the money supply in September 1979.[25] This belief in a framework to provide stability invoked elements of Keynes (herd behaviour) and 'rational expectations' thinking (investors need confidence in likely medium term interest rates). The MTFS set out a number of monetary and PSBR targets that were intended to give markets confidence in the British economy.

Documents regarding the MTFS hint at how economic policy was formulated in the first Thatcher government and also the influence of neoliberals. Special advisor to the chancellor Adam Ridley communicated a message on 18 February 1980 that he had spoken to two monetary economists, Brian Griffiths and Tim Congdon, who said they were broadly supportive of the government policies.[26] The government, however, was coming under pressure from journalists to publish monetary targets for the succeeding years. This included Samuel Brittan (who was 'quite friendly' with both Nigel Lawson and Terry Burns at the Treasury) in the *Financial Times* on the 20 and 28 February.[27] Geoffrey Howe wrote to Margaret Thatcher saying, 'I have been considering whether it would be possible to present our monetary and financial strategy for the medium term in a manner and context that would strengthen its credibility'.[28]

Against the liberal economic policymakers and commentators, however, was considerable opposition. Regarding the MTFS the prime minister and chancellor received several notes, on 22 February saying the Governor of the Bank of England had 'serious misgivings', from head of the Central Policy Review Staff (CPRS) Sir Kenneth Berrill on 25 February 'doubting the wisdom of the MTFS', from Cabinet Secretary Robert Armstrong on 26 February saying it 'would give the Government very little room for manoeuvre' and last even by the Chief Secretary to the Treasury – and arch-monetarist – John Biffen.[29] Writing to Howe, Biffen despaired on 4 March that 'the demand for such a Financial Strategy comes from journalists, academics and commentators rather than those in the commercial world'.[30] These documents give an insight into how few people within government were guiding economic policy during the first Thatcher term and suggest that neoliberals did indeed exert some influence over them. It also showed that both Geoffrey Howe and Margaret Thatcher had to act steadfastly in the face of opposition to the strategy they were pursuing.

The early economic policy of the Thatcher government, designed to squeeze inflation out of the economy, had a number of ideological interpretations. Milton Friedman was well-known for being a proponent of economic 'shock therapy'. Typical of his thinking was the 1977 speech, 'The Road to Economic Freedom: The Steps from Here to There'. Friedman set out two courses: 'gradualism' and 'shock treatment'.[31] Gradualism could steadily reduce inflation in an economy that exhibited single figure price rises but higher figures needed more drastic action. Friedman used two examples: post-war West Germany under the guidance of Ludwig Erhard and 1970s Chile.[32] Friedman stated that the British case was somewhere between a stable economy such as the United States and the more extreme examples of West Germany and Chile. He therefore believed 'modified shock treatment' was appropriate for Britain using instruments such as reduced government spending, lower tax rates, denationalization of state industries and reduced government bureaucracy.[33]

Friedman also believed in using the central bank to control money in the economy by using aggregates. It was this latter point that was most anathema to Austrian neoliberals like Hayek. By advocating the gold standard, then choice in currencies, the Austrian fell back upon the School's idea that markets will move towards equilibrium. The result would have been even more of a shock to the economy in terms of short-term employment.[34] Monetary policy was another example of how Hayek represented a more idealistic form of neoliberalism, closer to 'market fundamentalism' than Friedman's more pragmatic ideas, despite the widespread criticism the latter received from the left. Other Austrian thinkers may have considered Hayek as compromising some of the School's beliefs, but nevertheless his ideas were often distinct to other strands of neoliberalism such as the Chicago School.[35] It may have been that Hayek, buoyed by his Nobel prize, became more radical in his old age. In 1975, when he visited Chile, Hayek made a speech advocating abolishing all trade restrictions, income tax and the central bank itself. Arnold Harberger, of the Chicago School, described him at this time as 'remote from the real world'.[36] Mark Skousen wrote that Hayek was 'shockingly impractical and idealistic'.[37]

The first two years of economic policy of the Thatcher government was loosely based on a Friedmanite aggregate model, or the monetary base. Although not entirely true to their respective positions, David Willetts (then a researcher for Nigel Lawson), later said 'though we were trying to do Friedman, we were actually doing Hayek'.[38] This was presumably because there was a sharp rise in unemployment during this early phase of monetary control. Even monetary economist Tim Congdon thought interest rates were too high, that 'policy was too tight in much of 80 ... I objected to the severity of policy'.[39] These theoretical positions and the drastic impact of the Thatcher government's early economic measures were the backdrop of the 1981 Budget.

The controversial budget saw a reduction in the PSBR and an increase in taxation. Criticized for being deflationary in a time of recession, most famously in a letter to *The Times* signed by 364 economists, this juncture signified the determination of Howe and Thatcher that the battle against inflation was of primary importance. It also marked a shift from strict monetary control to a more concerted effort to reduce the deficit. The driving force behind the budget, however, has been contested and in particular the role of the prime minister's advisor Alan Walters. A diary entry made by Walters shortly before the budget was announced suggests it was the prime minister who demanded a tougher stance from Howe on reducing the PSBR. 'Saw MT at 10.00. What should she do about Geoffrey. Who could she promote. No-one.'[40] Shortly afterwards Walters reported on a discussion with Tim Lankester that echoed these sentiments: 'He (Tim) said PM told GH that he must get the PSBR down or "you are for the chop" – very unlike her.'[41] Despite this early example of the tension that would build between Thatcher and Howe, they continued to work together to pass the tough 1981 Budget.

The 1981 Budget, however, saw a shift that has often been neglected. Monetary aggregates remained important but the emphasis moved towards reducing the deficit. This was in keeping with 'rational expectations' thinking, that focused on the inflationary outlook based on likely interest rates. Friedman had previously shed light upon this work, citing in particular John Muth's 'Rational Expectations and the Theory of Price Movements' (1961) and Robert Lucas's 'Econometric Testing of the Natural Rate Hypothesis' (1972).[42] Adam Ridley believed that rational expectations was known and understood by only 'a very small proportion of the policymaking world' but that the work of Alan Budd and Terry Burns at the LBS in the 1970s was important in this respect.[43] By the time of the 1981 Budget Burns was Chief Economic Advisor to the Treasury.

Another advocate of rational expectations, Patrick Minford, thought the crucial turning point however was when Alan Walters entered the fray prior to the 1981 Budget and 'threw his considerable influence into the rational expectations monetarist camp and engineered a very large contraction in the budget deficit'.[44] Endorsing the rational expectations approach, Walters later said that after the 1981 Budget 'at first gradually, then much more rapidly, expectations adjusted to the reduced rates of inflation'.[45] What do these theoretical positions tell us about the economic policy of the first Thatcher government? First, it was broadly neoliberal and had shifted away from Keynesian orthodoxy. Second, although the techniques differed from MBC to deficit reduction, the chief contemporary influence was Milton Friedman and his ideas on monetarism. The use of empirical evidence, monetary aggregates and interest rate manipulation all follow the methods set by the second Chicago School. Although the unemployment that resulted from this strategy led some to say the government was 'doing Hayek', it can be concluded that the actual policy owed little to the work of the Austrian School.

The cost of these methods, however, was high. Thatcher liked the 'scientific' certainty of ideas like monetarism but was criticized as being attracted to 'gimmicks and dogma' in trying to solve complex and subtle economic problems.[46] Unemployment and factory closures soared, while interest rates and inflation remained high. A strong pound, buoyed by its petrocurrency status, made British exports uncompetitive, intensifying these difficulties. Inflation had been seemingly tamed in 1983 but the structural impact (or adjustment) done to the British economy was to prove intractable in some regions. Several of her own ministers were doubtful about the prime minister's path. Jim Prior said of both Margaret Thatcher and Keith Joseph that they saw Hayek and Friedman as 'gurus'.[47] Yet Margaret Thatcher made her reputation during this first term by remaining resolute in the face of overwhelming pressure, and in 1982, the Argentine junta which invaded the Falklands. Geoffrey Howe's determination to follow through on the government's strategy to reduce inflation was equally important. It was he, as well as the prime minister, who came up against resistance from within his own party as well as the establishment. Margaret Thatcher made the decision to trust in Howe's judgement.

Monetary targets were effectively abandoned during the second Thatcher government when Nigel Lawson took over as Chancellor of the Exchequer. Lawson, from 1985, pursued a policy of shadowing the Deutschmark (in a different attempt to maintain stability and as a precursor to joining the European Exchange Rate Mechanism).[48] He later believed that the MTFS worked better on the fiscal rather than on the monetary side.[49] Lawson's thinking was that market credibility was paramount, which had been achieved by monetary targets in the early 1980s but by the middle of the decade a new method was required.[50]

It was this transitory commitment to their principles that incensed monetary economists in the mid to late 1980s. Shadowing the Deutschmark, as well as easier credit, fuelled the 'Lawson Boom' of the latter part of the decade and caused a surge in asset prices.[51] £M3 aggregates increased by 20 per cent between June 1987 and June 1988.[52] This in turn led to high inflation in 1989 and 1990, punitive interest rates that effected homeowners and a recession in the early 1990s.[53] Monetary economists Tim Congdon and Gordon Pepper had warned of swollen asset prices between 1986 and 1988 and were proved correct in their inflationary predictions.[54]

Why was monetarism abandoned, allowing the inflationary cycle to return in the late 1980s? Tim Congdon, interviewed in 2012, said that 'deep down, British economists don't believe in monetarism'.[55] Congdon said that Nigel Lawson repeated the mistakes of the Heath-Barber boom of the early 1970s and that the prime minister, too dependent on Alan Walters (an economic advisor to Margaret Thatcher at several points during her premiership) did not really understand the technicalities.[56] Congdon said of Lawson and monetarism, 'I don't think he believed in it at all'.[57]

Notwithstanding monetarist criticism, limiting price rises has clearly become a prime goal of British governments. After almost reaching 10 per cent in 1989, inflation did not exceed 5 per cent in the UK in the 15 years from 1991. Prioritizing low inflationary conditions are a legacy of the Thatcher government, despite the surge at the end of the 1980s. Terry Burns said in 2011 that the monetary control 'we (the LBS) preached ... became orthodoxy'.[58] After the 1981 Budget, fiscal policy (according to Tim Congdon) was neutralized until 2008, as a clear result of the influence of monetarism.[59] The primacy of monetary policy, however, has not reached the heights of the first Thatcher government, although the MTFS remained Conservative policy, under the influence of Burns as Permanent Secretary to the Treasury.[60] Both Nigel Lawson and Geoffrey Howe, with reputations as 'dry' economic liberals, have both distanced themselves from monetarism. Some neoliberals, meanwhile, have advanced monetarist explanations for the 2007–8 financial crisis.[61] The response to the crisis, according to them, allowed the supply of money to contract too quickly and the resulting recession worse.[62] The early economic policy of the Thatcher government was influenced by neoliberal thinkers like

Milton Friedman and his Chicago School, think-tanks like the IEA, academics like those at the LBS and journalists like Samuel Brittan.

The impact of monetarism on the British economy during and since Thatcherism has meant low inflationary conditions are a key aim of policy-makers. Peter A. Hall, in 'Policy Paradigms, Social Learning, and the State' (1993) examined the shift from Keynesian to monetarist macroeconomic policymaking in Britain. Hall explored how ideas came to impact on institutions and policymakers. He identified the role of the media and to a lesser extent 'experts' in the 1970s, as well as competition for power between the political parties – particularly one that suited long-term Conservative objectives like lower public spending – as important.[63] Hall wrote that the shift in economic policy instruments, as well the hierarchy of objectives, represented a change in 'policy paradigm' so that independent ideas managed to 'induce changes in institutional routines'.[64] In this way, the changing methods and aims of economic policy during Thatcherism represented a 'retasking' of the role of the state. It can also be seen in its approach to the nationalized industries, trades unions and other areas of the public sector.

Conclusion

The Thatcher government did introduce some far-reaching economic reforms. Inflation was drastically reduced for much of the 1980s, this monetary climate provided a degree of economic stability and a basis for growth. The assault on inflation was ideologically-based and made a priority from the beginning of the Thatcher years. In ideological terms this was most closely linked with the neo-liberalism of Milton Friedman and the Chicago School, using the state to create stable monetary conditions and incentives to promote markets and economic activity. Friedman was concerned with a shift towards more liberal societies and economies. In this respect he was more willing to engage with the world as it really was, particularly the state, than his more idealistic Austrian counterparts. This was most clearly seen in the techniques he advocated to provide stable monetary and inflationary conditions. Ordoliberal ideas like an interdependent central bank were not to feature during the Thatcher government, but were implemented perhaps surprisingly under New Labour. Nevertheless, stable monetary conditions were clearly a prime objective for neoliberals of all stripes, and became a priority in government for the Conservatives under Margaret Thatcher, as well as her successors.

Notes

1 See Ernest Mandel's provocatively titled *Late Capitalism* (1978). In Britain Trotskyism had some influence in left wing groups in the 1970s such as the Socialist Worker's Party and Anti-Nazi League.
2 Kenneth Morgan, *Callaghan: A Life* (Oxford: Oxford University Press, 1997), 697.
3 Martin Holmes, *The First Thatcher Government. 1979–83* (Brighton: Wheatsheaf, 1985), 68.

4 *Guardian*, 'Inflation since 1948', accessed 7 May 2013. www.guardian.co.uk/news/datablog/2009/mar/09/inflation-economics.

5 Norman Barry, *The New Right* (Beckenham: Croom Helm, 1987), 23.

6 Wernhard Möschel, 'The Proper Scope of Government Viewed from an Ordo-liberal Perspective: The Example of Competition Policy', *Journal of Institutional and Theoretical Economics (JITE)/Zeitschrift für die gesamte Staatswissenschaft* 157:1 (2001), 10.

7 Milton Friedman, *Capitalism and Freedom* (Chicago, IL: University of Chicago Press, 1962), 38.

8 Milton Friedman, *Inflation and Unemployment: The New Dimension of Politics. The 1976 Alfred Nobel Memorial Lecture* (London: IEA, Occasional Paper 51, 1977), 12.

9 Milton Friedman and Anna Schwartz, *A Monetary History of the United States* (Princeton, NJ: Princeton University Press, first published 1963).

10 Friedman, *Inflation*, 12–23.

11 Sir Adam Ridley, personal correspondence with the author, 2 May 2013.

12 Ibid.

13 Interview with Lord Burns, 12 May 2011.

14 Ibid. Burns said that the IMF accepted monetary control 'early'. Adam Ridley also acknowledged the role of the IMF.

15 Tim Congdon, *Money in A Free Society. Keynes, Friedman, and the New Crisis in Capitalism* (London: Encounter Books, 2011), 247.

16 Records of the Prime Minister's Office: Correspondence and Papers, 1979–1997 (The National Archives: Public Record Office, Kew, hereafter PREM19), PREM19/33, paper by Peter Middleton, 18 July 1979 concerning monetary approaches.

17 Ibid.

18 Margaret Thatcher Foundation (hereafter MTF) 113283 – Lawson minute to Howe ('A Medium Term Financial Plan') [what it should contain], 24 September 1979; Robin Harris, *Not for Turning. The Life of Margaret Thatcher* (London: Bantam Press, 2013), 173–174; Congdon, *Money*, 376; Charles Moore, *Margaret Thatcher. The Authorized Biography. Volume One: Not for Turning* (London: Penguin, 2013), 523–524.

19 MTF117203, letter from Hayek to Arthur Seldon, 13 May 1985. Hayek wrote, 'I do regard the abandonment of the whole macroeconomics nonsense as very important … I have long regretted my failure to take time to criticize Friedman's Positive Economics'.

20 F. A. Hayek, *The Constitution of Liberty* (London: Routledge, 2006 [1960]), 291; F. A. Hayek, *Choice in Currency. A Way to Stop Inflation* (London: IEA, 1976), 14–22.

21 Victoria Curzon Price, 'Structural Aspects of the Thatcher Experiment. How to Put the Cart before the Horse and (Perhaps) Survive', *ORDO. Jahrbuch für die Ordnung von Wirtschaft und Gesellschaft* [Ordo Yearbook of Economic and Social Order] (Stuttgart: Gustav Fischer Verlag, Band 33, 1982), 60; Michael Parkin, 'Mrs. Thatcher's Monetary Policy', *ORDO. Jahrbuch für die Ordnung von Wirtschaft und Gesellschaft* [Ordo Yearbook of Economic and Social Order] (Stuttgart: Gustav Fischer Verlag, Band 33, 1982), 79–80.

22 Lord Howe of Aberavon, 'Can 364 Economists all be Wrong?' in *The Chancellors' Tales. Managing the British Economy*, ed. Howard Davies (Cambridge: Polity, 2006), 105–106.

23 MTF114507, *The Times*, 'Economists criticize Government', 10 March 1981.

24 Nigel Lawson, *Parliamentary Debates* (Commons), 908, 31 March 1976, 1511–37.

25 MTF 113283, 24 Sept 1979.

26 PREM19/177 on MTFS. Note from Adam Ridley to Douglas Wass 18 February 1980, articles by Samuel Brittan in *Financial Times* 20 February 1980 and 28 February 1980.

27 Interview with Lord Burns.

28 PREM19/177. Note from Howe to Thatcher 22 February 1980.

29 Ibid. Notes from Howe to Thatcher, 22 February 1980, Berrill to Thatcher on 25 February 1980 and Armstrong to Thatcher on 26 February 1980.

30 Ibid. Note from Biffen to Howe, 4 March 1980.

31 Milton Friedman, 'The Road to Economic Freedom: The Steps from Here to There', in *From Galbraith to Economic Freedom* (London: IEA, 1977), 43–44.

32 Friedman, 'Road', 43–44.

33 Friedman, 'Road', 43–48.

34 Mark Skousen, *Vienna & Chicago. Friends or Foes? A Tale of Two Schools of Free-Market Economics* (Washington, DC: Capital Press, 2005), 7–8, 37.

35 Walter Block, 'Hayek's Road to Serfdom', *Journal of Libertarian Studies* 12:2 (Fall 1996), 342, 365.

36 Skousen, *Vienna & Chicago*, 112.

37 Skousen, *Vienna & Chicago*, 112.

38 Moore, *Thatcher vol one*, 624.

39 Interview with Tim Congdon, 24 February 2012.

40 MTF114203, Alan Walters diary, 19 January 1981.

41 MTF114204, Alan Walters diary, 23 February 1981.

42 Milton Friedman, *Price Theory* (London: AldineTransaction, 2007 [1962, 2nd edn 1976]), 230–231; see also Esther-Mirjam Sent, *The Evolving Rationality of Rational Expectations: An Assessment of Thomas Sargent's Achievements* (Cambridge: Cambridge University Press, 1998).

43 Sir Adam Ridley, personal correspondence with the author, 2 May 2013.

44 Patrick Minford, 'Inflation, Unemployment and the Pound', in *Margaret Thatcher's Revolution. How it Happened and What it Means*, ed. S. Roy and J. Clarke (London: Continuum, 2005), 53.

45 John Ranelagh, *Thatcher's People. An Insider's Account of the Politics, the Power and the Personalities* (London: HarperCollins, 1991), 235.

46 John Campbell, *Margaret Thatcher. Volume Two: The Iron Lady* (London: Pimlico, 2004), 81.

47 Jim Prior, *A Balance of Power* (London: Hamish Hamilton, 1986), 104.

48 M. J. Oliver, 'The Macroeconomic Policies of Mr Lawson' *Contemporary British History* 13:1 (1999), 175.

49 Oliver, 'Mr Lawson', 174.

50 Lord Lawson of Blaby, 'Changing the Consensus', in *The Chancellors' Tales. Managing the British Economy*, ed. Howard Davies (Cambridge: Polity, 2006), 119.

51 Oliver, 'Mr Lawson', 175.

52 Ibid., 178.

53 A. Gamble, *Britain in Decline* (London: Macmillan, 1994a), 190.

54 Oliver, 'Mr Lawson', 178.

55 Interview with Tim Congdon CBE, 24 February 2012.

56 Ibid.

57 Ibid.

58 Interview with Lord Burns, 12 May 2011.

59 Interview with Tim Congdon, 24 February 2012.

60 Ibid.

61 Philip Booth, *Verdict on the Crash. Causes and Policy Implications* (London: IEA, 2009), 27.

62 Interview with Tim Congdon, 24 February 2012.

63 Peter A. Hall, 'Policy Paradigms, Social Learning, and the State: The Case of Economic Policymaking in Britain', *Comparative Politics* 25:3 (April 1993), 288–289.

64 Hall, 'Policy Paradigms', 279, 290.

4 Liberalization?

Exchange controls and enterprise zones

The Thatcher government made economic recovery its priority following the 'stagflation' of the 1970s. The manner in which familiar Keynesian instruments were abandoned demonstrated how Thatcherism broke with accepted orthodoxy. Chapter 3 demonstrated how neoliberal influence was present in the prioritization of monetary control between 1979 and 1983. If a more stable monetary environment was a primary goal then liberalization and deregulation were other objectives for the Thatcher government. Neoliberals had set out how the stimulation of economic growth through private enterprise and markets required state action. In so far as the Thatcher government went about market orientated policies it pursued liberalization and deregulation in selective ways. This chapter will explore two examples of this: the removal of exchange controls and enterprise zones. Both policies had a potent signalling effect, which is to say that the Thatcher government was pro-market, despite the continuing role of the state. The term deregulation, as so often with Thatcherism and neoliberalism, is somewhat misleading.

The policies of the first term paved the way for later reforms. Geoffrey Howe (Chancellor from 1979–83) introduced significant changes rapidly when he came into office based on the ideas of economic liberals. Exchange controls were abolished in 1979 and monetary targets quickly introduced. Margaret Thatcher described the former as showing the rhetorical commitment to the market would be matched by action, and Howe initiated the idea he had enthused about in opposition, enterprise zones.[1] Howe, influenced by Professor Peter Hall at the University of Reading and aided by the Bow Group had built on ideas from a 1961 series on urban renewal relating to New Towns.[2] The policy transformed the derelict Docklands area into a world financial centre during the 1980s.

Enterprise zones

Although less prominent compared to reforms like privatization, enterprise zones were another idea that became closely linked with Thatcherism. In March 1979 Labour MP Bruce George remarked that a Conservative proposal that 'free enterprise will move into ... inner urban areas' exposed the 'hand of Friedman'.[3] Although the Chicagoan did consistently eulogize pro-enterprise city states such as Hong Kong and Singapore, the enterprise zone idea had a much more diverse lineage. Its development was closely associated with Geoffrey Howe and the Bow Group, promoted business by incentivization and satisfied several neoliberal themes, such as reduced state intrusion, wealth creation and lower taxation. Enterprise zones were taken from a number of strands of thought and policies of the post-war period, although not specifically thinkers like Friedman. The Bow Group was a key influence but the planning concept of 'New Towns', Fabian academic Professor Peter Hall and the economic success of Singapore and Hong Kong were all important contributors to the eventual 1980 legislation. Although not exclusively neoliberal, enterprise zones were a good example of the impact of ideas on the Thatcher government, and particularly in this case on Geoffrey Howe. In terms of neoliberalism, however, enterprise zones were pro-business without necessarily being liberalizing or an act of free market deregulation. The more radical elements of Hall's initial model, such as the removal of immigration controls in the zones, were heavily watered down or excluded from the eventual legislation. This follows several of the Thatcher government's 'pro-market' policies.

Policy development

The New Towns Act of 1946 was part of the post-war housing strategy and over the subsequent 25 years a number of houses were built to absorb the growing UK population. This was very much in keeping with the programme of the Attlee government, where policy, from health to housing, was the result of state planning. Geoffrey Howe saw New Towns as one of the successes of planning. Howe, a long-standing liberal, viewed the allocation of land for certain purposes as a potentially positive role for the state.[4] Enterprise zones were earmarked for disused state-owned land in urban and inner city areas. A 1962 article in *Crossbow* (the Bow Group periodical) by journalist Godfrey Hodgson, *Wigan Delenda Est*, has been cited as a precursor to the enterprise zones idea.[5] It was part of a series on urban renewal after New Towns and concentrated on publically owned derelict land.[6] Labour governments had – with the 1967 Land Commission and 1976 Community Land Acts – attempted to manipulate the cost of land or nationalize it. The enterprise zone principle also tried to influence the use of land but rather than claiming it for government purposes, providing incentives on disused areas that the state already owned.

The other element in the development of enterprise zones was deregulation. The rapid growth of the Asian Tiger economies, such as Hong Kong, in the post-war period acted as an ideal for economic liberals. Through deregulation, low taxation, minimal building restrictions and ease of starting a business, ports like Hong Kong and Singapore developed rapidly.[7] Export-led growth unleashed the potential of enterprise and trade alongside a strong central authority (the Asian Tigers were not democracies). Some proponents of capitalism, as well as more unlikely figures saw this as a model. An academic from the University of Reading and a former chairman of the Fabian Society, Professor Peter Hall, used the examples of the Asian Tigers. He co-wrote 'Nonplan: An Experiment in Freedom' in 1969 and gave an influential paper in June 1977 setting out his idea of 'freeports'.[8] Hall described a freeport as an area exempt from certain regulations, like Hong Kong and Singapore, that could provide incentives for business and trade. Geoffrey Howe said he was 'delighted' that 'distinguished Socialist Professor Peter Hall' had begun to 'reach for the same prescription' as him.[9] Howe said, 'why not aim to recreate the Hong Kong of the 1950s inside Inner Liverpool or Inner Glasgow?'[10]

As Shadow chancellor between 1975 and 1979 Howe developed the enterprise zone idea. He has also cited future Conservative Cabinet member Nick Ridley's work done on 'non-planning agreement(s)' as influential: that an area of land may be exempt of regulation to increase productivity and attract business.[11] John Hoskyns, while working on the Stepping Stones project in the late 1970s, described a meeting he had with Howe in August 1977. Hoskyns said of Howe that a key policy was to 'create a liberal economic climate' and that he was 'very keen on an interesting idea from someone called Peter Hall for tax exempt, planning regulation exempt areas – e.g. regional, inner urban decay areas – where entrepreneurs could really let rip as in Singapore (and) Hong Kong'.[12] At first Margaret Thatcher was not convinced. A document from 1979 shows how Howe tried to win over the Conservative leader. 'Can I have another go at persuading you to endorse my "enterprise zone" proposal as something we should put forward in the Election?' Howe also attached an article written by the conservative US think-tank Heritage Foundation ('Enterprise Zone: A Solution to the Urban Crisis?') which came out in support of both the idea and the then Shadow chancellor himself. Peter Hall later said, however, that the Conservatives rendered his radical idea 'harmless' by omitting his proposals regarding free migration and exemption from mainstream legislation within the zone.[13] Hall thought these inner city areas required such an overhaul they needed to be 'completely open to immigration of entrepreneurs and capital' and 'effectively outside the UK's normal legislation and controls'.[14] Despite his Fabian links Hall demonstrated a radical anti-state and internationalist sentiment.

Howe had made a set piece speech regarding the policy in June the previous year. Speaking on the Isle of Dogs, site of a proposed pilot scheme, the Shadow chancellor proposed 'New Enterprise Zones'. He had asked for help from the Bow Group with the formulation of this idea two years earlier. Enterprise zones were to give free rein to construction, providing exemptions from planning permissions and reducing the bureaucratic process. Taxation on business would be lower, both local and central government control reduced. Howe described the dereliction of cities like London, Manchester and Glasgow and how they were ideally placed to reverse the process by their innate advantages: nearby commercial centres, often close to rivers and housing communities that yearned for jobs.[15] The policy of enterprise zones was to transform some of these areas and satisfied some neoliberal themes. As we have seen, however, other, more radical ones were not included.

Enterprise zones and the ethos of neoliberalism

Enterprise zones were important in setting the general tone of the policies of the Thatcher government and aligned it with some of the tenets of economic liberalism. Primarily, the shift that the idea encapsulated was an emphasis on favouring business and wealth creation over redistribution and producer interests such as trades unions. Enterprise zones represented the importance the Thatcher government attributed to economic growth and entrepreneurship. On the face of things the idea also incorporated some themes of Public Choice theory, such as incentivization and a reduced role for the state. Only a few years later Canary Wharf, in the enterprise zone set up on the Isle of Dogs, invoked a Hong Kong in miniature with high-rise neon towers hosting successful global financial companies. Canary Wharf became an iconic image of the Thatcher years. To supporters and critics alike it represented private sector resurgence. From the viewpoint of a 'model' market it can be said the policy reduced barriers to entry for producers and using the example of Canary Wharf, which drew in foreign direct investment, increased consumer choice and competition.[16] This in turn drove up economic activity in the enterprise zone and surrounding economy and widened ownership at the expense of previously publically owned land.[17]

Implementation

Enterprise zones were not included in the 1979 manifesto, possibly because Margaret Thatcher thought the idea had 'Heathian overtones' and was regional policy by another name.[18] Nevertheless the initial enterprise zone legislation was introduced in 1980 and was incorporated in two acts: the Local Government Planning and Land Act, and the Finance Act. Chancellor of the Exchequer Geoffrey Howe had announced the scheme and Michael Heseltine as Secretary of State for the Environment helped implement the policy. Six enterprise zones were initially allocated in 1980 and were given tax concessions, simplified planning procedures and rates exemptions.[19] These areas included the Isle of Dogs, Salford in Manchester and Clydebank in Glasgow.

In the early part of the first Thatcher government Britain sank into a deep recession. The prime minister and chancellor's focus on reducing inflation meant that numerous factories faced closure and many jobs were lost. As unemployment soared to three million and social unrest flared in 1981, the government came under pressure to act. The government attempted to paint enterprise zones as a palliative in areas particularly affected by recession.[20] On the Isle of Dogs the enterprise zone fell into the area controlled by the newly created London Docklands Development Corporation (LDDC), an example of an Urban Development Corporation (UDC). The LDDC had wide-ranging powers and access to public funding, encouraged by Heseltine and initially resisted by Geoffrey Howe and Keith Joseph.[21] The role the state played in the regeneration of Docklands was important. For example, the LDDC helped clear sites, build infrastructure projects such as the Docklands Light Railway (DLR) and make land available to private developers.[22] Certainly the business activity in the enterprise zone was assisted by this government-led action. In this respect, the state acted as a 'pump-primer' for the private sector and sits comfortably with Harvey's post-1970s neoliberal model, that the state creates the conditions for markets.[23]

Geoffrey Howe described the enterprise zones idea as his 'hobby horse' and he expanded the scheme in 1981–82, designating another ten zones, and a further 13 during 1983–86.[24] Both Geoffrey Howe and Michael Heseltine were reluctant to expand the policy any further during this time. Letters to the prime minister state that enterprise zones were 'experimental' and that expansion should wait.[25] Howe did target some of the areas that had been particularly affected by the government's austere economic policies, such as Liverpool, Tyneside and Clydebank. In this respect the scheme had a highly political element. Howe believed that 'Thatcherism', including enterprise zones, was a British export that was taken up by other governments during this period.[26] In this way Howe later proclaimed the Thatcher government had acted as the world's leading export agency for free market ideas and that it had 'set about making the whole of Britain into one massive "enterprise zone."'[27] Enterprise zones were one idea (albeit lesser known compared to a policy such as privatization) that was used by other governments. Geoffrey Howe said in 1988 that 'the United States has proved to be the main importer of the enterprise zones concept' and gave examples such as Ohio (which had allocated 51 zones) and Pennsylvania (26 zones).[28] Perhaps the most significant example of the use of enterprise zones was in China. In essence, Deng Xiaoping's economic reforms were state orchestrated capitalism focused on export-led growth.[29] China, with an eye on the success of Hong Kong, implemented their own enterprise zones (known as Special Economic Zones [SEZs]) in Shenzen and Zhuhai.[30]

Enterprise zones: analysis

Economic growth, creation of jobs through incentivization of the private sector as well as attracting foreign investment all satisfy the philosophy of the Thatcher government and neoliberalism.[31] As an example of deregulation, however, enterprise zones have not worn as well as some of the other policies of Thatcherism. In the UK they were not extended after their initial roll-out and were not considered an option by the Major government. In addition, and unlike some of the other policy areas looked at in this study, New Labour did not take up the idea. In 1987 an article in *Economic Affairs* (the IEA's periodical) wrote that there was no evidence to suggest enterprise zones had addressed the significant imbalances in employment rates in the UK.[32]

The policy met with other criticism. Opponents of enterprise zones charged that new jobs were just transferred from one area to another, and questioned whether businesses were being started or just moving.[33] Enterprise zones were said to favour large and mobile businesses and therefore acted as a barrier to smaller businesses.[34] Last, the location of enterprise zones has been criticized. Canary Wharf played its part in solidifying and increasing the comparative wealth of London and the South East, while the lesser-known zones tended to be situated in areas that were most badly affected by the government's economic policies. That enterprise zones were unevenly distributed and targeted in this way could also lead to the conclusion that this was regional policy (government assistance to less prosperous areas) by another name.[35] Last, the role of the state such as the 'pump-priming' by the LDDC has often been overlooked.

In summary, although enterprise zones have had their critics they were important as a signal of intent. The policy showed that the Thatcher government would favour the private over the public sector, and that economic liberalization measures would be one of its preferred tools. The lineage of the idea was a combination of the broad ethos of liberal economics but with a role for the state in fostering markets, while simultaneously attempting to draw back the role of government. In this respect enterprise zones were a good example of a neoliberal policy. As other writers have identified, the nominal rise in neoliberal influence often translated into pro-business rather than pro-market policies.[36] Enterprise zones looked less a 'market fundamentalist' measure in the Austrian tradition, which implementation of Hall's model could have resembled, than a political compromise. Another early indicator that the Thatcher governments would back markets to restore Britain's economy to health, and consistently cited as crucial by neoliberals, was the abolition of exchange controls.[37]

Exchange control removal

Exchange controls still existed in Britain in 1979. More open trade, and the removal of barriers to this such as exchange controls, were strongly advocated by neoliberals. German Ordoliberal Wilhelm Röpke, for instance, thought that post-war British currency devaluations were insufficient without 'abolition of exchange controls and the free convertibility of the Pound'.[38] Therefore the removal of exchange controls in 1979, according to Geoffrey Howe, 'sent out a message to the world about our commitment to liberal economics as the means of reviving Britain'.[39] Howe wrote in his memoirs that the decision was the only occasion he lost a night's sleep due to politics.[40] Howe made a clear case for abolishing the controls, saying the system had 'cost us dear' by stifling financial markets and competition.[41] He cited a pamphlet published by the IEA, written by John Wood and Robert Miller in February 1979, which helped break the 'intellectual icepack'.[42] Adam Ridley said the two main reasons for removal were the increasing cost of operating them and 'the long standing liberal economic tradition of open markets and freedom from control'.[43] Nigel Lawson also favoured abolishing exchange controls, including the issue in his maiden speech in the House of Commons in 1977 and wrote to Margaret Thatcher about it in October 1978: 'Removal of exchange control would be highly beneficial in itself.'[44] Geoffrey Howe relaxed investment restrictions in summer 1979 and then completely abolished them in October later that year.

Exchange controls were introduced in 1939 as a means of buttressing the pound and preventing capital flight. They existed as part of the 'sterling area' that consisted of British Empire and its dominions. This was what Geoffrey Howe described as further evidence that the UK was 'statist', using measures that were intended to protect British interests but actually acted as an impediment to enterprise. The controls also led to a layer of bureaucracy in Whitehall and Customs (at a cost according to Nigel Lawson of 750 staff and £14.5 million per year) that monitored the controls.[45] Permission was required for importing and exporting, curtailing investment and trade. Other Western European countries had removed their exchange controls after the Second World War but there was strong institutional resistance to ending them in Britain.[46] The country's entry into the European Community, however, made a tacit commitment to remove controls.[47] In her memoirs Margaret Thatcher said the reason for exchange controls was 'in the hope of increasing industrial investment in Britain and of resisting pressures on sterling'.[48] She said that the controls had not, if ever, achieved their objectives and by 1979 'with sterling buoyant and Britain beginning to enjoy the economic benefits of North Sea oil, the time had come to abolish them entirely'.[49] The former prime minister, however, omitted the fact that she equivocated over whether to impose inflow controls in 1980 and 1981.

Removing exchange controls exposed British industry and companies to international markets. This was potentially a problem for unproductive UK firms but not a plausible ideological reason for a government committed to the virtues of capitalism, as well as the associated instability. The more difficult issue was the impact of North Sea oil and the government's monetary policy. A CPRS paper in the first week after the 1979 election described Britain as being potentially at risk of the 'Dutch disease'. The report said that this would mean 'the tendency for oil and gas revenues to raise the exchange rate and so, in the short term at least, to lower competiveness. The Government's commitment to a strict monetary and fiscal stance will reinforce the strength of sterling'.[50]

The exchange rate began to rise as the benefits of North Sea oil started to be felt, affecting Britain's export capacity. Removing exchange controls caused sterling to appreciate and the strong currency exacerbated factory closures and the manufacturing collapse in the recession of the early 1980s.

Geoffrey Howe is said to have initially favoured liberalizing exchange controls solely on capital outflows to prevent North Sea oil tax revenues rising too far.[51] Exchange control abolition did play havoc with the government's economic strategy, making monetary aggregates harder to predict due to easier movement of capital.[52]

The removal of exchange controls in 1979 has not been studied in as great detail as the flagship reforms of Thatcherism. The policy, however, was consistent with several neoliberal themes and important in charting the general direction of the government. Removing controls reduced bureaucracy in Whitehall and in the customs service. In his memoirs, Lord Howe quipped: 'the consequent loss of jobs for 750 controllers at the Bank of England, so far from being a cause for concern, provoked the production of a celebratory tie, which I wear to this day.'[53] Nigel Lawson said of those 750 that 'some took early retirement and others were redeployed, most finding jobs in the City'.[54]

The policy was also an example of how market forces were given priority by the Conservative government in an attempt to promote wealth creation, economic growth and to allow markets to function more efficiently. Removing exchange controls reduced barriers to entry and therefore theoretically increased producers in a particular market. In this respect removing exchange controls satisfied all strands of neoliberal thinking. Hayek had stated in *The Road to Serfdom* that government control of 'foreign exchange' was a 'decisive advance on the path to totalitarianism and the suppression of individual liberty'.[55]

Also important, and in a similar way to enterprise zones, abolishing exchange controls acted as a signal of the policies of the Thatcher government and showed a faith in liberal economics. Geoffrey Howe said 'it *was* an act of faith, but it worked'.[56] It also showed the dynamic of the early cautiousness of the prime minister compared to her more committed pro-market ministers, such as Howe. Despite Margaret Thatcher's firmness in her own memoirs, Lord Howe's opinion was consistent with other accounts of the early years of the government. After the initial relaxation in summer 1979 a full move to abolition was urged by the chancellor. Margaret Thatcher's 'initial reaction was against further action'.[57] Nigel Lawson went further by suggesting that Howe was also 'cautious' in moving to complete abolition (which Lawson favoured) while the prime minister was 'even more hesitant'.[58] In any case, the combination of pragmatism and commitment to economic liberalism led to a result that was satisfactory to neoliberals such as Milton Friedman, who believed it was the precondition for later reforms.[59] Exchange controls also show a tension between nationalism and economic liberalism. Nationalist sentiment in the government might well have been attracted to a measure that protected British interests. In this case though, a commitment to free markets was preferred over protectionism. Geoffrey Howe wrote, 'Abolition improved the return on capital, and thus the efficiency of our economy. It enabled us to build up huge overseas assets and earn a substantial income from them'.[60]

Last, although only a relatively small measure in one economy – albeit still a major one despite all the talk of decline – removal of exchange controls can be seen as providing impetus to the globalization of trade. A number of catalysts can be identified in this trend. The end of the Bretton Woods system in 1971, when US President Nixon ended the convertibility of the dollar to gold (allowing floating exchange rates and accelerating international trade and finance) was an earlier, and crucial, step in this process. Geoffrey Howe said 'the success of that approach (removing exchange controls) helped fortify the commitment of other countries, not least those in the European Community, to the same course'.[61] The 1986 Big Bang in the City continued this trend.

The 1980/1 wobble

Documents from the first Thatcher government indicate the second thoughts some, including the prime minister, had about the blanket removal of exchange controls. This was due to the appreciating exchange rate caused by North Sea oil and the effects this was having in worsening the recession. The prime minister's private secretary, Tim Lankester, sent a note to Chancellor Geoffrey Howe on 14 February 1980 saying that 'the Prime Minister is concerned about the upward pressure on sterling which the current level of interest rates appear to be causing, and has asked whether we should not be urgently considering the imposition of controls on inward flows'.[62] In addition, Robin Ibbs (head of the CPRS) wrote to the prime minister in October that year urging reconsideration of inflow controls: 'I suggested that in considering ways in which industry can be helped high priority should be given to finding methods of reducing the exchange rate. Some system of inflow controls might provide necessary relief.'[63] Different viewpoints among economic liberals could also be seen. Monetarist economist Gordon Pepper's main concern was stable monetary conditions. Lankester wrote to the prime minister: 'I spoke to Gordon Pepper this evening. He is very worried about the continued upward pressure on Sterling, and thinks the Treasury should be seriously considering introducing exchange controls and/or negative interest rates on inward flows.'[64] Alan Walters, however, saw matters in a more free market way. He also wrote to Thatcher about the issue in 1981 stating concern about the rumours that controls were about to be reimposed. Walters said that would be 'very damaging'.[65]

The chancellor, however, would not be moved on the subject. He wrote to the prime minister towards the end of 1980 saying:

> I do not see inflow controls as offering a secure or apt way forward. I understand very well the concern which the CPRS expressed. This sort of device is not simply one that I find philosophically unattractive; it can offer no substitute for the far reaching changes we need in the economy (which will inevitably have to come to terms with a higher real exchange rate than in the past because of the fact of our North Sea oil).[66]

This revealed some of the dynamics in the first Thatcher government. Geoffrey Howe often behaved as the most steadfast economic liberal in the Cabinet (including Keith Joseph) and invested most faith in market forces. Margaret Thatcher too had some commitment to neoliberal ideas but was more constrained by political expediency. Her claim that she was 'not for turning' was in some cases a presentational device with the historical shadow of the Heath government in mind. Behind the scenes the prime minister could equivocate about policy decisions. On several neoliberal measures, such as enterprise zones and exchange control abolition, it was Geoffrey Howe that seemed most committed to reform.

The abolition of exchange controls was the forerunner of the 1986 Big Bang when financial markets in the City of London were liberalized. In his memoirs Lord Howe said that removing controls 'forced the City to become more competitive, and helped consolidate it as a world financial centre'.[67] Former Chairman of the London Stock Exchange (LSE), Nicholas Goodison, said the catalyst for financial deregulation and later Big Bang was this early act of the Thatcher government: 'The real cause I think was the abolition of exchange controls in 1979, because that completely freed international capital markets as far as London was concerned.'[68] The early liberalization measures were important in the process of globalization and acted as significant indicators on how the government intended to proceed.[69]

Conclusion

Both exchange control abolition and enterprise zones acted as important signals that Britain was once more a place to do business, showed a faith in the processes of capitalism and a shift towards wealth creation over state directed policies. Although not strictly a policy inspired by neoliberals, enterprise zones displayed many of its hallmarks: the state being utilized to create conditions for business if not necessarily freer markets. Exchange control removal, on the other hand, was a measure that broadly satisfied neoliberalism for its effect on more open trade, markets and movement of capital. Chapter 5 will explore the most famous act of deregulation of the Thatcher years: Big Bang in the City of London.

Notes

1 Margaret Thatcher, *The Downing Street Years* (London: HarperCollins, 1993), 40.
2 Interview with Lord Howe, 13 July 2009.
3 Bruce George MP, *Parliamentary Debates* (Commons), 964, 12 March 1979, 55–173.
4 Sir Geoffrey Howe, 'Speech to the Bow Group at The Waterman's Arms, Isle of Dogs', 26 June 1978, in *The Right Angle. Three Studies in Conservatism. Enterprise Zones* (London: Bow Group, 1978), 12.
5 Interview with Lord Howe, 13 July 2009. *Wigan Delenda Est* translated as Wigan must be destroyed, a play on *Carthage Delenda Est*.
6 Ibid.

7 Milton Friedman and Rose Friedman, *Free to Choose* (London: Pan Books, 1990 [1980]), 34.

8 S. M. Butler, *Enterprise Zones: Greenling the Inner Cities* (London: Heinemann, 1982), 95; Peter Hall, 'The British Enterprise Zones', in *Enterprise Zones. New Directions in Economic Development*, ed. Roy Green (London: Sage, 1991), 179.

9 Howe, 'Bow Group speech 1978', 16.

10 Ibid., 16.

11 Interview with Lord Howe, 13 July 2009.

12 The Papers of Sir John Hoskyns (Cambridge: Churchill Archives, hereafter HOSK), 1/33, Detailed notes by Hoskyns for Norman Strauss and Terry Price relating to his meeting with Geoffrey Howe on 2 August 1977, written 31 August 1977.

13 Hall, 'British', 184; Daniel Stedman-Jones, *Masters of the Universe. Hayek, Friedman, and the Birth of Neoliberal Politics* (Oxford: Princeton University Press, 2012), 317.

14 Hall, 'British', 180.

15 Howe, 'Bow Group speech 1978,' 15.

16 Defined using microeconomic principles of the Austrian School: free entry into a market, perfect information, high number of producers and consumers, price as key signal. Taken from Norman Barry, *The New Right* (Beckenham: Croom Helm, 1987), 35–36.

17 For 'surrounding area' substitute the South East region of England. Critics have pointed out how the financial success of the Docklands area has not made a significant difference to the residents of surrounding London boroughs.

18 Geoffrey Howe, *Conflict of Loyalty* (Basingstoke: Macmillan, 1994), 110.

19 Martin Holmes, *The First Thatcher Government. 1979–83* (Brighton: Wheatsheaf, 1985), 54.

20 Records of the Prime Minister's Office: Correspondence and Papers, 1979–1997 (The National Archives: Public Record Office, Kew, hereafter PREM19), PREM19/576. Note by CPRS on Liverpool, 18 March 1981, urging Howe to implement more zones; he counselled patience.

21 Jack Brown, 'The London Docklands Development Corporation: 1979–1981' (London: Queen Mary University of London, unpublished MA thesis, 2012), 1, 15, 52–53.

22 Brown, 'Docklands', 54.

23 Brown, 'Docklands', 54; David Harvey, *A Brief History of Neoliberalism* (Oxford: Oxford University Press, 2005), 2, 21.

24 Sir Geoffrey Howe, *Enterprise Zones and the Enterprise Culture* (London: Bow Group, 1988), 17.

25 PREM19/576. Notes from the CPRS, Michael Heseltine and Sir Geoffrey Howe to Margaret Thatcher.

26 Howe, *Enterprise Zones*, 22.

27 Howe, *Enterprise Zones*, 16–22.

28 Howe, *Enterprise Zones*, 22.

29 Again fitting Andrew Gamble's idea of the 'free market and the strong state'.

30 Howe, *Enterprise Zones*, 22.

31 In his 1988 speech, Geoffrey Howe extolled the success of enterprise zones, using the Isle of Dogs as the example. Howe quoted the employment figures in the area, from 641 in 1982 to 3700 in 1987, while the number of firms grew from 105 in 1982 to 270 in 1987 (James Barr, *The Bow Group. A History* (London: Politicos, 2001), 199).

32 Peter Stoney, 'Enterprise Zone: Incentive or Intervention?', *Economic Affairs* 8:1 (October/November 1987), 30.

33 Butler, *Enterprise Zones*, 115.

34 Butler, *Enterprise Zones*, 127.

35 Butler, *Enterprise Zones*, 127; *The Economist*, 12–18 March 2011, 15.

36 Neil Rollings, 'Cracks in the Post-War Keynesian Settlement? The Role of Organized Business in Britain in the Rise of Neoliberalism before Margaret Thatcher', *Twentieth Century British History* 24:4 (2013), 637–659; Ben Jackson, 'The Think-Tank Archipelago: Thatcherism and Neoliberalism', in *Making Thatcher's Britain*, ed. Ben Jackson and Robert Saunders (Cambridge: Cambridge University Press, 2012), 47–49.

37 Richard Vinen, *Thatcher's Britain. The Politics and Social Upheaval of the 1980s* (London: Simon and Schuster), 108.

38 The Papers of Wilhelm Röpke, Institut für Wirtschaftspolitik, Cologne, Germany (hereafter RÖPKE), letter from Röpke to Veronica Wedgwood, deputy editor of *Time and Tide*, 20 September 1949.

39 Howe, *Conflict*, 143.

40 Ibid., 142.

41 Ibid., 140–141.

42 Ibid., 141.

43 Sir Adam Ridley, personal correspondence with the author, 15 May 2013.

44 Nigel Lawson, *The View from No. 11* (London: Corgi Books, 1993), 38, The Papers of Margaret Thatcher (Cambridge: Churchill Archives, hereafter THCR), 2/1/2/12A, paper written by Nigel Lawson to Margaret Thatcher on 30 October 1978, regarding the European Monetary System.

45 Lawson, *View*, 40.

46 In her memoirs Margaret Thatcher described her position in the memorable phrase, 'not every capitalist had my confidence in capitalism'. One City expert allegedly exclaimed 'Steady on!' when they heard of the plans to remove exchange controls (Thatcher, *Downing Street Years*, 44).

47 John Campbell, *Edward Heath. A Biography* (London: Pimlico, 1993), 355–357.

48 Thatcher, *Downing Street Years*, 44.

49 Ibid., 44.

50 PREM19/37. CPRS 'Paper on the Economy of the UK', 8 May 1979.

51 HOSK/1/33.

52 John Campbell, *Margaret Thatcher. Volume Two: The Iron Lady* (London: Pimlico, 2004), 51.

53 Howe, *Conflict*, 143.

54 Lawson, *View*, 41.

55 F. A. Hayek, *The Road to Serfdom* (London: Routledge, 2007 [1944]), 127.

56 Howe, *Conflict*, 143.

57 Ibid., 142.

58 Lawson, *View*, 40.

59 Milton Friedman commented that 'the most important thing that Margaret Thatcher did was … to end foreign exchange control. That was a precondition for other measures'. *Margaret Thatcher's Revolution. How it Happened and What it Meant*, ed. S. Roy and J. Clarke (London: Continuum, 2005), 66.

60 Howe, *Conflict*, 143.

61 Howe, *Conflict*, 143.

62 PREM19/437 Note from Tim Lankester to Geoffrey Howe, 14 February 1980.

63 PREM19/437. Note from Robin Ibbs to Margaret Thatcher, 6 October 1980.

64 PREM19/437. Note from Lankester to Margaret Thatcher, 14 February 1980.

65 PREM19/437. Letter from Alan Walters to Margaret Thatcher, 22 October 1981.

66 PREM19/437. Letter from Geoffrey Howe to Margaret Thatcher, 17 September 1980.

67 Howe, *Conflict*, 143.

68 M. D. Kandiah, 'Witness Seminar I, "Big Bang": The October 1986 Stock Market Deregulation', *Contemporary British History* (13:1 1999b), 104.

69 Lawson, *View*, 2–53.

5 Financial deregulation

As we have seen, neoliberalism and Thatcherism broadly aligned in a desire to prioritize stable monetary conditions at the expense of Keynesian counter-cyclical deficit spending. It has been widely assumed that the Thatcher government was 'pro-market', implementing liberalization and deregulation. Chapter 4 examined this in terms of a liberal measure – removing exchange controls – and another that promoted private enterprise through a number of state-guided incentivized enterprise zones. The following chapters build upon this analysis by asking the related question: to what extent did the Thatcher government reduce the influence of vested interests on the British economy? By framing the policies of Thatcherism in this way we will examine the elusive concept of a 'free market'. The primary reason this formulation has been chosen is because it was a prime concern for the early neoliberals, in particular European Ordoliberals. The results will cast doubt upon the premise that the Thatcher government was indeed pro-market.

Part of the neoliberal critique of the 1970s the British economy rested upon was the impediment to economic freedom posed by entrenched interests. This can be seen most clearly during the Winter of Discontent. To Austrians like Friedrich Hayek and Ludwig von Mises this was also a by-product of democracy, where organized groups managed to exert influence over politicians who then attempted to satisfy their demands.[1] This was most obvious in the Labour Party's relationship with the trades unions as well as other 'producer' groups. Influence of this kind would, according to neoliberals, trigger government action that would distort markets and prices, and drive up inflation and potentially unemployment.

A leading member of the Treasury for most of the Thatcher years, Lord Burns, has said the prime minister and Nigel Lawson were naturally sceptical to organized entities in general, whether this was the CBI or the trades unions.[2] In addition, one of the broad aims of Thatcherism was reasserting order and government autonomy. This included reducing the kind of disorder seen during picketing in strikes and allowing government to make decisions without overwhelming pressure from a variety of interest groups. It is this dual purpose identified by Andrew Gamble in his (1994b) critique of Thatcherism: 'The Free Market and the Strong State'. This made a link between the Thatcher government and Freiburg neoliberals of the 1930s and 1940s. Indeed, Thatcherites characterized the British state in the 1970s as both too big and too weak.[3] Crucially though, Ordoliberals generally advocated measures that they considered 'market compatible'.[4] It may be, however, that by restructuring the British economy the Thatcher government reduced the power of some vested interests but created others. The following chapters aim to show that it ranged from effectively nullifying a previously powerful group's influence (trade union reform) to eliminating one but allowing another to appear (the City, privatization) and last, failing in its attempt to tackle one interest (the British Broadcasting Corporation [BBC]) yet permitting another to form (BSkyB).

Neoliberalism, vested interests and monopolies

Economic liberals dislike the impact of vested interests on markets. Groups influence policymakers, sometimes as a quid pro quo in the democratic process. They can behave as 'rent-seekers', elevate prices and raise barriers to market entry. Some liberals wanted to reduce the formation of monopolies, whether publicly or privately owned. Although theories of monopolies and competition in markets are complex, it is worth setting out some of the broad principles here.

Where the Hayekian and Friedmanite strands of thought converged was on the deleterious implications on markets of bureaucratic intervention. Although developing his own brand of economics, Friedman became an ardent proponent of the political principles found in *The Road to Serfdom*.[5] He explained one of the ways in which he thought government was 'the problem' through the influence of special interest groups: 'Government actions often provide substantial benefits to a few while imposing small costs on many.'[6] Austrians like Hayek thought that government acted as a civil association, when ideally it should simply *protect* civil association.[7] Likewise Hayek believed, and in this respect he agreed with Chicagoans, that monopolies were often created by governments, either directly or indirectly.[8] Once monopoly status was achieved, which the associated vested interest lobbying preserved, it could only worsen when an industry was state owned.

Early neoliberal thought, however, converged on the belief that monopolies should be prevented and competition promoted. Hayek, writing to Walter Lippman in the 1930s, did show some interest in using corporate law to limit the size of large corporations.[9] Hayek's contemporaries at the Freiburg School, the Ordoliberals, took a more activist line on these issues. The Ordoliberal model, used in part by post-war West German governments, had price and markets at its core, but believed the state should intervene to prevent monopoly formation.[10] Ordoliberals advocated competition rules embedded in law, rather than discretionary and often political decisions.[11] Wilhelm Röpke, in particular, had a lifelong interest in wanting to curb cartels and monopolies.[12] He believed that capitalism had fallen into disrepute because competition had been corrupted by monopoly, and because sectional interests had exploited state power.[13] The 'social market economy' constructed by the Ordoliberals had at its core a strong state, tasked with maintaining competition and monopoly, and constrained by law: the *Rechtsstaat*.[14] Daniel Stedman-Jones has identified the convergence between the Ordoliberals and the 'first' Chicago School of the 1930s. For instance, Chicagoan Henry Simons envisaged a role for the state in preventing monopoly.[15] Ben Jackson has also described how many of the early neoliberals, generally including Hayek but exempting Mises, produced literature in the 1930s and 1940s that advocated state regulation to break up large corporations.[16] Indeed Simons wrote in 1934 that 'the great enemy of democracy is monopoly, in all its forms'.[17]

This was to conflict markedly with later neoliberal thinking, which privileged the sovereignty of the individual over the wider community. The most prominent Ordoliberal politician, post-war German Finance Minister Ludwig Erhard, consistently put a free economy – unimpeded by vested interests – at the centre of his policies in government, or in his own formulation 'question number one'.[18] In a speech in 1948 Erhard said

> I do not regard myself as the representative of special interests, and certainly not as the representative of the interests of industry or trade.... To be responsible for economic policy means to be responsible to the people as a whole.[19]

The views of neoliberals towards monopolies and competition diverged in the 1950s. If the early neoliberal activist state became associated with German Ordoliberals both Austrians and Chicagoans subsequently took a more laissez-faire position. Hayek had included some minimal interventionist inclinations in *Road to Serfdom* but he came to represent more utopian thinking. Although Hayek feared state power, he never confronted private power and saw no need for antitrust and anti-monopoly policies. He believed that the power of large companies should be constrained by competition.[20] Other Austrian School thinkers articulated their belief that a monopoly like a trade union is more dangerous than an enterprise monopoly due to the former's legal privileges and powers of coercion.[21] Hayek thought the sort of models derived by Ordoliberals like Eucken would only serve to increasingly undermine the freedom of the individual.[22] Rather than enforcing competition, which Hayek thought 'absurd', Austrians believed the restraint of trade should be prevented.[23]

For Austrians, it was not monopoly but only the prevention of competition which was harmful.[24] Murray Rothbard, another neoliberal in the Austrian tradition, although by this time often deemed a 'libertarian', attacked the concept of 'natural monopoly' in the 1960s. Many thought that the provision of some essential public goods, such as water, were natural monopolies and should be controlled and administered by central government. This was dismissed by Rothbard, as well as the idea of 'collective goods', as fictions perpetuated by those with a vested interest in maintaining privileged positions.[25] Rothbard represented a newer generation of Austrian (in the tradition, not nationality) thinkers that took a more uncompromising line than predecessors like Hayek. Rothbard believed the state an 'anti-social instrument' that should be whittled down to its prime function of upholding the rule of law.[26]

The general stance of the Chicago School towards monopoly changed under the leadership of Milton Friedman after 1946, in part due to the 'Free Market Study Group' and 'Anti-Trust Project'.[27] Guided by George Stigler, Chicagoans came to believe that monopolies were sustained by government but that large companies could replicate the competition function.[28] As a result Friedman also became more relaxed about the appearance of monopolies, writing in 1962 that it is normal in most markets to observe 'giants and pygmies side by side'.[29] Chicagoans also advocated the best action to counter vested interests and monopoly was to reduce market entry barriers. According to Mark Skousen, however, the Austrian and Chicagoan positions differed because of their broader philosophical positions. Chicagoans generally believed in the possibilities of equilibrating 'perfect competition' while Austrians saw markets as dynamic, spontaneous and non-equilibrating.[30] Austrians saw attempts to restrict predatory practices by regulation or oversight as flawed, as 'inappropriate equilibrium theorizing' and serving only to impede information and efficiency in a particular market.[31] Bruce Caldwell has articulated the Austrian view that monopoly can be a reward for effective entrepreneurship, but that this situation is always impermanent.[32] So while the Austrians came to embody a position that advocated competition by reducing both entry barriers and regulation, the Chicagoans moved some way, but never fully to that ideal.[33] This was, according to Skousen, because Chicagoans sometimes supported policies prohibiting price fixing and mergers, and even worked directly with (the US) government in making 'anti-trust' laws.[34]

The various strands of neoliberalism, then, would agree that monopoly and vested interests had injurious effects on markets. They could also converge on the desirability of private rather than state ownership, as well as many producers operating in a market as possible. Last, information flows via the price mechanism would operate more efficiently if monopoly formation and special interest group influence were reduced. Each school, however, had a different approach as to how these objectives could be achieved. Ordoliberals believed action should be taken to break up monopolies while Friedman and Stigler thought reducing entry barriers was sufficient and moved away from the regulation of the 1950s. Austrians shared these liberalizing, rather than legislating, instincts, but often took a more utopian or 'hardline' point of view.[35]

A government committed to the tenets of economic liberalism may have been expected to confront vested interests and monopolies. There is, however, little evidence to suggest that the Thatcher government broadly set out to do this.[36] There was no master plan to tame vested interests, and some were actually among the Conservative Party's biggest supporters.[37] Given their association with neoliberalism, Conservative politicians like Geoffrey Howe and Keith Joseph appeared unconcerned by concentration of private economic power.[38] Nevertheless, economic liberals in the Conservative Party, not least the prime minister, did have a predisposition to this end. Adrian Williamson has written that many Tories wanted to promote competition in the 1970s as a means to reinvigorate the sluggish British economy.[39] The 1979 Conservative Manifesto talked of reviewing the roles of the Office of Fair Trading (OFT) and the Monopolies and Mergers Commission to 'ensure effective competition and fair pricing policies'.[40] Similarly the CPS had explicitly stated, in 1975, 'government has a clear responsibility to curtail restrictive practices and the abuse of monopoly power whether perpetrated by companies, trade unions, or professional associations'.[41]

The thinking of the party had long been influenced by the work of Edmund Burke, who stressed the importance of multiple sources of power and influence as well as of a pluralistic society.[42] The Conservatives were usually considered less beholden to special interests – at least beyond big business – in comparison with their counterparts in the Labour Party.[43] Indeed former Cabinet Minister in the Thatcher government, Kenneth Clarke, described in his memoirs one example of the prime minister's attitude towards industry lobbyists. Clarke was harangued by the pharmaceutical industry as he proposed a modest reform to reduce the number of branded products doctors could prescribe on the NHS. With Clarke unyielding a number of chief executives arranged a meeting with Thatcher in an attempt to quash the proposal, citing the funding that many of the companies gave to the Conservative Party. The prime minister told them 'funding was not to be abused for the purpose of obtaining private commercial advantage from the British government and the taxpayer' and 'sent them away with a flea in their ear'.[44]

With this combination of long-term Conservative thinking, the pressure exerted by trades unions in the 1970s, as well as the renewed interest in liberal economics by the time the Thatcher government came to power – as well as Thatcher's brusque attitude towards those requesting special treatment – it may have been anticipated that they would attempt to attenuate the influence of vested interests. This will be looked at by examining several such groups: trades unions, the nationalized industries, the BBC and the City of London. Margaret Thatcher had a long-standing antipathy to trades unions as well as the BBC.[45] Documents show how privatization of nationalized industries was a political objective from the early years of the Thatcher government while the emphasis on trade made financial liberalization another implicit goal. Taken together these policies may have represented a cross section of a broad, but ill-defined, effort to reduce the power of entrenched interests. These chapters explore to what extent this assertion was true.

'Big Bang'

Financial deregulation during the 1980s was a seemingly clear application of liberal economic ideas. The liberalization of the City of London (otherwise known as 'Big Bang') on 27 October 1986, was one of a series of measures, such as the removal of exchange controls, that apparently moved the British economy in a more pro-market direction.[46] Big Bang itself was probably the furthest reaching liberalization measure of Thatcherism for its impact on the flow of international financial capital, and globalization in general. Big Bang was one method of reducing the power of a vested interest: restrictive practices in the City of London. As with some of the other Thatcher reforms, however, one vested interest was emasculated only for another to take its place.

The City before Big Bang

For much of the twentieth century the City was inhabited by 'gentlemanly capitalists'.[47] The financial sector in London in the 1970s was considered a place of restrictive practices. As a former economic journalist Nigel Lawson talked of the 'old, clubby, City'.[48] It was one restrictive practice, the system of fixed minimum commissions (essentially limiting access to markets), that prompted the OFT to launch an investigation into the LSE in 1979. Another, the 'single capacity' rule regarding jobs (permitting one to act as either a stockbroker or a market maker) as well as effectively excluding all foreigners from LSE membership left the City, according to Lawson, undercapitalized and in danger of becoming a backwater.[49] Some felt the City a 'victim' of government action.[50] Peter Middleton, Permanent Secretary to the Treasury from 1983 to 1991, later noted the Bank of England too as a barrier to reform. He said 'the Bank's belief in orderly markets did get in the way of their belief in a liberal economic process'.[51]

The Chairman of the LSE, Nicholas Goodison, asked the OFT to call off its investigation if it promised to reform.[52] It was Cecil Parkinson in 1983, as Secretary of State at the Department of Trade and Industry (DTI), who launched the initiative (in conjunction with Goodison) that led to liberalization of the City.[53] A decision had to be made about whether to implement gradual or sudden change. Goodison believed it had to be the latter as the only way in obtaining his members' agreement in full.[54] Monetary economist Tim Congdon, however, believed Big Bang was part of a 'Bigger Bang', including an offshore revolution where companies and investors found that doing business in dollars in London increased returns. Congdon also saw financial deregulation as a natural step as levels of bank credit lent to the private sector grew in the early 1980s.[55]

27 October 1986

Restrictions on single capacity trading and fixed minimum commissions were lifted after Big Bang, and new hopefuls streamed into the City as trading in stocks and shares mushroomed. The government saw its role as setting out a regulatory framework to oversee the new-found financial freedom. The 1984 Gower Report proposed terms for investor protection but also stated that regulation could not 'seek to achieve the impossible task of protecting fools from their own folly'.[56] The regulatory bodies were outlined in the 1986 Financial Services Act, which formed self-regulatory organizations (SROs), (made up of 'providers and users of financial services who will have the knowledge and expertise to ensure that investors' interests are being properly looked after') and a Securities and Investment Board (SIB).[57] Nigel Lawson wrote in 2006 that this system was more bureaucratic than the government intended.[58] The IEA went much further. Despite Big Bang being an act of deregulation the think-tank, in the wake of the 2008 financial crisis, believed the 1986 framework was overly complex and created perverse incentives.[59] Neoliberals saw Big Bang, as well as providing some financial liberalization, as simultaneously an act of regulation.

Neoliberal rationale for Big Bang

Succeeding Cecil Parkinson at the DTI, Norman Tebbit argued for liberalization of financial services in 1984 in dry microeconomic terms: 'I see market forces as the most potent weapon available, and I propose to rely on them to the maximum extent feasible. There can be no effective play of market forces without good market information.'[60] Financial deregulation appeared to be a pure application of liberal economic ideas. It prioritized wealth creation, increased individual liberty and efficiency and lowered barriers to market entry. Alongside the growing revolution in communications and information technology, liberalization allowed quicker and more effective signalling and flow of information. Another example of deregulation was the ending of exchange controls in 1979. It was thought that controls had produced 'sub-optimal outcomes' and the same principle can be applied to the City, in particular the view that it was undercapitalized.[61] Hong Kong was often cited as a liberal economic model, despite the lack of political freedom in the city state. Milton Friedman, in his book *Free to Choose*, eulogized the Hong Kong system of low tax, minimal state and as a hub of global trade.[62] These measures of exchange control removal and Big Bang, as well as enterprise zones, all tie in with the neoliberal model of Hong Kong. One aspect of this strategy was that it exposed British firms to international competition, challenging in part the assertion that Margaret Thatcher's government was primarily nationalistic. In fact some in the City saw Big Bang as an act of betrayal by Thatcher as it allowed British-owned financial firms to be taken over by foreign banks.[63]

Impact of Big Bang

Big Bang had a number of consequences. One year after, the reform trade with customers in UK shares had nearly doubled while share prices had risen 46 per cent in the first seven months of 1987.[64] It led to rapid wealth accumulation in the City and the South East of the country in general. The changes enhanced London's status as a global financial hub and also caused social change in Britain itself. People from a variety of backgrounds came to work in the City, allowing many to enjoy previously unheard of affluence. Financial liberalization eroded some traditional class distinctions and had some impact in shaking up the old status quo. This was, perversely, at odds with the values of some Tories but precisely one of the goals of economic liberals.[65]

Into the latter part of the 1980s and then 1990s financial liberalization and deregulation, which Big Bang encapsulated, accelerated globalization. The rapid movement of finance capital across borders as well as an acceleration of global trade has been the major economic trend of the modern era. For some authors finance-led capitalism is what makes the neoliberal period distinctive.[66] At the same time it gave the City political power. Andrew Gamble has stated the view that the influence of the City has been exaggerated, that it is 'not large enough, coherent enough, or politically organized enough, to determine government policy'.[67] Lord Burns, however, said in 2011 that the prime minister was hostile to vested interests and organized entities. He believed that Margaret Thatcher generally managed to reduce the power of vested interests, with the exception of Big Bang, which created one: the financial services sector.[68] One subsequent effect of this was the attitude of New Labour towards the City. Gordon Brown courted the financial sector in the knowledge that, without income tax increases, receipts from the City were one of the only ways he could fund his domestic spending agenda. By the turn of the century the financial sector provided 25 per cent of the UK's corporate tax receipts.[69] Critics of financial deregulation believed the attitude and policies of Western governments from the 1980s, including ending the separation of investment and commercial banks, essentially allowed some to become 'too big to fail'.[70] The government's Policy Unit anticipated the impact of Big Bang in a paper, written by David Willetts and Brian Griffiths, in June 1986:

> If Big Bang goes off successfully, it will be seen as a showpiece for Government policy on deregulation and increased competition; if it leads to scandals and liquidations, it will be labelled the unacceptable face of unpopular capitalism.... Will we see boom and then bust?[71]

The economic liberal viewpoint, however, was that the regulatory framework itself sowed the seeds for later crises because policies were not sufficiently pro-market.[72] Hayekian thinking again viewed neoliberal deregulation as overbearing state involvement that distorted markets. With respect to Big Bang in 1986 the Thatcher government managed to end the restrictive practices of the old City system, only to replace it with a more powerful vested interest.

Conclusion

As with all the areas in this study, how far the Thatcher government reduced the influence of vested interests can be gauged in graduations, and according to which strain of liberalism one is discussing. For economic liberals vested interests distort market forces and reduce their efficiency. Thatcherism may have been expected to have reduced the power of these groups as far as possible. The policies towards the City and financial services show how the government attempted to reduce the power of a vested interest (restrictive practices in the City), only to create another (a reconstructed global financial hub). The 1986 Big Bang liberalized financial services in the City of London, sweeping away the old boys network of restrictive practices and bringing increased wealth to the South East of the country. Yet 'light-touch' regulation allowed huge financial institutions to form and created a new vested interest.

Notes

1 Norman Barry, *On Classical Liberalism and Libertarianism* (Basingstoke: Macmillan, 1986), 80. Hayek and Mises were wary of 'unlimited democracy' but accepted this as preferable to violence.
2 Interview with Lord Burns, 12 May 2011.
3 Richard Vinen, *Thatcher's Britain. The Politics and Social Upheaval of the 1980s* (London: Simon & Schuster, 2009), 282.
4 Christian Watrin, 'Alfred Müller-Armack – Economic Policy Maker and Sociologist of Religion', in *The Theory of Capitalism in the German Economic Tradition*, ed. Peter Koslowski (London: Springer, 2000), 209; Samuel Gregg, *Wilhelm Röpke's Political Economy* (Cheltenham: Edward Elgar, 2010), 89.
5 Milton Friedman, *Capitalism and Freedom* (Chicago, IL: University of Chicago Press, 2002 [1962]), 11.
6 Milton Friedman, *Why Government is the Problem* (Stanford, CA: Stanford University Press, 1993), 7.
7 Andrew Gamble, *Hayek. The Iron Cage of Liberty* (Cambridge: Polity Press, 1996), 189.
8 Alexander Shand, 'Austrian Policy for the Thatcher Government', *Economic Affairs* 4:1 (October 1983), 14.
9 Ben Jackson, 'Freedom, the Common Good, and the Rule of Law: Lippmann and Hayek on Economic Planning', *Journal of the History of Ideas* 73:1 (January 2012), 65.
10 Ralf Ptak, 'Neoliberalism in Germany. Revisiting the Ordoliberal Foundations of the Social Market Economy', in *The Road from Mont Pelerin. The Making of the Neoliberal Thought Collective*, ed. P. Mirowski and D. Plehwe (Harvard: Harvard University Press, 2009), 102; A. J. Nicholls, *Freedom with Responsibility. The Social Market Economy in Germany, 1918–1963* (Oxford: Oxford University Press, 1994), 395.

11 Wernhard Möschel, 'The Proper Scope of Government Viewed from an Ordoliberal Perspective: The Example of Competition Policy', *Journal of Institutional and Theoretical Economics (JITE)/Zeitschrift für die gesamte Staatswissenschaft* 157:1 (2001), 4.
12 Gregg, *Wilhelm Röpke*, 7.
13 Gregg, *Wilhelm Röpke*, 77.
14 Daniel Stedman-Jones, *Masters of the Universe. Hayek, Friedman, and the Birth of Neoliberal Politics* (Oxford: Princeton University Press, 2012), 122; Rachel S. Turner, *Neoliberal Ideology. History, Concepts and Policies* (Edinburgh: Edinburgh University Press, 2008), 219.
15 Stedman-Jones, *Masters*, 335.
16 Ben Jackson, 'At the Origins of Neoliberalism: The Free Economy and the Strong State, 1930–1947', *The Historical Journal* 53:1 (March 2010), 142.
17 Jackson, 'Origins', 142.
18 Alfred C. Mierzejewski, *Ludwig Erhard. A Biography* (London: University of North Carolina Press, 2004), 33.
19 Ludwig Erhard, *Prosperity through Competition*, translated by Edith Temple Roberts and John B. Wood (New York: Frederick A. Praeger, 1958), 101.
20 Gamble, *Hayek*, 72, 190.
21 Alexander Shand, *Free Market Morality. The Political Economy of the Austrian School* (London: Routledge, 1990), 176.
22 Artur Woll, 'Freiheit durch Ordnung: Die gesellschaftspolitische Leitidee im Denken von Walter Eucken und Friedrich A. von Hayek' [Freedom through Order: The Guiding Principle of Economic Policy in Walter Eucken's and Friedrich A. von Hayek's Thought], *ORDO. Jahrbuch für die Ordnung von Wirtschaft und Gesellschaft* [Ordo Yearbook of Economic and Social Order] (Stuttgart: Gustav Fischer Verlag, Band 40, 1989), 97.
23 Manfried E. Streit and Michael Wohlgemuth, 'The Market Economy and the State. Hayekian and Ordoliberal Conceptions', in *The Theory of Capitalism in the German Economic Tradition*, ed. Peter Koslowski (London: Springer, 2000), 244.
24 Alexander H. Shand, *The Capitalist Alternative: An Introduction to Neo-Austrian Economics* (Frome: Wheatsheaf, 1984), 130.
25 Thomas J. Dilorenzo, 'The Myth of Natural Monopoly', *Review of Austrian Economics* 9:2 (1996), 43; Shand, *Neo-Austrian*, 101–103.
26 Shand, *Neo-Austrian*, 182–183.
27 Daniel Stedman-Jones, 'The Influence of Transatlantic Neoliberal Politics', seminar at Queen Mary University of London, 22 October 2013.
28 Stedman-Jones, 'Influence', seminar.
29 Friedman, *Capitalism*, 121.
30 Mark Skousen, *Vienna & Chicago. Friends or Foes? A Tale of Two Schools of Free-Market Economics* (Washington, DC: Capital Press, 2005), 214.
31 Dominick T. Armentano, 'Antitrust Reform: Predatory Practices and the Competitive Process', *Review of Austrian Economics* 3 (1989), 72.
32 Bruce Caldwell, 'The Chicago School, Hayek and Neoliberalism', in *Building Chicago Economics: New Perspectives on the History of America's Most Powerful Economics Program*, ed. Robert Van Horn, Philip Mirowski and Thomas A. Stapleford (Cambridge: Cambridge University Press, 2011), 319.
33 Skousen, *Vienna & Chicago*, 218.
34 Skousen, *Vienna & Chicago*, 214, 218.
35 Skousen, *Vienna & Chicago*, 218.
36 Email correspondence with Sir Adam Ridley, 15 May 2013.
37 Charles Moore, *Margaret Thatcher. The Authorized Biography, Volume Two: Everything She Wants* (London: Allen Lane, 2015), 187.
38 Ben Jackson, 'Currents of Neo-Liberalism: British Political Ideologies and the New Right, c.1955–1979', *English Historical Review* 131 (2016), 842.

39 Adrian Williamson, *Conservative Economic Policymaking and the Birth of Thatcherism, 1964–1979* (Basingstoke: Palgrave Macmillan, 2015), 140, 155.
40 The 1979 Conservative Party election manifesto, accessed 2 June 2017, www.conservativemanifesto.com/1979/1979-conservative-manifesto.shtml
41 Centre for Policy Studies, 'Why Britain Needs a Social Market Economy' (Chichester: Barry Rose, 1975), 1–8.
42 Email correspondence with Sir Adam Ridley, 15 May 2013, Margaret Thatcher Foundation (hereafter MTF), 108087, Margaret Thatcher Speech to Scottish Conservative Party Conference, 12 May 1990.
43 Tim Bale, *The Conservatives Since 1945* (Oxford: Oxford University Press, 2012), 290; Norman Barry, *The New Right* (Beckenham: Croom Helm, 1987), 127.
44 Ken Clarke, *Kind of Blue: A Political Memoir* (London: Macmillan, 2016), 136.
45 Interview with Sir Alan Peacock, 26 January 2010; Charles Moore, *Margaret Thatcher. The Authorized Biography. Volume One: Not for Turning* (London: Allen Lane, 2013), 136.
46 Chairman of the London Stock Exchange Sir Nicholas Goodison later said that the 'real cause (of Big Bang) was the abolition of exchange controls'. From M. D. Kandiah, 'Witness Seminar I "Big Bang": The October 1986 Stock Market Deregulation', *Contemporary British History* 13:1 (1999b), 106.
47 E. H. H. Green, 'The Conservatives and the City', in *The British Government and the City of London in the Twentieth Century*, ed. R. Michie and P. Williamson (Cambridge: Cambridge University Press, 2011), 172.
48 Nigel Lawson, 'Foreword', in *Big Bang 20 Years on. New Challenges Facing the Financial Services Sector. Collected Essays* (London: CPS, 2006), ii.
49 Lawson, 'Foreword,' i–ii.
50 Philip Williamson, 'The City of London and Government in Modern Britain: Debates and Politics', in *The British Government and the City of London in the Twentieth Century*, ed. R. Michie and P. Williamson (Cambridge: Cambridge University Press, 2011), 10.
51 Sir Peter Middleton, cited in M. D. Kandiah, 'Witness Seminar I "Big Bang": The October 1986 Stock Market Deregulation', *Contemporary British History* 13:1 (1999b), 109.
52 Lawson, 'Foreword', I; David Kynaston, *City of London, The History*, ed. D. Miller (London: Chatto & Windus, 2011), 555.
53 Nigel Lawson, *The View from No. 11. Memoirs of a Tory Radical* (London: Corgi Books, 1993), 398–399; Kynaston, *City*, 556.
54 Lawson, *View*, 400.
55 Interview with Tim Congdon, 24 February 2012.
56 Lawson, *View*, 401.
57 Lawson, *View*, 402; Leon Brittan, *Parliamentary Debates* (Commons), 89, 14 January 1986, 938–1024.
58 Lawson, 'Foreword', iv.
59 Philip Booth, 'More Regulation, Less Regulation or Better Regulation?', in *Verdict on the Crash. Causes and Policy Implications*, ed. P. Booth (London: IEA, 2009), 169.
60 Lawson, 'Foreword', iv.
61 Ranald Michie, 'City and Government: Changing Relationship', in *The British Government and the City of London in the Twentieth Century*, ed. R. Michie and P. Williamson (Cambridge: Cambridge University Press, 2011), 55.
62 Milton and Rose Friedman, *Free to Choose* (London: Pan Books, 1990 [1980]), 34.
63 Michie, 'City', 51;, Kynaston, *City*, 575.
64 Virginia Preston, ' "Big Bang": Chronology of Events', *Contemporary British History* 13:1 (1999), 99.
65 Green, 'Conservatives', 173; Barry, *Liberalism*, 70.

66 Matthew Eagleton-Pierce, *Neoliberalism: The Key Concepts* (Abingdon: Routledge, 2016), 68–77.
67 Andrew Gamble, *The Free Economy and the Strong State: The Politics of Thatcherism* (Basingstoke: Palgrave Macmillan, 1994b), 130.
68 Interview with Lord Burns, 12 May 2011.
69 Alistair Darling, *Back From the Brink. 1,000 Days at Number 11* (London: Atlantic Books, 2012), 100.
70 Joseph Stiglitz, *Freefall. Free Markets and the Sinking of the Global Economy* (London: Penguin, 2010), 82–83.
71 Records of the Prime Minister's Office: Correspondence and Papers, 1979–1997 (The National Archives: Public Record Office, Kew, hereafter PREM19), PREM19/1718, 'Economic Policy: Gower Report on Investor Protection', David Willetts and Brian Griffiths, Policy Unit paper, 3 June 1986.
72 Eamonn Butler, 'The Financial Crisis: Blame Governments, not Banks', in *Verdict on the Crash. Causes and Policy Implications*, ed. P. Booth (London: Institute for Economic Affairs, 2009), 52–56.

6   Trade union reform

No study of vested interests and Thatcherism would be complete without an examination of trade union policy. Although it might be perceived that neoliberals were uniformly hostile to organized labour, there were a number of different approaches to industrial relations. Chapter 5 outlined a number of core positions taken by the different schools of neoliberalism towards vested interests, monopolies and competition. We will now look at how the Thatcher government sought to reduce the influence of trade union power.

Conservative politicians in the 1970s may not have been uniformly economic liberal but most could unite around the issue of trade union reform. The influence of trades unions had increased over the twentieth century to the point when one of the abiding memories of 1978 and 1979 in Britain remains of widespread strikes, from Ford workers to gravediggers to refuse collectors. Revisionist historians have questioned the commonly held assumption that unions wielded as much power as has often been thought, or if there was even a series of crises in the 1970s.[1] That assertion, however, is at odds with the statistics, and that both Labour and Conservative leaders were 'governing against pressure' from the unions.[2] The amount of days lost due to strikes over this period, for example, was 31 times greater in 1972, compared to 1991.[3] In addition, successive incomes policies and the high position in political life accorded to trade union leaders reflected their pre-Thatcher influence. Working through the issues of the day over 'beer and sandwiches' at Downing Street was a cliché of corporatist Britain, but a telling one nevertheless. What is clear, however, is that the economic problems of the 1970s – in particular the strikes of 1978 and 1979 – gave the Conservative Party the opportunity to demonize the unions and play on the public's widespread frustration with them. Robert Saunders has identified the importance of the 'crisis' narrative formulated by Margaret Thatcher in the 1970s and how her political programme was initially based on its diagnostic, rather than prescriptive nature.[4] This crisis narrative was exploited remorselessly over the next decade, while the antipathy towards trades unions helped to discredit the Labour Party for a generation.[5]

Development of the trade union movement

The rise of the trade union movement from the mid-1800s was consolidated by legislation in granting it privileges in 1871 and 1875, and in particular the 1906 Trade Disputes Act.[6] The latter was cited by Friedrich Hayek as the key law liberals needed to repeal.[7] Union influence increased as nationalization advanced, particularly in the post-1945 period. During its time in government between 1951 and 1964, Conservative leaders were charged with showing a degree of accommodation and cooperation with trade union leaders not seen before or after. The dominant One Nation strand of the party wanted good relations with unions, between employers and management and refrained from legislating in this area.[8] One Nation Tories may have sought to limit the inequality that could threaten capitalism and parliamentary democracy and drive some towards Marxism. It was in keeping with ideas of enlightened self-interest to mollify the trades unions.[9] Former civil servant and author Alec Cairncross, however, believed the Conservatives' relationship was not as harmonious during this era and that the party 'was never able to obtain the agreement of the trade unions … to a period of wage restraint'.[10] Some in the Conservative Party were concerned at the growth in union influence in their 13 years in government. In 1958 the Inns of Court Conservative Association produced *A Giant's Strength*, which advocated taming growing trade union power.[11] During the following decades, 'wildcat' strikes began to proliferate.[12] Days lost through strikes rose from 2.277 million days in 1964 to 4.69 million in 1968 and to a peak of 23.909 million during 1972.[13] From the legislation of the late nineteenth century until the 1970s, trades unions appeared to be exerting ever greater influence over political decisions. Hayek had identified the growth in power he believed organized labour increasingly enjoyed were steps towards excessive state control, while warning of the effects of 'unlimited democracy' on individual freedom.[14]

Harold Wilson, recognizing that industrial relations needed improvement, backed Barbara Castle's 1969 White Paper, *In Place of Strife*. It aimed to bring unofficial strikes to an end by proposing ballots before action, and also made provision for an Industrial Relations Court to settle disputes. There was vehement opposition to *In Place of Strife*, from trade union leaders and within the Labour Party itself. Margaret Thatcher later wrote, outlining the neoliberal linkage between vested interests and politics, that Callaghan 'had built his career on giving the trade unions whatever they wanted. So I felt that he was to blame, in a uniquely personal way, for the scenes of the winter of 1978/79'.[15] Wilson's relatively moderate stance was not helped by growing left wing inclinations within his party and the trade union movement as a whole during this period.[16]

The 1970s: widespread strikes and the crises of state power

The governments of the 1960s had attempted to restrain wage demands but nevertheless failed to prevent strikes. After winning the 1970 election the Conservatives attempted to deal with the issue in one piece of legislation, the 1971 Industrial Relations Act. Put together by then Solicitor General Geoffrey Howe and Secretary of State for Employment Robert Carr, the Act covered much the same ground as *In Place of Strife*, while also limiting authorized strike action. The law was not widely enforced, however, undermining the credibility of the Heath government and added to the growing divide between it and the trade union movement.

After changing course at the end of 1971 – one of several derided 'U-turns' – the Heath government struggled to control inflation through a prices and incomes policy. The government was fatally damaged by the National Union of Mineworkers (NUM) strikes between 1972 and 1974, in conjunction with the 1973 oil crisis that caused a further surge in inflation and increased the cost of energy. For a time in the late 1970s, James Callaghan's Labour government had managed to reduce inflation with a nominal 5 per cent wage limit, during the 'social contract' period. The policy unravelled in late 1978 as the Winter of Discontent took hold amid widespread strikes. This gave Margaret Thatcher the rhetorical space to appear to offer an alternative.[17]

Neoliberalism and trades unions

The Conservatives in the late 1970s were guarded about how they would tackle trade union militancy. While in other areas they would overtly profess interest in liberal economic recommendations, such as monetarist economics, when it came to industrial relations the party had to tread carefully. Conservative politicians were scarred by the humiliation of the Heath government. Nevertheless, if there was one topic on which neoliberals had produced reams of material it was trade union reform.

During the 1960s and 1970s, the IEA concentrated primarily on two issues: monetarism to combat high inflation and trade union reform.[18] In 1975, the IEA reprinted a pamphlet titled *The Theory of Collective Bargaining* by a neoliberal contemporary of Hayek, W. H. Hutt. Originally written in 1931, it was claimed by Hutt that trades unions had operated as a 'regressive and impoverishing influence' and that the strike threat had led to a diminishing of Britain's power in the world. Hutt said that the main beneficiaries had been union hierarchies, in which leaders were well paid in comparison with the rank and file, and the politicians who profited by supporting them.[19] Targeting union leaders and not rank and file members was a consistent neoliberal device. Friedrich Hayek criticized unions as being organized minorities pursuing self-interest at the expense of the wider community, who pay in terms of both monopoly prices and disorder. Hayek also said that collective bargaining worsened conditions for highly-skilled workers who had the same position as others in the union.[20]

As we have seen, the CPS, founded in 1974 by Keith Joseph, was initially charged with examining the West German *Soziale Marktwirtschaft* (social market economy). Interestingly in light of how the Thatcher government would treat monopoly and competition, Joseph initially planned to name the CPS the 'Erhard Foundation', after the West German leader and political embodiment of Ordoliberalism.[21] Joseph identified good industrial relations as key to West Germany's success.[22] Nigel Lawson also showed interest in the German model of 'work's councils', although the subsequent Thatcher government's attitude to industrial relations looked very different from the more consensual German approach.[23] Joseph addressed the Bow Group in 1979 by framing the issue in a long-term and declinist narrative. 'If the debate is to be productive and honest, setting the union problem in the context of our economic decline, rather than at the centre of today's crisis [is crucial].'[24] The Bow Group, particularly under the leadership of Peter Lilley, also identified the importance of reducing union influence. The group formulated an 'Alternative Manifesto' ahead of the February 1974 election and later 'Lessons for Power' that argued against incomes policies.[25]

Pro-market economists and writers targeted trade union reform as an urgent priority in the 1960s and 1970s for a number of reasons. The most obvious one was that Britain suffered a series of debilitating strikes that hampered the economy and caused social unrest. The second was that excessive wage demands fuelled inflation. According to neoliberals like Milton Friedman, intervention in the economy from government would cause inflation, and therefore drive wage demands upwards.[26] In this respect there was a fundamental difference between Hayekians and Friedmanites as to whether trades unions mattered at all.[27] For the latter, the monetary environment was of far greater importance.

Neoliberals thought vested interests affected markets in a number of ways. The collective power of trades unions restricted market entry to other producers through practices such as the closed shop, excessive wage demands and potentially by picketing. Unions collectively prevented competition and therefore choice for consumers. Barriers to entry would hamper productivity and cause price distortions. Power rested with the producer. Liberals wanted to shift this emphasis towards the consumer. Trades unions also impacted on liberal themes of maintaining the sanctity of contracts and respecting the sovereignty of the individual. Some neoliberals believed that unions priced out new labour and had an impoverishing effect, while impeding the growth of the economy as a whole. These last points were adopted by Margaret Thatcher in the 1970s.[28]

Trade union reform: the Conservative Party in opposition

The 1970s strikes energized the Conservative Party. Cecil Parkinson later wrote that the coal mining industry in particular 'was given a privileged position and it abused the privilege'.[29] When returned to opposition many in the party were keen not to alienate voters with tough rhetoric towards the unions, but behind the scenes there was furious debate on how they should be tackled. The work done by the Conservatives in opposition between 1974 and 1979 is documented in detail elsewhere in this book. *The Right Approach* (1976) and *The Right Approach to the Economy* (1977) were both relatively subdued on the issue of trade union reform. They sought to end incomes policy and, in the case of a 'direct *political* challenge to a newly elected Conservative government, we say now quite plainly that they will be resisted firmly and decisively'.[30] The unpublished Stepping Stones project was more combative and forthright towards industrial relations.

John Hoskyns, in charge of Stepping Stones, believed the trade union issue had to be dealt with urgently and comprehensively. Richard Ryder, then political secretary to Margaret Thatcher, described Hoskyns's approach (as well as that of Alfred Sherman at the CPS) as 'hard at it' and impatient for change compared to many in the party.[31] Chris Patten, head of the CRD did not want to estrange voters and thought the emphasis should be on other policies.[32] Hoskyns accused Patten, in a 1978 letter, of ignoring the union issue.[33] Shadow Secretary for Employment, Jim Prior, also took a more moderate stance towards the unions. This was at odds with Conservatives such as Geoffrey Howe, Nigel Lawson and Keith Joseph who wanted to confront the unions, Lawson wrote a letter to Joseph in 1978 complaining that the unions should be higher up the agenda and that the Stepping Stones project was drifting.[34] Geoffrey Howe set out a key component of the Conservative trade union strategy as early as 1977. It echoed the thoughts of Hutt in the 1975 IEA pamphlet. Howe thought that a fruitful tactic could be to identify 'enemies' in the battle with the unions. He said that both trade union leaders and the Labour government should be singled out as adversaries, whereas rank and file trade union members and Labour supporters should be framed separately.[35] This became a key element in the policy of the Thatcher government. Although it was the prime minister herself who was often viewed as identifying enemies and relishing battles here it can be seen that the apparently more placid Howe was articulating this strategy.[36] In addition, the insinuation itself, that trade union members were more moderate than their leaders, may have been false.[37]

Although attempting to appear reasonable towards trades unions in opposition, Margaret Thatcher's real thoughts on them were much tougher. A document from 1978 demonstrated how the future prime minister underlined text from a speech from Friedrich Hayek that berated the unions, such as that 'nobody ought to have the right to force others to strike' and that unions were 'abusing this power which the law has granted to them'.[38] The 1979 Conservative election manifesto said trades unions were a 'single powerful interest group', led by 'a minority of extremists' that Labour had allowed to 'abuse individual liberties and to thwart Britain's chances of success'.[39] The manifesto made three proposals. First the limiting of picketing, second a review of the closed shop and third a wider use of secret ballots, provided for by public funds. Coming soon after the Winter of Discontent, the issue of industrial relations was clearly a major one in 1979.

The first Thatcher government's trade union reforms

James Prior continued in the role he had held in opposition and became Margaret Thatcher's first Secretary for Employment in 1979. Prior was seen as more open to compromise with trade union leaders and less hostile than others in the party, including the prime minister. He described his difficult task of introducing reform in his memoirs.

> I was having to fight on two fronts – I was striving to impose some form of legislation on the unions while repelling the right wing demands for extreme measures ... [it] made me look the reasonable man and therefore difficult for the TUC to attack.[40]

While in opposition, Nicholas Ridley chaired a group on the nationalized industries. Ridley had written a report on the trades unions after the demise of the Heath government, which was leaked to *The Economist* in 1978. The report concluded that a new Conservative government would face a union challenge within its initial two years in power, probably from coal, electricity or dock workers. The government was advised to choose its opponents carefully, preferably British Leyland, the railways or civil service. The Ridley Report also outlined the need for mobile police tactics.[41] Leonard Neal advised Margaret Thatcher on union reform early in the first term and did not see eye to eye with Prior.[42] Lord Ryder, as we have seen, explained how free market liberals close to the prime minister like Alfred Sherman and John Hoskyns, urged a tough stance towards the trades unions.[43] The pressure on Prior (as well as Margaret Thatcher) from the likes of Ridley, Neal, Sherman and Hoskyns as well as Nigel Lawson, was strong. Yet Prior used this to his advantage and the union leaders may have been more flexible as a result.

After the fact there has been some suggestion that the Thatcher government had a pre-planned strategy towards trade union reform. Prior wrote in his memoirs that he argued for 'step-by-step' reform.[44] There is, however, little evidence that this was part of a preconceived grand plan.[45] What we can say, however, is that the Conservatives proceeded with some caution and gradually eroded union privileges when the opportunity arose. The first step was the 1980 Employment Act.

1980 Employment Act

There was some evidence to show the public backed trade union reform. Polls sent by party researcher Keith Britto to the prime minister in November 1979 suggested a majority of union members themselves backed the proposed government reforms.[46] A 1980 CRD report carried out by Party Chairman Peter Thorneycroft, later commented on by *The Times*, showed many rank and file trades unionists supported change. It stated that 47 per cent of union members (against 43 per cent that disagreed) believed reform of trade union law to be in the best interests of the country. The paper also showed strong support to ban secondary picketing in both non-trade unionists (70 per cent) as well as union members (59 per cent).[47] This may have been less to do with market liberalization than the hope that a repeat of the Winter of Discontent might be avoided and frustration at the loss of income suffered when workers were forced out in supposed solidarity with fellow trades unionists with whom, in reality, they had little sympathy.

Jim Prior himself mused on the opposition's failure in government, alluding to the weight of the vested interest on its closest political representatives:

> It may be that because of the Labour Party's relationship with the unions it is not possible for a Labour Government ever to take the necessary steps, even though in their hearts many members of Labour Governments know that they should do so.[48]

Prior, mindful of the failure of the 1971 Act, charted a more moderate course. The eventual legislation modified the law on the closed shop, made most secondary picketing illegal, removed immunity from trade union officials organizing certain secondary strikes and provided public money for secret ballots.[49] Prior devised legislation that was politically possible at that point with the recent past in mind. In this sense, like so much else in Thatcherism, the policy was opportunistic.

The legislation introduced by the Thatcher government was part of a wider strategy that reduced trade union influence and would satisfy most strains of neoliberalism. After two years of Conservative government, however, Hayek was unhappy at the progress being made on the issue. He commented on trade union reform on the BBC programme *Panorama* in March 1981, criticizing Prior. 'The minister in charge of it is not in favour of radical alteration. I have no hope that so long as the matter is in his hands the necessary things will be done.'[50] What was not appreciated by many at the time, however, was that Prior's role and the incremental approach, intended or otherwise, was important in reducing the power of organized labour. There were several other components that reduced its power as a vested interest, but that this early legislation survived played one part.

Prior was succeeded at the Department of Employment by the more Thatcherite Norman Tebbit, who later wrote that the 1982 Employment Act was the highlight of his political career, concentrating the legislation on union immunity from liability in tort.[51] Tebbit wrote, 'I have no doubt that the (1982) Act was my greatest achievement in Government and I believe it has been one of the principal pillars on which the Thatcher economic reforms have been built'.[52] The Act introduced stricter controls on the closed shop and narrowed the definition of a 'trade dispute' to reduce the legal protection available to union officials. It removed the immunity from trades unions in four cases: when action was outside the new definition of a dispute, unlawful picketing, unlawful secondary picketing and if it was taken to impose union membership. The 1982 law was significant because it removed privileges that had existed since the 1906 Trades Disputes Act.[53] The 1982 legislation saw a tightening of that which was introduced in 1980 and signified the next step in Conservative trade union reform. Despite the hostile protestations from Labour, the opposition was in disarray by 1982.

The gradual erosion of the ability of organized labour to disrupt the economy through legislation may appear to be an example of the 'free economy–strong state' thesis. The importance of the changes in law, however, have not been considered crucial by some historians. Martin Holmes thought that the 1980 and 1982 Employment Acts were not as significant on industrial relations as the abandonment of both corporatism and an incomes policy during the first Thatcher government.[54] Certainly the ending of the arrangement between government and industry about setting prices and income levels was important in giving the market more credence. It was also clear that the influence of a vested interest like the trades unions was not going to be as close to central policy making, as well as setting the government on a more adversarial course as communication ceased with union leaders. The 1980 and 1982 Acts, however, demonstrated that the government was going to take legal steps to reduce union power and the strike threat to the country and its economy. The legislation showed that agreement and voluntarism could not be trusted without the force of law. They rolled back the privileges of 1906 that had – according to Hayek[55] – been the core component of union militancy throughout the century and partially curbed the restrictive practices of the closed shop, strikes without secret ballots and secondary picketing. In addition, like the ending of exchange controls in 1979 economic policy, the legislation acted as a signal that the government was going to reduce the power of trades unions and privilege market forces. The 1980 and 1982 Acts were reinforced by subsequent legislation.

The 1984 Trade Union Act set out that industrial action could only be taken after a majority in a secret ballot, made every voting member of a union's governing body be re-elected after five years and insisted unions keep a register of all members' names and addresses.[56] The erosion of union power was to culminate in the miners' strikes. It took longer than the Ridley Report envisaged, five years as opposed to two, but the NUM took on the government in 1984. In the popular consciousness, this was the focal point of the confrontation between the Thatcher government and the trade union movement.

The National Coal Board (NCB)'s announcement of accelerated pit closures prompted strikes, incited by NUM leader Arthur Scargill, across the country in March 1984. The action lasted for a year and violent picketing reached a peak at Orgreave in Yorkshire in June 1984. The violence was robustly fought by 'mobile policing', as had also been recommended in the Ridley Report. The schism in the union between the UDM (Union of Democratic Mineworkers) and NUM in Nottinghamshire and South Derbyshire, the lack of a ballot for action and Scargill's belligerent stance gave credence to the long-standing Conservative assertion that union leaders were extreme and did not represent the views of rank and file members.[57] Trade union legislation itself was not necessarily crucial in the strike as secondary picketing laws were generally ignored.[58] Secretary of State for Energy Peter Walker prevented use of the recent laws as he thought this could increase sympathy for the striking miners from other workers.[59] Another important factor proved to be that – after 1979 – courts were more inclined to interpret the previous legislation (for instance the police had the same powers in 1984 and 1985 as they did before 1979) in a way that restricted the privileges that unions enjoyed.[60] The determination of the government to support the police during the strike does give more credence to the 'strong state' principle. The new laws were to be more important subsequently. The resolve of the government, the police methods used and the flawed strategy of the NUM were all central. The identification of the union leadership as 'enemies' and the tactics of Scargill himself (calling a strike in the spring, without a ballot and encouraging violent picketing) all played their part in the eventual outcome. Defeating the miners was of huge significance to the overall programme of Thatcherism. David Owen, leader of the SDP after splitting from Labour in 1981 – identified the prime minister's role in this in April 1989:

> Until Arthur Scargill was soundly and humiliatingly defeated, the spectre of 1979's Winter of Discontent hung over the country. It was Mrs Thatcher who, virtually alone, understood this.[61]

The wider strategy to curb union influence

In addition to legislation and the defeat of the miners' strike there were other efforts to reduce the power of the trades unions. The privatization of several industries moved employees out of the state sector, although many retained union membership. The amount of workers belonging to a union decreased during the 1980s, falling to fewer than nine million members in 1990 from a high of over 12 million in 1979.[62] This was also connected to the sharp rise in unemployment in the early 1980s. Many people found jobs in the service sector where the norm was to be non-unionized.[63] The realignment of the British economy had the effect of reducing union power. Another strategy the Thatcher government pursued was that of 'contracting out', which meant that services nominally provided by the state (such as cleaning in hospitals or refuse collection) were put out to tender to private companies. This contract work also reduced the power of union members to wield influence in the state sector.[64] Contracting out acted as a half-way house to increase competition in public utilities.[65] Again this had its liberal critics. The IEA, for instance, believed contracting out tended to cause rent seeking behaviour as once gained, there were no commercial pressures to improve performance.[66] Austrians also thought contracting out did little to address liberal objectives such as greater efficiency or greater individual liberty.[67]

It has also been argued that class-consciousness and class-based solidarities waned during the 1980s.[68] There may have been splintering of the working class, facilitated by social and economic policy that led to a flexible and skilled 'top end' working class, leaving the worse-off poorer by 1990.[69] This was assisted by policies such as Right to Buy, where council house sales may have helped to convert some traditional Labour supporters into property owning Conservative voters. Other trends, such as an increasingly right-leaning media (from tabloids like the *Sun* and the *Daily Mail* to broadsheets like the *Daily Telegraph*) supported many Thatcherite policies, became hostile to both the European Community and the 'Loony Left' characterized by Labour politicians like Derek Hatton and Ken Livingstone. In summary, the 1980s saw an erosion of the solidarity for trade union action through a combination of long-term trends and the policies of the Thatcher government.

Trade union policy after the miners' strike

The miners' strike was not the end of industrial unrest in Britain. The teaching unions NUT (National Union of Teachers) and NASUWT (National Association of Schoolmasters/Union of Women's Teachers) were on strike intermittently between 1985 and 1987. More significantly, strikes broke out when News International moved its printing operation from Fleet Street to Wapping in the London Docklands in 1986. Rupert Murdoch had built up a large multinational media empire that included British newspapers like *The Sun*, the *News of the World* and *The Times*. In 1986 the group moved its offices to Wapping and as a result, 6000 of its workers went on strike in protest. The national union called action amid redundancies but despite the strikes lasting for over a year, production of the newspapers continued. Industrial relations had been notoriously bad in newspaper printing and this dispute, not the miners' strike, was where the laws enacted by the Thatcher government were initially put to use.[70]

The Conservatives introduced two more pieces of trade union legislation under Margaret Thatcher, the 1988 Employment Act (when Norman Fowler was Secretary for Employment) and its 1990 counterpart, by Michael Howard. The 1988 Act removed all statutory support for the closed shop, tightened balloting procedures and removed sanctions that unions could levy on members for breaking strikes.[71] It was not until the 1990 law, however, that the government attempted to eliminate the closed shop altogether.[72] It also made all secondary action unlawful and unions responsible for unofficial strikes liable for the acts of all of their officials.[73]

Union influence as a vested interest was drastically reduced by 1990, in effect becoming an 'outsider' group excluded from the policymaking process.[74] The Thatcher government achieved this through a combination of policies, laws, confrontation with the NUM and other long-term trends. Although as already noted this was not all by pre-planned design, some writers have said the trade union strategy of Thatcherism bore some semblance to tactics outlined in Stepping Stones.[75]

Within the Labour Party, Neil Kinnock had managed to reduce union influence there too, reasserting the primacy of the Parliamentary Labour Party (PLP) over party policy.[76] From a liberal economic point of view markets received less pressure from unions as a vested interest. The rise of non-unionized jobs in the service sector allowed for the more flexible labour market favoured by liberals. In 2013 *The Economist* described Britain's labour market as 'Europe's most flexible'.[77] The Labour governments of Tony Blair and Gordon Brown did not repeal any of the Conservative trade union legislation, while attempting to appear business-friendly.[78] In this respect Thatcherism achieved one of its, and neoliberalism's, long-term goals of reducing trade union influence on political and economic processes. Trade union reform was the clearest example of how the Thatcher government tamed a vested interest.

Conclusion

The most effective example of how the Thatcher government reduced the influence of a vested interest was trade union reform. Unions had wielded particular influence over both the British economy and policymakers over the previous 20 years. Although for the most part improvised, the 'step-by-step' and 'divide and rule' (separating union leaders from the rank and file) approach greatly reduced this influence and created a more flexible labour market. Trade union reform was both economic and political in its aim. The demoralization of the trades unions had a severe impact on certain areas of the country and was one of the key reasons many in Britain took a visceral dislike to both the prime minister and her administration. For pro-market thinkers, however, trade union policy forced much-needed liberalization and structural reform on the British economy.

Notes

1 David Marsh, *The New Politics of British Trade Unionism. Union Power and the Thatcher Legacy* (Basingstoke: Macmillan Press, 1992), 52. Marsh wrote that union power was limited even at its height and that the assertions of overwhelming power enjoyed by the unions between 1974 and 1979 were exaggerated; Ken Clarke, *Kind of Blue: A Political Memoir* (London: Macmillan, 2016), 79. Clarke summed up the Tory analysis: 'Economic policy involved a lurch towards a syndicalist system dominated by increasingly powerful trade unions and interest groups'.

2 J. P. F. Thomsen, *British Politics and Trade Unions in the 1980s: Governing against Pressure* (Aldershot: Dartmouth, 1996), 230.

3 Figures taken from www.unionancestors.co.uk, accessed 20 September 2011.

4 Robert Saunders, '"Crisis? What Crisis?": Thatcherism and the Seventies', in *Making Thatcher's Britain*, ed. Ben Jackson and Robert Saunders (Cambridge: Cambridge University Press, 2012), 25, 42.

5 Matthias Matthijs, *Ideas and Economic Crises in Britain from Attlee to Blair (1945–2005)* (Abingdon: Routledge, 2011), 115.

6 Sidney and Beatrice Webb, *A History of Trade Unionism 1666–1920* (Edinburgh: R & R. Clark, 1920), 180–232; M. Davis, '"New Model" Unionism', TUC History Online, accessed 19 September 2011. www.unionhistory.info/time line/1850_1880.php.

7 Friedrich Hayek, Letter to *The Times*, 'Trade union immunity under the law', 21 July 1977, 15.

8 Peter Dorey, *British Conservatism and Trade Unionism, 1945–1964* (Farnham: Ashgate, 2009), 168.

9 Dorey, *British*, 170.

10 Alec Cairncross, *The British Economy since 1945* (Oxford: Blackwell, 1995), 112.

11 Tim Bale, *The Conservatives since 1945* (Oxford: Oxford University Press, 2012), 139; Margaret Thatcher, *The Path to Power* (London: HarperCollins, 1995), 110.

12 Dorey, *British*, 175–179. A 'wildcat' strike is an action taken by workers without the consent of the union leadership.

13 Figures taken from www.unionancestors.co.uk, accessed 1 August 2017.

14 F. A. Hayek, *Social Justice, Socialism & Democracy. Three Australian Lectures by F. A. Hayek* (Turramurra, NSW: Centre for Independent Studies, 1979), 39–45; F. A. Hayek, *The Road to Serfdom* (London: Routledge, 2007 [1944]), 204; Ben Jackson, 'At the Origins of Neoliberalism: The Free Economy and the Strong State, 1930–1947', *The Historical Journal* 53:1 (March 2010), 145.

15 Thatcher, *Path*, 444.

16 Seamus Milne, *The Enemy within. The Secret War against the Miners* (London: Verso, 2004), 14; Richard Hyman, 'Trade Unions, the Left and the Communist Party in Great Britain', in *Comrades and Brothers: Communism and Trade Unions in Europe*, ed. W. Waller, S. Courtois and M. Lazar (London: Frank Cass, 1991), 148, 156–57.

17 Thatcher, *Path*, 395.

18 Richard Cockett, *Thinking the Unthinkable. Think-Tanks and the Economic Counter-Revolution, 1931–83* (London: Harper Collins, 1995), 148.

19 W. H. Hutt, *The Theory of Collective Bargaining 1930–75* (London: IEA, 1975 [1931]), 124–25.

20 Shirley Robin Letwin, *The Anatomy of Thatcherism* (London: HarperCollins, 1992), 142.

21 Margaret Thatcher Foundation (hereafter MTF), MTF 114760, 'Sir Keith Joseph note ('The Erhard Foundation')', 21 March 1974.

22 Richard Vinen, *Thatcher's Britain. The Politics and Social Upheaval of the 1980s* (London: Simon and Schuster), 92.

23 Vinen, *Thatcher's Britain*, 89.

24 The Papers of Margaret Thatcher (Cambridge: Churchill Archives, hereafter THCR), 2/6/2/93, 'Talk to the Bow Group' by Sir Keith Joseph, on 5 February 1979.

25 Interview with Peter Lilley, 7 February 2011.

26 Milton Friedman, *Inflation and Unemployment: The New Dimension of Politics. The 1976 Alfred Nobel Memorial Lecture* (London: IEA, Occasional Paper 51, 1977), 1–18.

27 Adrian Williamson, *Conservative Economic Policymaking and the Birth of Thatcherism, 1964–1979* (Basingstoke: Palgrave Macmillan, 2015), 170.

28 Thatcher, *Path*, 140.
29 Cecil Parkinson, *Right at the Centre* (London: Weidenfeld and Nicolson, 1992), 281.
30 MTF 109439, *The Right Approach*. Conservative Policy Statement (London, 1976), 38; MTF 112551, *The Right Approach to the Economy*. Conservative Policy Statement (London, 1977), 16.
31 Interview with Lord Ryder, 23 February 2011.
32 The Papers of John Hoskyns (Cambridge: Churchill Archives, hereafter HOSK), 1/79. 'A note by Christopher Patten, further thoughts on strategy' on 23 February 1978.
33 HOSK 1/80, 'Copy of a letter by John Hoskyns to Keith Joseph relating to a note by Christopher Patten', 27 February 1978.
34 HOSK 1/98, 'Copy of a letter on 27 March 1978 by Nigel Lawson to Sir Keith Joseph relating to the Policy Search Group meeting', 20 March 1978.
35 HOSK1/33, 'Detailed notes by Hoskyns for Norman Strauss and Terry Price relating to a meeting with Geoffrey Howe', 26 August 1977.
36 John Campbell, *Margaret Thatcher. Volume Two: The Iron Lady* (London: Pimlico, 2004), 361–362.
37 '1971: Workers Down Tools over Union Rights', BBC online, accessed 4 October 2011. http://news.bbc.co.uk/onthisday/hi/dates/stories/march/1/newsid_2514000/2514033.stm.
38 THCR 2/2/1/14, A series of three lectures by Professor F. A. Hayek. 3: 'The Exploitation of Workers by Workers', transmitted 12 August 1978, interview with Lord Ryder, 23 February 2011. Ryder and John Hoskyns both subsequently said that Thatcher's underlining of text usually represented an interest in a document. Hoskyns's comment came on a Radio 4 programme on release of new Thatcher documents in December, 2011.
39 Conservative Party Manifesto 1979, accessed 27 September 2011. www.conservative-party.net/manifestos/1979/1979-conservative-manifesto.shtml.
40 James Prior, *A Balance of Power* (London: Hamish Hamilton, 1986), 154–155.
41 Geoffrey Fry, *The Politics of The Thatcher Revolution. An Interpretation of British Politics, 1979–90* (Basingstoke: Palgrave Macmillan, 2008), 100.
42 Cockett, *Thinking*, 267, 298.
43 Interview with Lord Ryder 23 February 2011.
44 Prior, *Balance*, 156.
45 Marsh, *New*, 80–81'; Bale, *Conservatives*, 289.
46 MTF 112198, 'Memo by Keith Britto', 21 November 1979, 'Public Opinion after the First Seven Months of the New Government', accessed 10 October 2011. www.margaretthatcher.org/document/112198.
47 THCR 2/6/2/174, CRD Paper led by Peter Thorneycroft on a survey regarding trade union reform.
48 James Prior, *Parliamentary Debates* (Commons), 976, 17 December 1979, 58–174.
49 C. G. Hanson, *Taming the Trade Unions. A Guide to the Thatcher Government's Employment Reforms, 1980–90* (Basingstoke: Macmillan, 1991), 17.
50 MTF 114507, 'Economists criticize Government', *The Times*, 10 March 1981, accessed 12 September 2012. www.Margaretthatcher.org/document/114507.
51 Norman Tebbit, *Upwardly Mobile* (London: Weidenfeld and Nicolson, 1988), 182–184.
52 Tebbit, *Upwardly*, 184.
53 Hanson, *Taming*, 17–18.
54 Martin Holmes, *The First Thatcher Government, 1979–83* (Brighton: Wheatsheaf, 1985), 34, 203.
55 Adrian Williamson, *Conservative Economic Policymaking and the Birth of Thatcherism, 1964–1979* (Basingstoke: Palgrave Macmillan, 2015), 169.

56 Hanson, *Taming*, 18.
57 Paul Willman, Tim Morris and Beverly Aston, *Union Business: Trade Union Organization and Financial Reform in the Thatcher Years* (Cambridge: Cambridge University Press, 1993), 124.
58 Hanson, *Taming*, 45.
59 Vinen, *Thatcher's Britain*, 165.
60 Marsh, *New*, 108–109.
61 David Owen, writing in *The Times*, 19 April 1989, in Hanson, *Taming*, 111.
62 BBC online, 'TUC Membership 1940–2002', accessed 4 October 2011. http://news.bbc.co.uk/1/hi/business/3526917.stm#membership%20graph.
63 Joseph Stiglitz, 'Employment, Social Justice and Societal Well-Being', *International Labour Review* 141:1–2 (2002), 13.
64 Thomsen, *British*, 240.
65 Celia Veljanovski, 'Privatization: Monopoly Money or Competition?', in *Privatization and Competition. A Market Prospectus*, ed. C. Veljanovski (London: IEA Hobart Paperback 28, 1989), 48.
66 John Blundell, 'Privatization – by Political Process or Consumer Preference?', *Affairs* 7:1 (October–November 1986), 62.
67 Bruce L. Benson, 'Third Thoughts on Contracting Out', *Journal of Libertarian Studies* 11:1 (Fall 1994), 46–47.
68 Heather Nunn and Anita Biressi, 'Shameless? Picturing the "Underclass" after Thatcherism,' in *Thatcher and after. Margaret Thatcher and her Afterlife in Contemporary Culture*, ed. L. Hadley and E. Ho (Basingstoke: Palgrave Macmillan, 2010), 137–138.
69 Nunn and Biressi, 'Shameless?', 138.
70 Hanson, *Taming*, 74.
71 Hanson, *Taming*, 18.
72 Vinen, *Thatcher's Britain*, 121.
73 Hanson, *Taming*, 19.
74 Thomsen, *British*, 233.
75 Matthijs, *Ideas and Economic Crises*, 132.
76 Marsh, *New*, 162.
77 *The Economist*, 'British immigration. You're welcome', 21 December 2013, accessed 26 December 2013. www.economist.com/news/leaders/21591865-open-letter-citizens-bulgaria-and-romania-youre-welcome.
78 For instance Peter Mandelson's remark in 1998 that New Labour was 'intensely relaxed about people getting filthy rich as long as they pay their taxes', or Gordon Brown's courtship of the City while chancellor.

7 Electricity privatization

Competition is a core neoliberal principle.[1] How competition is achieved, however, differs between the different neoliberal strands. Privatization was one of the flagship policies of Thatcherism and appears to satisfy neoliberal thinking by removing nationalized monopolies and exposing them to competition in the private sector. In addition, privatization was also one of the most prominent Thatcherite policy exports. The Know-How Fund for Eastern Europe in the late 1980s and early 1990s specifically offered the advice of British experts in how to sell state assets. The scheme was incremental during the 1980s and grew after early sales of smaller companies. With little opposition to these, renewed political capital after the Falklands War and 1983 election as well as the success of Right to Buy, the Thatcher government privatized large utilities like British Gas and BT. The British Electricity Authority (BEA) was privatized at the end of the Thatcher years, and was completed after the prime minister herself had stepped down. The results may not have satisfied some economic liberal thinking but privatization was an ideological policy. This was because it went to one of the core themes of liberalism: ownership and private property rights. Even when answering criticism of the project, that electricity was rushed through for political expediency and that competition was not created, Nigel Lawson saw the primary goal of the policy as changing the terms of ownership.[2]

What happened to these bodies when they became privately owned has been the subject of much debate. Ordoliberals advocated the breaking up of monopolies and promotion of competition, Austrians as little government intervention as possible and entry barriers reduced. Chicagoans were closer to the latter, tolerating monopolies but accepting some state action to create market conditions if necessary. The Thatcher government will be shown to be closest to Friedman and Stigler's position although showing some inclinations towards Ordoliberal competition enforcement during electricity privatization.[3]

Electricity privatization built on the experience of previous asset sales and as such is a convenient lens through which to view the strategy as a whole. The promise of putting the industry into the private sector came in the 1987 election manifesto and was finally implemented during 1990 and 1991. One of the challenges of electricity privatization was that it existed in the state sector as a series of regional monopolies. How would shares be sold in 12 different (regionally based) companies? How could competition be created in both supply and generation of electricity and what would happen to the politically sensitive issue of nuclear power? The eventual system, power supplied by the private sector and watched over by a regulator was to have its critics. Energy privatization, internationally as well as in Britain, was sometimes viewed as providing little benefit to consumers or worse allowing them to be prey to unscrupulous companies.[4] In Britain windfall taxes on power companies were levied during the first Labour government of Tony Blair, while pensioners were subsidized by the government with a 'winter fuel allowance' from 1997. Ed Miliband's pledge – as Labour Party leader – to freeze energy prices in 2013 caused a furore. The policy was later mimicked by Theresa May's Conservative Party.[5] Clearly energy privatization and deregulation have not been universally popular.

Nationalization after 1945

The BEA was formed in 1948 when it amalgamated over 600 small companies into 14 regional bodies and one central authority, the Central Electricity Generating Board (CEGB), responsible for generation. It formed part of the wider programme of nationalization by the Attlee government. Many of these utilities were considered natural monopolies by policymakers, for instance water, although this concept has been opposed by some neoliberals.[6] Alfred Sherman, director of the CPS in the 1970s, wrote that nationalization was counterproductive, that it became a parasitic burden on the economy that awarded privileged conditions of employment to selected, highly unionized groups.[7]

The Attlee government succeeded in nationalizing all the major industries except steel, which was moved late in the government's tenure and reversed by the Churchill government. It was later re-nationalized by Harold Wilson in 1967. Edward Heath vowed to prevent further movement of industry into the state sector, the 1970 election manifesto saying 'We are totally opposed to further nationalisation of British industry'.[8] Heath reneged on this when his government felt forced to nationalize the ailing Rolls-Royce company in 1973. The 1974–9 Labour governments of Harold Wilson and James Callaghan were themselves committed to more nationalization, under pressure from an increasingly vociferous left in the party. It was one area where Keith Joseph pursued his 'ratchet effect' thesis as more companies moved into the public sector. Despite this, there is little evidence to show the British public were in favour of reversing this process in 1979.[9]

The neoliberal critique of state ownership

A key debate in the 1970s centred on ownership. Those on the left and in both main political parties accepted the orthodoxy that large state utilities and industry were more effectively owned in the public sector, in part because of economies of scale. Neoliberals, however, refuted this principle and produced literature in the 1970s and 1980s that called for a decoupling of government and industry of all kinds. Economic liberals generally accepted the state should provide security and enforce the law, but should intervene only in cases of market failure and market asymmetries. The 'market fundamentalist' brand of liberalism – which would include some Austrian thinkers like Rothbard – would reject the latter, seeking market-based solutions to most issues. The majority of British industry, according to neoliberals, therefore did not require government control. Pro-market thinkers regularly wrote about the 'sanctity' of private property rights. The editorial stance of publications such as *The Economist* changed in the 1970s and this reflected a shift in emphasis over ownership.[10] The work of John Locke and Adam Smith often provided the intellectual justification. Only if privately owned, it was argued, can business and industry operate efficiently, productively and with accountability. A poorly run and unprofitable firm will collapse if privately owned. There was never this threat with state-owned industry. A study at Liverpool University by Richard Pryke examined public and private productivity between 1958–68 and 1968–78. The second period was found less productive for both but particularly the public sector.[11] Pryke commented that 'public ownership provides a comfortable life and destroys the commercial ethic'.[12]

The primacy of property rights tied in with other neoliberal themes: Public Choice theory and theories of monopoly. Public Choice theory, the 'economics of politics', examined the workings of government and bureaucracy. Thinkers such as Gordon Tullock and James Buchanan identified waste, inefficiency and low productivity as endemic in the public sector. They also characterized how they believed bureaucrats had a natural tendency to expand their field of influence and also towards rent seeking behaviour. Keith Joseph echoed this when he described a 'ratchet effect', that government will grow if left unchecked. The problems posed by Public Choice theorists amounted to what think-tanks such as the IEA, CPS and ASI, as well as other neoliberals, deemed 'government failure'.[13] This was deliberately put in economic terms to compare it with that of market failure. The acceptance of this ideological tenet was one that could justify privatization.[14] As a result, even a monopoly in the private sector – according to Conservatives like Nigel Lawson – had more incentive to make a profit than its state-owned counterpart.[15] Some on the pro-market right believed that even so-called natural monopolies were better in the private sector where there was the threat of bankruptcy.[16] Chicago School thinkers, such as George Stigler, went further by suggesting private monopolies could replicate the competition function within a large organization.[17]

Economic liberal Jack Wiseman evoked the principles of *Road to Serfdom* when he criticized nationalized industries:

> [T]he case is weak. First, their arguments of principle against private property per se are implausible and unconvincing. Second, the destruction of

private property must imply the concentration of political and economic power in the same hands. This must be expected to result, and has in the past resulted, in a severe curtailment of individual freedom.[18]

Both Austrians and Chicagoans believed that monopolies should not be legislated against, only that government should reduce barriers to market entry.[19] Not all liberals, though, were so relaxed about privately owned monopolies. Adam Smith wrote that monopolies maintained high prices and kept markets under-stocked.[20] Nevertheless, the prime goal for neoliberals was the withdrawal of the state from ownership of utilities and industry.

There was a growing sympathy for these thoughts in the Conservative Party in the 1970s. Even in the 1950s Margaret Thatcher had said that consumers should be given priority over producers. Party policy had consistently spoken out against nationalization.[21] By the late 1970s Geoffrey Howe believed that the Morrisonian Corporation was 'constitutionally irresponsible'.[22] There was some, if limited, mention of (what was to become) privatization in the 1979 election manifesto:

> We will offer to sell back to private ownership the recently nationalized aerospace and shipbuilding concerns, giving their employees the opportunity to purchase shares. We aim to sell shares in the National Freight Corporation to the general public in order to achieve substantial private investment in it.[23]

This amounted to a pledge to overturn recent Labour nationalizations and not to commit any further industry into the public sector. It was not, however, a programme of broad-ranging privatization and echoed the similar sentiments in other post-war Conservative election manifestos.

Privatization and the first Thatcher government

The Thatcher government was not the first to move a state-owned industry into the private sector. The Churchill government had denationalized steel in 1953, although this was reversed in 1967.[24] During this process Conservatives had been concerned at the lack of response from investors and the subsequent performance of the industry in private hands.[25] Under Margaret Thatcher it was only when more economic liberals moved into the top government positions and into a Cabinet majority after 1981 that privatization gained momentum. In addition, the political opportunity existed after the Falklands War and with the economy growing after 1982. Nigel Lawson's claim, however, that 'denationalization' was a 'central plank of our policy right from the start' was also exaggerated.[26] Andrew Gamble believed the process was improvised, while Lord Burns said it was opportunistic.[27] It was true that the 1977 Ridley Report, concerning state-owned industry, did mention denationalization. It did not, however, recommend 'a frontal attack on this situation' rather 'a policy of preparing the industries for partial return to the private sector, more or less by stealth'.[28] One pertinent example of this was British Leyland. The company was broken up, saw a rise in productivity and was sold into the private sector in 1986.[29] Privatization was initially incremental. Monopolies would make the process more problematic.

Several smaller state-owned assets were moved into the private sector during the first term. These included the National Freight Company, Britoil and Amersham International. What was notable about these sales was the lack of opposition to them from the public.[30] This, along with the unexpected amount of interest in buying shares by small investors (the sale of Amersham International was the example often cited) gave ministers confidence to extend the programme. In stark contrast to denationalization in the 1950s, the Amersham share offer was oversubscribed by 24 to 1 and raised £65 million for the Treasury.[31] Employees were offered free shares and were told they would see their shares matched by the government up to certain levels (the first 350 shares purchased by each employee in the case of Amersham).[32] This strategy was a template for later schemes.

Nigel Lawson, in particular, was emboldened by the privatizations between 1980 and 1982.[33] If the smaller privatizations of the first term were an unpredicted success then the major policy in promoting private ownership was the Right to Buy scheme, selling council houses to tenants. These early policies which appeared to illustrate the aspiration to own capital could be utilized further. To reflect this, the Number 10 Policy Unit (the prime minister's 'think-tank') under John Redwood claimed to have coined the term 'popular capitalism' in 1983.[34] In more practical terms the CPRS produced a paper in October 1982 that set out how monopolies might be privatized as regulated businesses.[35] The role of regulation would prove important. In addition, the Nationalised Industries Study Group article 'Switching Direction' in 1982 influenced the eventual privatization of BT.[36] This study group, the Policy Unit and the CPRS all had an impact on the development of privatization.

By 1983 the opportunity presented itself to privatize a large utility. Lord Burns, then Chief Economic Advisor to the Treasury said that privatization 'took advantage of the moment' while the *Official History of Privatization* stated that only by 1983 were there sufficient investors to launch large asset sales.[37] Others believed that the overwhelming desire to reduce the PSBR was the prime motivation behind privatization, by both a windfall for the Treasury and removing continuing state subsidization.[38] Andrew Gamble wrote that among the key aims of privatization, along with choice, competition and efficiency, were: to control public sector pay, reducing the PSBR; to weaken the trades unions; and to remove decisions from the political process.[39] The last point demonstrated how privatization could lessen the influence of a vested interest on government, a key neoliberal aim.[40] Privatization was one of several liberalization measures, or supply-side reforms, that furthered the political goals of Thatcherism.[41] David Owen, then leader of the SDP and at the vanguard of the eventual ideological shift from old to New Labour, wrote in *Economic Affairs* in 1983 that there was some merit to privatization, but little where a state monopoly becomes a private one.[42] The latter point was a recurring argument from across the political spectrum and could be applied to the larger privatizations of the second term. Indeed, the 1983 Conservative Party election manifesto made the same argument.[43]

BT was privatized in 1984, British Gas in 1986. They made sizeable profits for the Treasury (£5 billion for BT, £9 billion for British Gas) and appeared to capture the public imagination. Furthermore, privatization acted as an influential Thatcherite export. Lord Burns said privatization 'led the world' while Lord Ryder (Conservative MP and Margaret Thatcher's political secretary in the first term) called it one of Thatcherism's 'greatest achievements'.[44] In liberal economic terms however, how pro-market were these privatizations?

Criticisms of privatization 1984–6

A repeated criticism of privatization was that it simply shifted a monopoly from public to private sector. As we have seen, many neoliberals still thought this was preferable to public ownership. Others considered a monopoly worse in the private sector because dividends paid to shareholders could have been used for investment. The level of profit paid out has been described as 'economic rent'.[45] There were also questions surrounding the regulators put in place during the privatization process. By the end of the 1980s some neoliberals feared that in a monopolistic situation these regulators would be 'captured' by industry, while the scheme for British Gas had been 'hastily' put together.[46] Indeed, the prime minister herself wanted to avoid a repetition of the BT scheme – that is to say selling off a monopoly into the private sector without breaking it up – but this was obstructed by Secretary of State for Energy, Peter Walker, and Chairman of the Gas Corporation, Denis Rooke.[47]

The speed of privatization was attributed to the electoral cycle.[48] These points, in keeping with neoliberalism as a whole, still put the emphasis on the nature of state intervention, rather than private ownership itself. The regulatory framework was to blame, according to neoliberals, rather than the dynamics of monopolies in the private sector.[49] Last, privatization from one monopoly to another was criticized in terms of information flows. This was an argument from the left that utilized neoliberal microeconomic principles. Monopolies, with no need to compete, were blamed for withholding information in order to maximize profits.[50] Therefore, for some, the change in ownership and regulatory system in gas and telecoms did not do enough to promote competition and efficient markets. If the regulators of these private monopolies really were captured, with little competition, the process could hardly be labelled liberal.

There were more positive opinions of privatization. Standards of service and labour productivity were considered to have improved after privatization.[51] There was also a fall in prices. It was claimed that there was a 35 per cent reduction in BT's main prices in real terms between 1984 and 1994. Prices of British Gas were also estimated to have fallen by 3 per cent.[52] All these issues were important when formulating the last major privatization of the Thatcher years, that of electricity. The government wanted a successful sale as well as improvements in efficiency for consumers, but economic liberals were also concerned about encouraging competition and setting up an independent and effective regulator.

Electricity privatization 1987–91

The Conservatives announced their intention to privatize electricity in the 1987 election manifesto, 'following the success of gas privatization' and 'the benefits it brought to employees and millions of consumers'.[53] Nigel Lawson, as Secretary of State for Energy in 1983, had asked Coopers and Lybrand (a multinational accountancy firm) to produce a report on electricity privatization.[54] The process then stalled when Peter Walker (a 'wet' who Thatcher consistently accommodated in her Cabinet) moved to the Energy ministry and was not to accelerate until Cecil Parkinson took over after the 1987 election. Parkinson was keenly aware of the criticism of previous privatizations:

> I was determined that we would not follow the pattern set by BT and British Gas and take it to the market as a highly regulated monopoly. I wanted to introduce competition where possible and regulation where it was not.[55]

Lawson's last major undertaking as Secretary of State for Energy was the 1983 Energy Act, which attempted to introduce some degree of competition into the industry. One IEA critic, however, wrote that this failed because the CEGB abused its dominant position.[56] Lawson had helped diversify Britain's supply of energy, for example initiating the 'dash for gas'.[57] He also helped stockpile coal in the strategy to resist a miners strike. Cecil Parkinson also wrote that expanding production of nuclear energy was crucial during the subsequent strike.[58]

Electricity was described, however, as unsuitable for privatization because of its regional structure.[59] What was to stop privatization simply becoming 14 regional (12 in England and Wales, two in Scotland) monopolies in the private sector? Once privatization of electricity was put into the 1987 manifesto through the 1989 Act up until implementation in 1990–1, the issue of competition dogged the scheme. In this respect, with liberal commentators as well as Cecil Parkinson aware of the issue, the government's thinking began to move towards Ordoliberal ideas, that of the state ensuring competitive markets. Using legislation and a regulatory framework to enforce competition and prevent monopolies forming echoed the sentiments of the 1930s and 1940s Freiburg neoliberals.

One critic, Michael Parker, stated there was no pressure for privatization after the miners' strike was defeated and oil prices plummeted in 1986.[60] Despite efficiency gains during the 1980s,[61] it was feared that these would be outweighed by the higher transaction costs in trading, metering and securing supply under smaller private companies.[62] There was also the problem of how to treat nuclear power and this was initially included in the privatization plans. Asset sales were criticized as being short-termist and dominated by the financial markets in the City of London, which benefited significantly from privatization.[63] Last, there were concerns about effective regulation and that the process would be completed too hastily to fit in with the electoral cycle.[64] Cecil Parkinson confirmed this latter point, stating that from the early meetings about the policy it was agreed privatization had to be completed by summer 1991, before the next probable election.[65]

The 1989 Electricity Act and its implementation

The British Electricity industry was finally privatized after the 1989 Electricity Act, following Cecil Parkinson's 1988 White Paper. The supply of electricity was sold off as 12 regional companies, with the two Scottish companies following in 1991. There was some debate about whether to split the CEGB, the power generator, into several companies (Margaret Thatcher and Cecil Parkinson said in their respective memoirs that four or five companies were floated) but in the end it was just two, in a 70 per cent–30 per cent split as National Power and PowerGen.[66] This crucial objective, of creating competition in generation, was strongly resisted by the head of CEGB, Lord Marshall.[67] Nuclear power, because of the costs and the political implications, was excluded from the privatization process. There was also some disagreement over how to sell the shares. Other schemes had involved just one share, representing the giant company that was essentially a monopoly. The difficulty with electricity was that the supply companies would be numerous. Kleinwort Benson, the bank that advised the government during this privatization, suggested the 'exploding share', whereby an investor would buy one share that would then split into 12 components, representing the 12 regional companies.[68] The fear was that some of the new companies would be more subscribed than others and the government was anxious that the privatization be a success. A similar question arose over selling shares in regional water boards, which took place around the same time. In his memoirs Nigel Lawson described being unimpressed by the 'exploding share' idea and felt it too complex for the public.[69] Lawson said that Kleinwort Benson went some way in persuading Cecil Parkinson and subsequently leaked the idea to the press.[70] In the end though, the water sale went ahead first and sold shares in its ten different companies separately. The exploding share scheme was then forgotten. Electricity privatization took place in 1990 and 1991 and the proceeds made £9 billion for the Treasury.[71]

Electricity privatization: analysis

Privatizing the electricity industry in Britain had – according to its backers – a number of benefits. First, standards of service apparently improved.[72] Office hours were extended and appointments were kept within a specified waiting time.[73] Second, prices went down. The figure claimed was a 3 per cent decrease (over five years).[74] There was, however, also criticism. The most pertinent point was that a monopoly situation had been retained in the private sector. Cecil Parkinson, on introducing the White Paper, said 'competition is the best guarantee of customers' interests'. He also wrote that Nigel Lawson, in particular, insisted on the importance of competition.[75] Liberals believed the lack of competition in generation hampered the process.[76] Lawson, the most committed proponent of privatization in the Thatcher government, reserved a whole section of his autobiography to rebut the critics of privatization.

Responding to criticism that privatization was a short-term strategy to deal with government borrowing difficulties and bring funds into the Treasury (former Prime Minister Harold Macmillan supposedly said the government was 'selling off the family silver'), Lawson denied that this was the prime motive.[77] The prime minister, however, had written in a note in May 1979 that 'the sale of assets could provide a significant contribution to getting the PSBR down'.[78] The actual share prices during the privatization programme also proved contentious. Even in 1979 monetary economist Gordon Pepper wrote to Margaret Thatcher regarding the sale of BP saying that 'publicly owned assets ought not to be sold at knock down prices'.[79]

Lawson went on to write that the battle of ideas was of critical importance, in particular in widening share ownership.[80] Lawson believed there was no evidence that investors were looking to make a quick gain and that electricity shareholders were in for the long term.[81] He also rebuked the suggestion that competition mattered more than ownership, and that the latter 'would itself set up pressures for more competition and other structural changes'.[82] Answering the charge that state-owned industry improved productivity in the 1980s regardless of ownership Lawson said that this was unsurprising because the prospect of privatization acted as a motivation. He concluded by saying, 'neglect of the economic consequences of ownership is every bit as ideological as the neglect of competition'.[83] Nevertheless, one proponent of Thatcherism and head of the No. 10 Policy Unit in the mid-1980s, John Redwood, later admitted that the government was 'weaker on competition than we should have been … competition … produces the magic'.[84]

There was a clear political dimension to privatization. Geoffrey Howe described the benefits of selling shares to the public during privatization: [The process] 'had the political advantage of increasing the numbers of those with a vested interest in our success'.[85] It also decreased the likelihood of Labour reversing the policy when it returned to government.[86] One critic believed that the biggest losers of privatization were trade union members.[87]

In a 1989 Hobart Paper by the IEA, there was a pertinent critique of the government's privatization programme. George Yarrow, in his chapter 'Does Ownership Matter?', wrote that at a microeconomic level privatization had most notably promoted economic efficiency.[88] Yarrow went on to say that the initial phase of privatization between 1979 and 1984 involved (for instance Cable and Wireless, National Freight, Amersham International, British Aerospace, Britoil and Enterprise Oil) 'the transfer to the private sector of firms that operated in reasonably competitive product markets'.[89] The same could not be said for the monopoly industries privatized in the second and third terms, where the government was, according to Yarrow, 'distinctly less pro-competitive than would have been desirable'.[90] Yarrow concluded that the key to better performance in the large utilities was 'to get competition and regulation working in tandem to provide improved information flows and better incentive structures'.[91] In 2013 the IEA returned to the British energy market. Colin Robinson stated that electricity privatization had done little in the short term to introduce competition of the market.[92] By the turn of the millennium, however, the regulator's effort to reduce entry barriers had managed to improve market conditions for consumers by allowing increased competition.[93] This was then eroded, according to Robinson, because of increased government legislation and the collusion of the new energy companies with the regulator, essentially raising market entry barriers and price.[94] Robinson suggests that liberalization can only be temporary such is the ingrained process of special interest groups wanting to protect their privileged position, whether trades unions, large companies or others.[95] This sentiment also reflected the Ordoliberal belief that *Ordnungspolitik* (economic order) was a permanent task.[96] Robinson's paper therefore insists that the contemporary debate around energy prices is because of the leading companies acting in concert, effectively colluding to restrict competition.[97]

When the 2017 Conservative Party general election manifesto appeared to mimic Ed Miliband's call for an energy price cap, Britain's free market think-tanks reacted in similar fashion. The IEA railed against market intervention, claiming that a price cap would backfire, while the ASI set out its opinion that the 'real solution to high energy prices is more competition'.[98] The IEA has stated that politicians attempted to deal with the symptoms of high energy prices rather than the cause and this can be traced back to the privatization process that occurred during Thatcherism.[99] The think-tank characteristically calls for 'less government action and more competition'.[100]

Effective regulation as well as competition has been difficult to ensure in some industries. Yet the spirit of the times meant that less government was in vogue and that 'light-touch' regulation was desirable. Loose regulation, regulators captured by an industry or rules that created perverse incentives were the key components that prevented privatization satisfying more consumers, as well as more neoliberals. Privatization again may have shifted the power of vested interests from one (state-owned) monopoly to another (privately owned) that both had influence and in some cases subsidies, from central government. In this way privatization, even of electricity, began to look like Friedmanite neoliberalism. That is to say the state helped to create the conditions for a market, and then retreated from the Ordoliberal goal of enforcing competition. Austrians still saw many barriers to more efficient markets. Like other policies of the Thatcher government it satisfied neoliberal's primary aims (private property rights, wider capital ownership, some increased efficiency and productivity, less government) but not the specifically Austrian or micro-themes that allow a market to operate effectively. This included lack of competition, preventing information flow to consumers, monopoly, lack of producers entering the market, price distortions, continued government intervention due to a flawed system or 'market failures'.

Conclusion

Privatization achieved some of the broad aims of neoliberals. Several principles found in liberal economic thinking made the case for the policy: Public Choice theory, government failure, monopoly theory, and the 'ratchet effect' of the state. Privatization shifted ownership of utilities and state-owned industry into the private sector, creating millions of new shareholders with their own vested interest in its success. Efficiency was – according to the policy's supporters – generally raised and in some cases prices went down, benefiting the consumer. The main liberal difficulty with privatization, however, was the lack of competition, effectively converting public monopolies into private ones. In privatizing the electricity industry, the new privately owned companies in some cases became regional monopolies. There was also the issue that regulators could be 'captured' by the privately run companies. The problem of creating competition in power stemmed from the fact that only supply, not generation, was effectively vying for consumers.

In summary, privatization satisfied some neoliberal thinking and did allow markets to function more efficiently. It would have been preferable to economic liberals if more competition had been introduced. Ordoliberal principles would have been invoked by implementing a regulatory or law-based framework that enforced competition and set out to impede monopoly formation. This appeared to be the direction Cecil Parkinson and Nigel Lawson were heading with electricity privatization. The end result, however, fell short of many liberals' stated aim of a competitive industry and looked to be somewhere between the Austrians and Ordoliberals, a potentially 'captured' regulator and a market that was not fully liberalized. A vested interest was reduced, that of state-owned monopolies, but reappeared to a lesser degree in the private sector. This is indicative of a number of case studies in this book. The IEA has suggested that liberalization is only temporary before vested interests emerge once more, and by implication is a process rather than a series of one-off acts.[101] This fits the pattern for much of these 'liberalizing' policies of Thatcherism, which appeared to reduce the impact of special interest groups.

Notes

1 Matthew Eagleton-Pierce, *Neoliberalism: The Key Concepts* (Abingdon: Routledge, 2016), 33–37.

2 Nigel Lawson, *The View from No. 11. Memoirs of a Tory Radical* (London: Corgi Books, 1993), 239.

3 Mark Skousen, *Vienna & Chicago. Friends or Foes? A Tale of Two Schools of Free-Market Economics* (Washington, DC: Capital Press, 2005), 214, 218.

4 Warwick Funnell, Robert Jupe and Jane Andrew, *In Government We Trust. Market Failure and the Delusions of Privatization* (London: Pluto Press, 2009), 190–195, 200–209. Besides the UK, Funnel *et al.* pay particular attention to the deregulation of electricity in New Zealand in the early 1990s and the Enron scandal at the end of the decade.

5 Anushka Asthana and Adam Vaughan, 'Theresa May to promise price cap on energy bills in Tory manifesto', *Guardian*, 9 May 2017, accessed 5 June 2017. www.theguardian.com/money/2017/may/08/theresa-may-to-promise-price-cap-on-energy-bills-in-tory-manifesto.

6 Sir Adam Ridley, personal correspondence with the author, 15 May 2013. Ridley stated that 'it being the old standard view (never properly spelt out) that most of these utilities were intrinsic monopolies'; Thomas J. Dilorenzo, 'The Myth of Natural Monopoly', *Review of Austrian Economics* 9:2 (1996), 43.

7 Alfred Sherman, *Paradoxes of Power*, ed. Mark Garnett (Exeter: Imprint Academic, 2005), 72.

8 Conservative Party 1970 Election Manifesto, accessed 7 November 2011. www.conservative-party.net/manifestos/1970/1970-conservative-manifesto.shtml.

9 Andrew Gamble, 'Privatization, Thatcherism and the British State', in *Thatcher's Law*, ed. Andrew Gamble and Celia Wells (Oxford: Blackwell, 1989), 4.

10 David Parker, *The Official History of Privatisation. Volume 1: The Formative Years 1970–87* (London: Routledge, 2009), 25.

11 Richard Pryke, *The Nationalized Industries. Polices and Performance since 1968* (Oxford: Martin Robertson, 1981), 250–257.

12 Brian Dick, *Privatization in the UK: The Free Market versus State Control* (York: Longman, 1988), 22.

13 Parker, *Official*, 400.

14 Funnell *et al.*, *In Government*, 9, 39.

15 Lawson, *View*, 239.

16 Dennis Swann, *Retreat of the State* (Hemel Hempstead: Wheatsheaf, 1988), 298, 303.

17 Daniel Stedman-Jones, 'The Influence of Transatlantic Neoliberal Politics', seminar, Queen Mary University London, 22 October 2013.

18 Jack Wiseman, 'Growing without Nationalization', in *Privatization and Competition. A Market Prospectus*, ed. C. Veljanovski (London: IEA Hobart Paperback 28, 1989), 4.

19 Norman Barry, 'Austrian Challenge to Orthodoxy', *Economic Affairs* 4:3 (April–June 1984), 61.

20 Adam Smith, *The Wealth of Nations Books I–III* (London: Penguin, 1986 [1776]), 164.

21 Lecture given by David Willetts MP, 'Inaugural John Ramsden Memorial Lecture, Liberal Conservatism', Queen Mary University, London, 10 May 2011.

22 Parker, *Official*, 17.

23 Conservative Party Manifesto 1979, accessed 22 December 2012. www.conservative-party.net/manifestos/1979/1979-conservative-manifesto.shtml.

24 Kathleen Burk, *The First Privatization. The Politicians, the City, and the Denationalization of Steel* (London: The Historians' Press, 1988), 140.

25 Burk, *First*, 140.
26 Geoffrey Fry, *The Politics of the Thatcher Revolution. An Interpretation of British Politics, 1979–90* (Basingstoke: Palgrave Macmillan, 2008), 95.
27 Gamble, 'Privatization', 4–7; Interview with Lord Burns, 12 May 2011.
28 Margaret Thatcher Foundation (hereafter MTF), MTF 110795, 'Report of Nationalized Industries Policy Group', 30 June 1977, 15.
29 John Campbell, *Margaret Thatcher. Volume Two: The Iron Lady* (London: Pimlico, 2004), 101.
30 Parker, *Official*, 399.
31 'Privatization. The Facts' (Price Waterhouse, 1987), 6–8.
32 Ibid., 6–8.
33 Fry, *Politics*, 97.
34 John Redwood, *Singing the Blues* (London: Politico, 2004), 69.
35 Parker, *Official*, 402.
36 Cockett, *Thinking*, 302.
37 Interview with Lord Burns, 12 May 2011; Parker, *Official*, 159.
38 Dick, *Privatization*, 1.
39 Gamble, 'Privatization,' 11.
40 F. A. Hayek, *Social Justice, Socialism & Democracy. Three Australian Lectures by F. A. Hayek.* (Turramurra, NSW: Centre for Independent Studies, 1979), 39–45.
41 Dick, *Privatization*, 1.
42 David Owen, 'Agenda for Competitiveness with Compassion', *Economic Affairs* 4:1 (October 1983), 28.
43 Conservative General Election Manifesto 1983; MTF 110859, accessed 19 June 2017. www.margaretthatcher.org/document/110859.
44 Interview with Lord Burns, 12 May 2011; interview with Lord Ryder, 23 February 2011.
45 Mike Parker, 'General Conclusions and Lessons', in *The British Electricity Experiment. Privatization: The Record, the Issues, the Lessons*, ed. J. Surrey (London: Earthscan, 1996), 298.
46 Colin Robinson, *Competition in Electricity? The Government's Proposals for Privatizing Electricity Supply* (London: IEA, 1988), 7, 18.
47 Charles Moore, *Margaret Thatcher The Authorized Biography, Volume Two: Everything She Wants* (London: Allen Lane, 2015), 195.
48 Parker, 'General', 298.
49 Philip Booth, 'More Regulation, Less Regulation or Better Regulation?', in *Verdict on the Crash. Causes and Policy Implications*, ed. P. Booth (London: IEA, 2009), 169.
50 Funnell *et al.*, *In Government*, 46; Swann, *Retreat*, 16.
51 Parker, 'General', 297.
52 Angela Browning, *Privatization 1979–1994. Everyone's a Winner* (London: Conservative Political Centre, 1994), 20–24.
53 Conservative Party Manifesto 1987, accessed 23 December 2011. www.conservative-party.net/manifestos/1987/1987-conservative-manifesto.shtml.
54 Lawson, *View*, 234.
55 Cecil Parkinson, *Right at the Centre* (London: Weidenfeld and Nicolson, 1992), 260.
56 Celia Veljanovski, 'Privatization: Monopoly Money or Competition?', in *Privatization and Competition. A Market Prospectus*, ed. C. Veljanovski (London: IEA Hobart Paperback 28, 1989), 26.
57 Parker, 'General', 297.
58 Parkinson, *Right*, 274.
59 Browning, *Winner*, 22.
60 Parker, 'General', 296.

61 This was possibly because of the Thatcher government's more rigorous manage-ment style, influenced by Sir Derek Rayner's task force in the first term and later by that of Robin Ibbs.

62 Peter Hennessy, *Whitehall* (London: Fontana, 1990), 593; Tim Bale, *The Conser-vatives since 1945* (Oxford: Oxford University Press, 2012), 276; John Surrey, 'Introduction', in *The British Electricity Experiment. Privatization: The Record, the Issues, the Lessons*, ed. J. Surrey (London: Earthscan, 1996), 10.

63 Parker, 'General', 303.

64 Robinson, *Competition*, 7.

65 Parkinson, *Right*, 265.

66 Margaret Thatcher, *The Downing Street Years* (London: HarperCollins, 1993), 683–684.

67 Parkinson, *Right*, 263.

68 Lawson, *View*, 234.

69 Lawson, *View*, 234.

70 Lawson, *View*, 234.

71 Lawson, *View*, 235.

72 Parker, 'General', 302.

73 Browning, *Winner*, 23–24.

74 Browning, *Winner*, 23.

75 Parkinson, *Right*, 265, 277.

76 Robinson, *Competition*, 22.

77 Harold Macmillan (then Lord Stockton) was paraphrased; he actually said (to the House of Lords on 13 November, 1984), 'The sale of assets is common with individuals and states when they run into financial difficulties. First, all the Geor-gian silver goes, and then all that nice furniture that used to be in the saloon. Then the Canalettos go'.

78 The Papers of Margaret Thatcher (Cambridge: Churchill Archives, hereafter THCR); THCR 2/6/2/48, note from Tim Lankester, 16 May 1979.

79 THCR 19/529, letter from Gordon Pepper to Margaret Thatcher 16 May 1979.

80 Lawson, *View*, 238.

81 Lawson, *View*, 238.

82 Lawson, *View*, 239.

83 Lawson, *View*, 239–240.

84 Moore, *Volume Two*, 220.

85 Geoffrey Howe, *Conflict of Loyalty* (Basingstoke: Macmillan, 1994), 460.

86 Parker, 'Official', 430.

87 Swann, *Retreat*, 317.

88 George Yarrow, 'Does Ownership Matter?', in *Privatization and Competition. A Market Prospectus*, ed. C. Veljanovski (London: IEA Hobart Paperback 28, 1989), 52.

89 Yarrow, 'Ownership', 56.

90 Yarrow, 'Ownership', 69.

91 Yarrow, 'Ownership', 69.

92 Colin Robinson, *From Nationalization to State Control. The Return of Centralised Energy Planning*, IEA Discussion Paper No. 49 (London: IEA, 2013), accessed 26 December 2013, 8. www.iea.org.uk/sites/default/files/publications/files/From %20Nationalisation%20to%20State%20Control_web.pdf.

93 Robinson, *From*, 9.

94 Robinson, *From*, 11–12.

95 Robinson, *From*, 11.

96 Peter Oberender, 'Der Einfluss ordnungstheoretischer Prinzipien Walter Euckens auf die deutsche Wirtschaftspolitik nach dem Zweiten Weltkrieg: Eine ordnungs politische Analyse' [Walter Eucken's Influence on German Economic Policy

after World War II], in *ORDO. Jahrbuch für die Ordnung von Wirtschaft und Gesell-schaft* (Stuttgart: Gustav Fischer Verlag, Band 40, 1989), 350.

97 Robinson, *From*, 6–7, 11–14.

98 Sam Dumitriu, 'Theresa May's energy price cap will backfire', Adam Smith Institute, 9 May 2017, accessed 2 July 2017. www.adamsmith.org/news/theresa-mays-energy-price-cap-will-backfire; Institute of Economic Affairs, 'Energy price cap will not guarantee lower bills', accessed 3 July 2017. https://iea.org.uk/media/energy-price-cap-will-not-guarantee-lower-bills/.

99 Robinson, *From*, 7.

100 Robinson, *From*, 7.

101 Robinson, *From*, 11.

8 Broadcasting policy

This book's final two chapters will examine policies – broadcasting, education vouchers and housing – that have received rather less attention than, for instance, privatization and Big Bang. The focus will remain on the neoliberal theme of competition and monopolies. In particular these final chapters will invoke the neoliberal theme of 'market distortion' in order to analyse the economic liberal instincts of the Thatcher government. As with the other case studies in this book, the Thatcher government will be shown to be partly neoliberal in its approach, with this commitment to free markets demonstrated by a confrontation with one vested interest, only to be brought into question by the preferential political treatment of a separate group.

The broadcasting policy of the Thatcher government

The strategy of the Thatcher government towards broadcasting exposed some of the tension in its wider programme: liberalism curtailed by politics, liberal but not libertarian, tackling one vested interest but creating another. Two key points in this narrative were the 1985 Peacock Report and the 1990 Broadcasting Act. The former examined funding of the BBC and the second paved the way for the boom in satellite television in the 1990s. If the Thatcher government wanted to reduce the power of a vested interest (the BBC) it did not succeed. In addition it helped create another, BSkyB.

The BBC was launched in 1927 and ever since has enjoyed a privileged position in British life. It had a monopoly on television programming until 1955, when Independent Television (ITV), which had an 11 per cent excise duty levied on its advertising by the government, began screening.[1] BBC2 was then launched in 1964 and subsequently Channel 4 in 1982. The latter was intended to satisfy fringe tastes and displeased some conservative opinion. Nevertheless, Willie Whitelaw – unnerved by the inner city violence of 1981 – remarked that 'he preferred to see and hear minority views on television than in riots and violence on the street'.[2] Others felt that one of the roles of Channel 4 was to provide competition and to shake up the BBC, which had become a sizeable vested interest.[3]

In 1981 the government passed the Broadcasting Act, a first step towards satellite television. The IBA (Independent Broadcasting Authority) subsequently took bids to provide the new medium in Britain. The first cable supplier of satellite television began a trial service in mainland Europe in October 1981, officially created as the Sky channel a year later. Rupert Murdoch's News International group, by and large supportive of the prime minister, gained control of Sky in 1983.[4] Sky and BSB (British Satellite Broadcasting) won the franchise bids from the IBA in 1986. Margaret Thatcher was an unyielding critic of the BBC, believing it unsympathetic to her government and that it represented much of the ethos she wanted to sweep away from Britain.[5] Reducing the influence of and providing alternatives to the corporation became one of the aims of the broadcasting policy of Thatcherism. John Campbell wrote that the prime minister disliked state-owned television on principle and thought that the BBC coverage of Northern Ireland, in particular, was unhelpful to her administration.[6] Furthermore, Thatcher believed the manner in which the 1981 riots were presented caused copycat incidents while the reporting of the Falklands War was disproportionate. The prime minister believed that one of the BBC's roles was to be on 'our side'.[7] Sir Alan Peacock (Chair of the 1985 report) said in 2010 that Margaret Thatcher had become annoyed with the BBC and wanted it to accept advertising and competition.[8] The catalyst for setting up the Peacock Report was the BBC's request for a 41 per cent increase in the licence fee in 1984, causing uproar in the press. This triggered the prime minister's move against the corporation.[9] In March 1985, Home Secretary Leon Brittan charged a committee, to be chaired by Peacock, with the task of examining the funding of the BBC.[10]

The Peacock Report

The Peacock Report was published in May 1986. Including liberal economic writer Samuel Brittan, the committee was thought to be sympathetic to the general philosophy of the government and was expected to decide that the licence fee should be abolished. That it did not, came as a surprise to many, infuriated the prime minister and was 'kicked into the long grass' by her private secretary Bernard Ingham.[11] Shadow Cabinet member Gerald Kaufman dryly said that Ingham's subsequent 'character assassination machine has so single-mindedly devoted its attention to Professor Peacock that one might have thought the poor man was a member of the Cabinet'.[12]

The report did make a number of recommendations: that the licence fee should be used to fund only Public Sector Broadcasting (PSB) and items of national interest, and that the BBC should have to compete for buying programmes. Peacock thought that the BBC's combined role as broadcaster and producer was not sufficiently impartial.[13] The report, reflecting the liberal and libertarian instincts of its authors, stated that viewers and listeners were the best ultimate judges of their own interest; and that all censorship should end.[14] The report also recommended indexation (to retail price inflation) of the BBC licence fee, direct subscription to the BBC to replace the main part of the fee and finally to encourage a multiplicity of choice with pay-per-view and pay-per-channel.[15] Home Secretary Douglas Hurd put a positive spin on the report, despite its rejecting abolishing the licence fee: 'The report obviously does not conceal the view that the days of the BBC licence fee system are numbered.'[16] Samuel Brittan believed the main reason the prime minister was irritated by the report was over censorship. Brittan said this 'exposed many of the contradictions in the Thatcherite espousal of market forces. They espoused the market system but disliked the libertarian value judgements'.[17] Hurd said that censorship reflected the 'peculiarly intrusive nature of broadcasting' which 'require[s] special regulatory arrangements'.[18] Here we see the evidence of small 'c' conservatism and more traditional Toryism still alive within the Thatcher government, and by association in Thatcherism.

The response of the BBC to the Peacock Committee was also crucial to its outcome. To prove it was indeed a potent vested interest the corporation commissioned and supervised research that demonstrated in impeccably 'dry' economic terms the impracticality of funding by advertising.[19] The BBC team considered each member of the committee's background and the best way to approach them. They were also effective campaigners behind the scenes.[20] The key to the BBC strategy was to make its income appear as indivisible as ITV's advertising revenues. It also stated that there would not be enough advertising to fund both channels.[21] This was a shrewd plan to overcome the danger the committee posed and in fact turned the attention from the BBC to ITV. Margaret Thatcher was 'greatly disappointed' by the Peacock Report's findings on the BBC. Colleagues like Hurd thought the prime minister was obsessed by the corporation.[22] Nevertheless, the BBC had proved itself a vested interest of some potency by diverting Thatcher's fire towards ITV.

The government was attracted by Peacock's proposals for ITV, notably the idea of auctioning its franchises and requiring Channel 4 to sell its own advertising. The Conservatives disliked ITV's monopoly on advertising and the channel also drew the prime minister's ire with its 1988 programme 'Death on the Rock', about the shooting of three IRA members by the SAS in Gibraltar.[23] The 1990 Broadcasting Act was to exert pressure on ITV, as did the growth of satellite television. This was one outcome of the Peacock Report. Former BBC producer Janet Jones believed the report 'refashioned television firmly within the domain of the market' and made direct payment for television a reality.[24] Peter Jay said that Alan Peacock's recommendations opened the door to an '"ideologically free" philosophy celebrating consumer sovereignty'.[25] The committee did force the BBC to change, even if not as drastically as Thatcher had hoped. Janet Jones said that the report 'created a far humbler, more innovative and democratic BBC, one that knew it must find a new rationale to survive as a public institution into the next century'.[26]

The 1990 Broadcasting Act

BBC funding survived the Peacock Report. It may have been forced into some changes but still retained its establishment position in British society. The aftermath of the Peacock Report, however, caused a revolution in commercial television. The committee paved the way for the expansion of satellite television and also exposed ITV to more pressure. Douglas Hurd introduced the 1988 White Paper by saying the government had 'been influenced at many points by the Peacock Report'.[27] The prime minister favoured an increased number of channels and competition for programmes, in part because she thought that it would weaken the BBC. The 1988 White Paper 'Broadcasting in the 90s: Competition, Choice and Quality' proposed that Channel 4 should be obliged to sell its own advertising and therefore provide rivalry with ITV.[28] It also allowed the expansion of satellite and cable television providers. The White Paper eventually became the 1990 Broadcasting Act, which encapsulated several themes of liberalization: the free market, deregulation, withdrawal of the state and removing market entry barriers to producers.[29] The Act looked at the theme of ownership. Douglas Hurd said in 1988, 'The ownership of commercial television and radio should be widely spread, not concentrated in the hands of a few groups or individuals and to prevent excessive media cross-ownership'.[30]

Yet there were two criticisms of the government's policy: first that instead of widening ownership it would actually lead to concentration of power. Second, that increased choice would mean decreased quality. One company in particular has been a recurring target for the left, that of Rupert Murdoch's News International group. Roy Hattersley said in 1988 of Hurd's White Paper: 'He asserts the need for ownership to be widespread. I make a prediction: they will not be regulations to which Mr. Rupert Murdoch takes exception.'[31] Returning to the policy the following year the then Home Secretary David Waddington attempted to reassure the public that this would not be the case. 'There must be ownership rules. There is no chance whatsoever of British broadcasting falling into the hands of a bunch of tycoons or a cluster of conglomerates.'[32] Again Hattersley poured scorn upon this suggestion.

> Already the Government have allowed Mr. Murdoch to acquire two national newspapers without the scrutiny of a Monopolies and Mergers Commission inquiry. In part, the Bill might have been dictated during one of Mr. Murdoch's cosy lunches with the Prime Minister.[33]

The reference to Rupert Murdoch's purchase of *The Times* newspapers in 1981 demonstrated another side to the prime minister's approach to special interests and concentration of power. As Murdoch sought to purchase the loss-making *Times* and *Sunday Times* from Thomson's – who threatened to close the papers if a buyer could not be found – the Secretary of State for Trade, John Biffen, considered referring the issue to the Monopolies and

Mergers Commission (MMC).[34] This was in line with the 1973 Fair Trading Act, which stated an MMC examination was required 'where the transfer of a newspaper to a newspaper proprietor will result in a combined circulation of 500,000 or more'.[35] Nevertheless, after Murdoch threatened to pull out of the acquisition and having met Margaret Thatcher in person, the sale was approved.[36] Kenneth Clarke later wrote that the prime minister intervened on Murdoch's behalf and 'bullied' Biffen to waive a referral to the MMC.[37] In this instance, Thatcher's approach to special interest groups looked inconsistent.

Can we say, however, that the Thatcher government in the late 1980s actively assisted Murdoch's companies in its broadcasting policy? As a market for satellite broadcasting did not exist at this time it is difficult to assert such a statement. The government had a problem, in so far as not restricting the growth of satellite television without drowning it at birth. It did not want to deter investors because the initial start-up costs were large. Satellites and the rockets to launch them do not come cheap, nor initially did distributing dishes and decoders. In addition, the very nature of satellite television meant it was essentially a transnational business that was more difficult to control than terrestrial broadcasting.[38] Both BSB and Murdoch's Sky launched packages in 1989. One difference between the two was that Sky used mainly American programmes (on the Sky One channel) and Hollywood films (on the Sky Movies channel). BSB collapsed in November and was swallowed up as BSkyB, launched in April 1991.[39] This outlined the difficulties with the government's insistence that competition would be ensured.

David Waddington bent the government's own rules to allow the merger between BSB and Sky. Newspaper owners were allowed to own only 20 per cent of television channels but by this point Murdoch controlled almost 50 per cent of satellite broadcasting.[40] John Campbell even wrote that Margaret Thatcher did everything she could to help Murdoch dominate the new medium.[41] By proclaiming that it wanted to prevent monopoly formation and promote competition in satellite broadcasting, but encouraging market forces, in the late 1980s the government invoked Ordoliberal principles. Essentially though, satellite television policy was again closer to Friedmanite neoliberalism. It utilized the state to liberalize or create a market, then retreated from it while tolerating monopoly. It implicitly took the position, as did the Chicagoans, that 'giants' in a market were acceptable as long as there was some liberalization.

Subscription-funded Sky mushroomed in popularity in the 1990s. The network attracted customers by buying the rights to repeats of old programmes (such as soaps like Coronation Street) and mainly by exclusively showing sporting events and films.[42] The advance of Sky has been matched by criticism of the quality of the material shown. David Waddington said in 1990 'I do not believe for a moment that anyone will be able to argue ... that we are creating a *philistines' charter* or *yob television*'.[43] Others, however, disagreed. Ian Gilmour, a regular critic of his own party, said the Act was 'sheer vandalism' while John Campbell said the broadcasting policy of the Thatcher government accelerated a decline in moral values by a 'mixture of crude free-market dogma spiked with political malice'.[44] This line of criticism exposed the contradictions outlined by Brittan: liberal but unable to accept libertarian value judgements.

The nature of television changed over this period. Murdoch's was one of several big organizations operating partly as rivals and partly as a cartel with shared strands of ownership. In the United States the media market came to be dominated by three American firms (Time Warner, Disney and Viacom) and four foreign ones (Seagram of Canada, Bertelsmann of Germany, Sony of Japan and News International). Material originating from one part of Murdoch's empire (in practice the United States) could be transmitted to audiences in all other parts of it.[45] Hence the accusations of homogenization, cartelization and the problem countries had in restricting overseas programmes.[46] Others saw the trend as a brand of calculating geopolitics or cultural imperialism. Des Freedman wrote in 2008 that 'recent US and UK governments have embraced globalization as an opportunity to secure increased economic benefits and cultural influence through the activities of their media industries'.[47] There is no evidence, however, to suggest the Thatcher government used media policy either as an extension of soft power in foreign affairs or to pursue a pro-market agenda. The broadcasting policy of the Thatcher government was designed for the domestic market but also a response to a rapidly changing world, much of which it could not control. It did try and tame the BBC but came up against a potent vested interest, again showing the limits of Thatcherism. By the twenty-first century the BBC was still an effective force – and not necessarily anti-Tory: Tony Blair's administration was described as 'at times, on a virtual war footing with the BBC'.[48]

The second phase of the Thatcher government's media strategy was to tackle commercial television. It was true that it managed to create a more competitive market in television and reduce the barriers to entry for producers. The growth of satellite and cable broadcasting has meant greater consumer choice. As with other policies of the Conservatives in the 1980s broad neoliberal aims were met. Other market principles, however, were not due to lack of competition. Legislation could not prevent, and may have encouraged, a near monopoly by Sky in satellite television. The Thatcher government provided some reforms that pro-market thinkers approved of but could not reduce the power of one vested interest, the BBC, and managed to create another, Sky. Although at times the government's rhetoric had an Ordoliberal approach to ownership, the reality was closer to Friedmanite neoliberalism. In addition, the Austrian and Chicagoan analysis that monopolies are vested interests often created and maintained by government, may also have been true of broadcasting policy even during Thatcherism.

Conclusion

At the time of writing there is still fierce debate over the influence and market share of Rupert Murdoch's media companies.[49] In June 2017, however, his attempt to take a majority share of Sky was surprisingly referred to the UK regulator by the Conservative government. Nevertheless the policies of the Thatcher government towards broadcasting align with the broad analytical narrative in this book. The Thatcher government attempted to reduce the power of a vested interest (the BBC), only to create another (BSkyB). The BBC showed its potency as a power broker by effectively defeating the government's plans to force advertising or abolition of the licence fee. It turned the prime minister's fire towards ITV and subsequent reforms allowed the growth of satellite television. BSkyB operated a near monopoly in this new medium and with a combined newspaper and broadcasting empire exerting influence over both the British consumer and consecutive governments.

Notes

1 Andrew Crisell, *An Introductory History of British Broadcasting* (London: Routledge, 2002), 108.
2 John Ranelagh, 'Channel 4: A View from Within', in *The Making of Channel 4*, ed. Peter Catterall (London: Frank Cass, 1999), 56.
3 Peter Catterall, 'Witness Seminar: The Origins of Channel 4', in *The Making of Channel 4*, ed. Peter Catterall (London: Frank Cass, 1999), 83.
4 Catterall, 'Witness', 230.
5 Charles Moore, *Margaret Thatcher The Authorized Biography, Volume Two: Everything She Wants* (London: Allen Lane, 2015), 529.
6 John Campbell, *Margaret Thatcher. Volume Two: The Iron Lady* (London: Pimlico, 2004), 401.
7 Campbell, *Iron Lady*, 401–402.
8 Interview with Sir Alan Peacock, 26 January 2010.
9 Crisell, *Introductory*, 234.
10 Campbell, *Iron Lady*, 404.
11 Interview with Sir Alan Peacock, 26 January 2010.
12 Gerald Kaufman, *Parliamentary Debates* (Commons), 100, 3 July 1986, 1180–1193.
13 Interview with Sir Alan Peacock, 26 January 2010.
14 Samuel Brittan, 'The Fight for Freedom in Broadcasting', in *The Peacock Committee and UK Broadcasting Policy*, ed. T. O'Malley and J. Jones (Basingstoke: Palgrave Macmillan, 2009), 107.
15 Brittan, 'Fight', 110.
16 Douglas Hurd, *Parliamentary Debates* (Commons), 100, 3 July 1986, 1180–1193.
17 Brittan, 'Fight', 102.
18 Douglas Hurd, *Parliamentary Debates* (Commons), 100, 3 July 1986, 1180–1193.
19 Jean Seaton and Anthony McNicholas, 'It was the BBC wot Won It. Winning the Peacock Report for the Corporation, or How the BBC Responded to the Peacock Committee', in *The Peacock Committee and UK Broadcasting Policy*, ed. T. O'Malley and J. Jones (Basingstoke: Palgrave Macmillan, 2009), 142.
20 Seaton and McNicholas, 'BBC', 142–143.
21 Seaton and McNicholas, 'BBC', 133.
22 Campbell, *Iron Lady*, 404–406.

23 Crisell, *Introductory*, 235.
24 Janet Jones, 'PSB 2.0 – UK Broadcasting Policy after Peacock', in *The Peacock Committee and UK Broadcasting Policy*, ed. T. O'Malley and J. Jones (Basingstoke: Palgrave Macmillan, 2009), 187, 191.
25 Jones, 'PSB', 191.
26 Jones, 'PSB', 205.
27 Douglas Hurd, *Parliamentary Debates* (Commons), 140, 7 November 1988, 29–46.
28 Crisell, *Introductory*, 236.
29 Jones, 'PSB', 192, 204. Douglas Hurd also said in the House of Commons in 1988 that 'The Government are determined to keep the market open to newcomers'.
30 Douglas Hurd, *Parliamentary Debates* (Commons), 140, 7 November 1988, 29–46.
31 Roy Hattersley, *Parliamentary Debates* (Commons), 140, 7 November 1988, 29–46. It is worth noting that after the 1986 Wapping printing dispute the Labour Party refused to deal with representatives of the Murdoch Papers: Moore, *Volume Two*, 529.
32 David Waddington, *Parliamentary Debates* (Commons), 164, 18 December 1989, 40–122.
33 Roy Hattersley, *Parliamentary Debates* (Commons), 164, 18 December 1989, 40–122.
34 For a more detailed account of this episode, from the vantage point of 2017, see Peter Preston, 'What the sale of the Times to Murdoch can teach us today', *Guardian*, 18 June 2017, accessed 18 June 2017. www.theguardian.com/media/2017/jun/18/what-sale-of-times-to-rupert-murdoch-can-teach-us.
35 PREM 19/1063, Times Newspapers Dispute, Biffen briefing to Thatcher, 26 January 1981.
36 PREM 19/1063, Murdoch met with Thatcher on 27 March 1981.
37 Ken Clarke, *Kind of Blue: A Political Memoir* (London: Macmillan, 2016), 259.
38 Crisell, *Introductory*, 232.
39 Crisell, *Introductory*, 231.
40 Campbell, *Iron Lady*, 572.
41 Campbell, *Iron Lady*, 572.
42 Crisell, *Introductory*, 258.
43 David Waddington, *Parliamentary Debates* (Commons), 164, 18 December 1989, 40–122.
44 Campbell, *Iron Lady*, 573.
45 Crisell, *Introductory*, 259–260.
46 Crisell, *Introductory*, 260.
47 Des Freedman, *The Politics of Media Policy* (Cambridge: Polity Press, 2008), 216.
48 Freedman, *Media*, 222.
49 Nils Pratley, 'Rupert Murdoch's Sky bid is now very likely to succeed', *Guardian*, 29 June 2017, accessed 29 June 2017. www.theguardian.com/business/nils-pratley-on-finance/2017/jun/29/rupert-murdoch-sky-bid-is-now-very-likely-to-succeed; Paul Sandle and Kate Holton, 'Britain says Fox bid for Sky risks giving Murdoch too much power', *Reuters*, 29 June 2017, accessed 29 June 2017. http://uk.reuters.com/article/uk-sky-m-a-fox-idUKKBN19K1D7.

9 Social policy

Education vouchers and housing

Neoliberal thinking had greater influence on the Thatcher government's economic strategy than on its social policy. This is unsurprising because of the neoliberal preoccupation with economics and free markets. Nevertheless, in neoliberal terms social policy impacted on the public finances and state spending. Ideologically, areas like education represented the contested role and view of the state. Social reform had the potential to introduce liberal principles such as competition, ownership and incentivization while realigning the broader political ethos away from the state and vested interests towards the individual. This chapter will examine two social policy case studies: education vouchers and housing. This will highlight the limits of liberal economic ideas on the policies of Thatcherism as well as reinforcing the idea that the Conservative Party helped foster new vested interests in Britain.

Matthijs has written that Margaret Thatcher saw a 'spreading network of corporatist institutions as the main obstacle to achieving a free economy'.[1] Indeed the Thatcher government had in its sights the central pillars of the post-war British state. The monolithic NHS, state education and social (council) housing were to present major resistance to change. Nevertheless they were subject to significant reorganization during the Thatcher years, although to different extents. Housing will be examined in order to show the perceived successes, failures and limits of liberal economic influence on the social policy of the Thatcher years.

Although initially focusing on inflation and trade union reform, the various components of post-war Britain subsequently proved targets for economic liberals. Neoliberals stressed several pervading themes that could be applied to these case studies: supply-side reforms that would increase productivity and efficiency; decreased bureaucracy and state intervention; increased competition and choice; a transfer of power from the producer to the consumer; increased ownership and individual responsibility; and emphasis on what makes the market effective such as lower entry barriers. This chapter will examine to what extent these principles were applied to education and housing policy.

The role of the state

A question that preoccupied liberals was the role of the state. Its role and scope has differed throughout modern British historical periods. For instance, in Victorian Britain there existed the idea of deserving and undeserving poor. Welfare was often administered by charities. Subsequently, Seebohm Rowntree's research on living conditions, *Poverty, a Study of Town Life* (published in 1901) acted as a catalyst to erode Victorian opinions. That poorer families might need assistance from the state to break out of poverty became accepted by the Liberal governments of Herbert Asquith and David Lloyd George. An expanding system of welfare insurance, some state built housing and schools existed until the Second World War. The 1942 Beveridge Report then marked another catalyst, as well as the results of central planning in the war, for the wider provisions of the welfare state constructed by the Attlee government. This phase, although promising assistance from 'cradle to grave', essentially set up a safety net or 'security from loss of wages'.[2] This was extended by the more complex interventions of the Labour government of Harold Wilson in the 1960s. Wilson came under pressure after the 1965 report by Peter Townsend and Brian Abel-Smith, *The Poor and the Poorest* indicated relative poverty was still widespread in the UK. This led to increased state involvement in welfare.[3] Economically, Keynesian counter-cyclical fiscal policy was nominally practised to maintain employment.[4] Intrusive prices and incomes policies were intended to hold back inflation and excessive wage demands. Planning was in vogue and, to some neoliberals, government virtually controlled where citizens should live, where their children went to school and how much businesses should charge for goods.

At the same time as collectivism appeared to be strengthening, social individualism was growing. In particular the 'permissive society' reforms of the 1960s allowed many in Britain to act in a more socially liberal and individualistic manner. These two trends – growing state planning in the economy and public services alongside increasing individualism – were set on a collision course in the 1970s and 1980s. In opposition the Conservatives bemoaned the intrusive nature of the state and the loss of morality and responsibility after the 'permissive society'. Matthew Grimley has identified Thatcherism as 'part of a wider reaction against permissiveness in 1970s Britain' while David Marquand identified a 'paradoxical continuation' of the social changes of the 1960s.[5] Florence Sutcliffe-Braithwaite has described a Conservative shift in opposition from 'paternalistic, state-centred policies to a radical skepticism about the virtues the state can inculate'.[6] In government Thatcherism utilized the growing desire for choice and individualism to change the role of the state. Council houses were sold to their tenants, parents were encouraged to actively choose from a variety of possible schools and personal taxation was reduced, allowing a higher percentage of take-home pay to be spent as each person desired. The size of the state, however, by some measurements did not alter much during the Thatcher years. Yet the constant battle by successive chancellors to reduce the PSBR and lower capital investment in the public sector suggested that the state did retreat from several areas of British life.

The oft-cited 'Victorian values' of Margaret Thatcher also altered the relationship between poverty and the role of the state. The concept of deserving and undeserving poor returned in the 1980s. Critics claimed Thatcher 'exploited and magnified popular resentments to redefine the welfare state'.[7] Arch-Thatcherite Norman Tebbit famously suggested that if someone could not find a job, they should emulate his father and 'get on their bike' and find one. Therefore this role altered for several reasons, including the social changes of the 1960s as well as the liberal critique of planning. The separate strands of neoliberal thinking viewed social policies in different ways. Ordoliberals saw social outcomes as of prime concern. To avoid 'proletarianization' of the working classes, markets could be utilized for social purposes, hence the idea of a 'social market economy'.[8] Austrians saw things in a more laissez-faire way. Although accepting some level of welfare Hayek was generally antagonistic to social policy. He once said that ' "social justice" is nothing more than an empty formula and intellectually disreputable' and that egalitarianism was 'fundamentally immoral'.[9] Others in or close to the Austrian tradition, such as Murray Rothbard and Robert Nozick went further in calling for a 'nightwatchman' or 'ultraminimal' state that did little apart from guarantee law and order.[10] Chicago School academics like Milton Friedman sought a more pragmatic path, sympathetic to the kind of liberal society Hayek envisaged but astute enough to provide practical recommendations. One example of this was Friedman's long-running support for education vouchers, which would have some impact on the Thatcher government.

Education vouchers

State education had long been criticized by economic liberals. The IEA has claimed it 'damaged the poor and led to lower literacy rates than those in pre 1870 Britain'.[11] One neoliberal idea to improve education, and a favourite policy recommendation of both Milton Friedman and the IEA, was education vouchers. It was one model that had taken form before 1979 and had some level of support in the UK in the shape of FEVER (Friends of the Education Voucher Experiment in Representative Regions). Education vouchers could have been introduced at the end of the first Thatcher term, while Keith Joseph was Secretary of State for Education. When this opportunity was missed it appeared the education voucher idea would be abandoned. Instead there were some attempts at creating competition and improving standards in the Education Reform Act of 1988.

Statutory state education can be traced back to the Elementary Education Act of 1870, which set out the provision of compulsory education, delivered by local boards, up to the age of 12. To this point schooling had been provided privately and as the quote above claimed, many liberals even today consider this to be a better way to deliver education for all. Typically Friedrich Hayek saw little role for government in providing education.[12]

State funded education was expanded in the twentieth century, crucially by Rab Butler's 1944 Education Act. This split state funded schools into three categories: grammar schools, secondary technical schools and secondary modern schools. Grammar schools proved to be the most contentious because they had a selection procedure, which only allowed pupils admission if they passed an exam. This selection, at age 11, was increasingly resisted by the Labour Party in the post-war period. They felt that the process discriminated against children from working-class or poorer backgrounds. From 1965, the Secretary of State for Education in Harold Wilson's government, Anthony Crosland, attempted to force local authorities to convert all schools to non-selective comprehensives. Crosland was vehemently opposed to grammar schools and most became comprehensives over the next 15 years, including many by a – reluctant – Margaret Thatcher as Education Secretary in the Heath government 1970–74. The end of the 'tripartite' schooling system (grammar, secondary technical and secondary modern schools) was associated by some with the general malaise in Britain by the 1970s and fitted in with the mood of declinism that was remorselessly exploited by the Conservatives, albeit after they had left office.[13]

Development of the education voucher idea

Liberal economic thinkers had an alternative to the state education system which developed over a number of years: the education voucher scheme. It appealed to Conservatives like Margaret Thatcher and Keith Joseph because it challenged what they saw as sedentary, LEA-organized comprehensives. In its basic form parents would be given a voucher, which they could use to send their children to a school of their choosing. The idea was intended to promote competition between schools, raise standards of teaching and induce some degree of market discipline into the state school system. It was initially proposed by Milton Friedman in 1955, in an article titled 'The Role of Government in Education'.[14] Friedman wrote that government-led education was neither 'required' nor 'justifiable in a predominantly free enterprise society'. He said a voucher scheme 'would be a sizeable reduction in the direct activities of government, yet a great widening in the educational opportunities open to our children'. Last, 'Government would serve its proper function of improving the operation of the invisible hand without substituting the dead hand of bureaucracy'. Friedman's idea was an example of the neoliberalism with which he came to be associated. That is to say that the state should act to promote market forces, creating markets if they did not exist. In this sense Friedman saw the potential of government as an enabler. Hayekians (or the more classical liberals of the Austrian School) saw no role for the state in education and that the private sector would operate effectively without government interference. In *The Constitution of Liberty*

Hayek applauded Friedman's voucher idea but nevertheless said that 'it would undoubtedly be possible to leave the organization and management of education entirely to private efforts' and that 'the case against the management of schools by government … [is] stronger than ever'.[15] It may have been another attempt to conceal the real differences Hayek had with his fellow Mont Pelerin member. Again we see similar thinking between Austrian and Chicago Schools, diverging with the former's more puritanical liberal view compared to Friedman's more practical engagement. The Chicagoan's support for vouchers – administered by government – was one reason he would have to defend himself against accusations of being 'statist' by more idealistic, or as he put it 'utopian', economic liberals.[16]

Alan Peacock and Jack Wiseman wrote a 1964 pamphlet for the IEA – *Education for Democrats. A Study of the Financing of Education in a Free Society* – supporting the voucher principle. Peacock, in 2010, said that he had been looking at post-war social policy and wanted to improve education for the poorest families in Britain. He originally looked at vouchers in health policy but thought this would be too controversial, subsequently transferring his focus to education. Peacock wanted to increase the power and choice of the consumer, in this case the parent.[17] He was a member of the Liberal Party at this time and later said that most Conservatives were against the idea when it was first suggested, with the exceptions of Keith Joseph and Geoffrey Howe.[18]

The IEA became closely associated with education vouchers from the 1960s, in particular with its President Arthur Seldon and his wife Marjorie, who was the Founder Chair of FEVER. The pressure group was set up in 1974 to promote the voucher scheme. During this period some Conservative MPs began to look at the idea, including Rhodes Boyson, who backed the scheme in a 1975 paper called *The Fight for Education*.[19] Milton Friedman returned to his idea in *Free to Choose* in 1980, and the accompanying television series devoted a whole episode to education vouchers.[20]

Like many liberal economic policy recommendations, education vouchers were seen by many as eccentric. What the voucher scheme attempted to do was represent the same amount of money that the state allocated to a child's education but in a mobile form that could follow the best performing and sought after schools. The intention was to force institutions and teachers to improve their standards. Vouchers were a typically neoliberal proposal, attempting to impose market forces and discipline on a state-run system, in the belief this would increase quality and productivity.

Education policy of the Conservative Party, 1979

It might have been expected that the Thatcher government would be keen to alter the status quo in education. Within Thatcherism's broader strategy there were several reasons for this, economic and political. Comprehensive schools were seen to be under the control of LEAs (Local Education Authorities).

Politically this layer of bureaucracy was deemed as being left-leaning and inclined to support Labour. From a neoliberal perspective LEAs would have been a target for advocates of Public Choice theory. LEAs had been seen as a particularly inflexible arm of government. Chancellor Nigel Lawson said in a speech in 1988 that he saw one of the central government's roles as empowering the individual. Regarding education, Lawson said that since local government (in most cases) showed no signs of divesting power voluntarily, central government had to step in. The aim was to transfer power from bureaucratic and often obstructive bodies directly to the people. This explained several reforms of the Thatcher government and why it wanted to reduce the influence of LEAs.[21] Public Choice theorist Gordon Tullock believed education vouchers could reduce the power and prestige of civil servants.[22] In addition, the Labour Party had become the champion of producer groups such as teachers. Economic liberals felt that education policy should be aimed at the consumers (parents and their children) and not the producers (teachers and bureaucrats). As with council house sales, education vouchers had the potential to reduce the influence of forces antagonistic to the Conservative Party. Unlike housing though, vouchers in education would not be a vote winner in the short term (particularly the electoral cycle) and would possibly take several years to produce results.

The Thatcher government's desire to reform education had another dimension. The prime minister herself has been characterized as being driven by the need to defeat 'enemies'. In his biography of Thatcher, John Campbell wrote a chapter, titled 'Enemies Within' that described a 'need for enemies' and a 'taste for confrontation'.[23] During her tenure Margaret Thatcher identified and took on, for the most part shrewdly, a number of individuals and groups that she saw as reactionary. The trade union movement and the coal miner's leader Arthur Scargill, the civil service, the communist world, the European Community: all were targets. Local authorities and the education establishment were seen as intransigent, another bastion of leftism in the UK. Education reforms that reduced their power, however, would increase the power of central government.

Therefore it is unsurprising the Thatcher government saw radical education reform as desirable and part of its wider objectives. Attacking the entrenched education establishment was not only an opportunity to improve school standards but also to shape British political thinking and practices to Thatcherism's broader programme. Secretary of State for Education between 1986 and 1989 Kenneth Baker summed up many Conservative's opinion of the education establishment. He believed there had been a deterioration in standards of education due to the '1960s ethos' of the Department of Education and Science (DES) which had left it 'rooted in [the] "progressive" orthodoxies' of the comprehensive system, and 'in league' with teaching unions.[24]

Education vouchers: Keith Joseph's opportunity

Keith Joseph had been Secretary of State for Industry from 1979, taking over from Mark Carlisle at education in 1981. He was perhaps the most ardently pro-market (intellectually if not in practice) of the politicians in the Thatcher government and was interested in the voucher scheme when he became education secretary.[25] He was also the closest politician to the IEA, who had pushed the scheme hard in the previous years. Subsequently, voucher proponent Arthur Seldon said that the possible phase for introducing the idea was between October 1982 and June 1983, when the government was riding high after the victory in the Falklands and the economy was coming out of recession.[26] The scheme was examined in this period but was eventually shelved. It was left to Kenneth Baker to present the key piece of education legislation during the Thatcher era, the 1988 Education Reform Act. If education vouchers were going to be introduced it would surely have been while the economically liberal Joseph was in charge of the department. Several reasons have been proffered as to why Joseph failed to implement education vouchers: that the DES proved too resistant to the scheme, that Joseph was an ineffective Secretary of State or that it was simply unworkable.

Keith Joseph had wholeheartedly embraced economic liberalism after 1974. In opposition he toured universities around Britain delivering numerous speeches that espoused liberal ideas, such as 'Monetarism is Not Enough'.[27] In 1974 he was the driving force behind the founding of the CPS, with the aim of trying to emulate the West German economic 'miracle'.[28] In 1976 Joseph allegedly provided Margaret Thatcher with a list of key liberal economic texts, such as Hayek.[29] One of the most original thinkers in the Thatcher government, his policymaking often changed course rapidly.[30] Kenneth Clarke, who worked with Joseph at the DTI, thought him 'indecisive' and 'not suited to being in charge of any complex organization'.[31] James Prior criticized his enthusiasm for 'hare-brained schemes' while even supporters like Milton Friedman expressed disquiet over Joseph's interventionist policies at the DTI.[32] The latter point was based around keeping British Leyland afloat but had been identified by Michael Heseltine as electorally crucial in the contested region of the West Midlands.[33] Some liberals, such as Alfred Sherman, believed Joseph became guided by his civil servants, who were resistant to change.[34] A one-time advisor, Alan Peacock, thought that vouchers would have stood more chance of success if the 'rougher' Rhodes Boyson had led the department.[35] The role of civil servants has consistently been cited as a reason education reform proved so drawn out. The prime minister apparently told Joseph that he headed 'an awful department'.[36]

While examining the possible voucher scheme Joseph asked Alan Peacock to make some recommendations on the policy.[37] Peacock was an economist who had been an advisor at the DTI under Joseph during the Heath government. Peacock subsequently believed he was obstructed by civil servants while attempting to fulfil his role.[38] He described most of the top civil servants at the Ministry of Education as against the voucher idea, that it would have lessened their power and that the Permanent Secretary was 'vehemently opposed'.[39] These revelations were of course meat and drink to Public Choice advocates. Milton Friedman later said that bureaucrats had overstepped their remit and should have helped policymaking, not be making it themselves.[40]

In 1982, after Rhodes Boyson announced that the government was looking into a voucher scheme in education, the civil service produced an internal paper called *Educational Vouchers. Some Thoughts from California*. A voucher system had at that time recently been introduced in parts of the state. It said that vouchers had met 'widespread opposition' but that the idea was unlikely to fade due to 'widespread public dissatisfaction with state education'.[41] It concluded with several criticisms, perhaps most pertinently that there was 'a real fear that the market mechanism is not appropriate in education' but also that vouchers could encourage separatism, that parents chose schools that strengthened their own views, inequalities would be reinforced, voucher supporters underestimated true costs involved (such as transport issues) and that the view of diligent parents researching competing schools was unrealistic.[42] Last, most parents just wanted and preferred a good local school.[43]

The electoral cycle, it should also be said, could have worked against a radical proposal. After the victory in the 1982 Falklands War and with inflation falling and the economy recovering, an election was planned for 1983. With this looming, unemployment still high and the slump of 1980–1 still fresh in the memory, the Conservative leadership may have seen a voucher experiment as an unnecessary risk. In addition, the idea of education vouchers was not canvassed hard enough within the Conservative Party and was simply 'not a high priority' for Margaret Thatcher, despite her apparently liking the policy.[44] Furthermore, critics declared education an inert market and by implication one of the areas where the state had to intervene. Arthur Seldon said that the economic basis for opposition to vouchers was based on this conclusion and the fear that school facilities would be inelastic to changing demand.[45] This critique, led by civil servants and teaching unions, was central in preventing the education voucher from being attempted by the Thatcher government. Ultimately Keith Joseph concluded that vouchers would have involved

> hugely controversial and complex legislation, splitting the Conservative Party, as well as creating a tumultuous split between the parties, alienating most teacher unions, most local authorities, perhaps the churches and leading if we went for a pilot scheme possibly to a mouse at the end.[46]

Nevertheless, choice in state education – although not specifically a voucher – was pursued by Kenneth Baker in the third Thatcher term, as well as by all subsequent governments, both Conservative and Labour. Milton Friedman's principle of using government to pursue liberal principles has been a durable one.

Council house sales

The sale of council houses to their tenants has been widely acknowledged as one of the most popular, if not the most popular, reform of the Thatcher government. Housing was, and still is, a defining feature of British life. The country is sometimes considered unique in its obsession with homeowner-ship.[47] As urban areas expanded in the 1800s, and through the twentieth century, how to improve housing for the poorest people had been of concern to policymakers and intellectuals, often in a paternalistic fashion. Some of the industrialists of the Victorian era provided homes for their employees. The Cadbury family, famous for its confectionary business in Birmingham, was one example: they built an entire village in Bourneville for the workers of their factory and very much in their image – the family were Quakers so pubs were prohibited and exercise was encouraged.

Government subsequently began to build social housing and this acceler-ated after each world war. The period after 1945 saw a huge increase in council house building, including the numerous 'new towns' allocated by the state. The situation for many who moved into these homes was a drastic improvement from inner city overcrowding. Yet post-war council housing was to lead to problems. The housing was mostly built in concentrated areas and, especially in the 1960s, in the architectural fashion of the time for 'bru-talism': huge tower blocks in a futuristic style that soon lost its allure. Marga-ret Thatcher, although no architecture critic, described post-war high-rise flats as 'badly designed monstrosities'.[48] Additionally, there was usually a waiting list to gain a place in a council home. Rents were cheap and once in a house there was little advantage in losing this (relatively) privileged position. Cheap rents also often meant low maintenance. This created a situation that was not propitious for labour mobility or a dynamic economy.

Labour mobility was a consistent liberal theme and often linked with a cri-tique of rent controls.[49] These were also branded a hindrance to good quality housing in Britain. The issue had been identified in the 1950s by Geoffrey Howe (and Colin Jones for the Bow Group in the 1956 pamphlet *Houses to Let*) as a problem and had other liberal critics over several years (Milton Fried-man and George Stigler as far back as 1946), including another future Chancel-lor of the Exchequer, Nigel Lawson.[50] The 1957 Rent Act was attacked for creating perverse incentives for landlords, who in return for artificially low rents meant they often did not maintain their properties. Rent controls were intro-duced in 1915 due to the wartime shortage but continued after 1918 as insuffi-cient houses were built.[51] In their 1956 pamphlet, Howe and Jones wrote that rent controls fed inflation elsewhere in the economy, removed an incentive for private enterprise to build houses and limited supply and quality.[52] They con-cluded that rent control 'betokens wastage of housing, distortion in the economy and injustice for many'.[53] Hayek wrote in *The Constitution of Liberty* that rent controls meant property was essentially 'expropriated' and led to 'weakening the respect for property and the sense of individual responsibility'.[54]

Limits on rents could be understood as a way of protecting tenants from exploitative landlords and to keep housing affordable, similar to subsidized building of council houses. Maintaining rent at below market levels, however, acted as a disincentive to the private construction of new property, therefore increasing demand on existing houses, which led to shortages and, to many, reduced quality. The state was then further relied upon to provide new homes. The Conservatives at their 1950 conference made a commitment to build more social housing than Labour – much of it in the public sector.[55] After the subsequent government's target was reached in 1953, however, the Conservatives turned more towards private housing provision. Nevertheless, though Labour was more inclined towards social housing than the Conservatives, council housing building continued at various levels until 1979.[56] Governments also continued to subsidize rents. These policies exposed one ideological divide between economic liberals and post-war socialists (or social democrats). In 1978 Margaret Thatcher said of rent control, 'Labour's policy in fact produced derelict property and more homeless people'.[57]

Hugh Rossi, one of the architects of the Right to Buy legislation, also commented on the decline of private rented property. 'The 1974 Rent Act was part of Labour's deliberate policy to break the private landlord, to drive him out of business and, at the same time, provide local authorities with the funds to buy him out.'[58] This assertion, however, has been disputed. Supporters of rent controls have consistently challenged whether the policy had negative effects on housing, claiming they made little or no difference.[59] It was a counterfactual claim that was difficult to quantify. Nevertheless, rented property was an issue that was important to economic liberals because it was closely aligned with labour mobility.[60]

Selling council houses to their tenants

One of the key ideas of classical economics was that private property was sacrosanct. For many on the left the principle was heretic, and land should be put into common ownership. The tension between these two positions appeared to lie behind housing policy in Britain. Council housing, built and owned by the state, allocated to those most in need was a project inspired by socialism and state planning. Some Conservatives believed Labour's council house building strategy in London was intended to gain political advantage, part of a 'longstanding gerrymander'.[61]

The vast expansion of trade during the industrial revolution and the huge improvements in quality of life for many in Britain, according to liberals, had been possible because human beings act in a self-interested way. Private property and the ability to enjoy the fruits of labour lay behind this rapid development. These instincts, according to neoliberals, would be reignited if ownership and private property could be expanded. Margaret Thatcher tellingly commented on a large council estate in Toxteth in Liverpool, that the residents took little pride in their neighbourhood, questioning 'how people could live in such circumstances without trying to clear up the mess and improve their surroundings'.[62] To this line of thinking private ownership could reverse these trends. Indeed Conservative activists claimed, following the Right to Buy scheme, they could tell who owned their home 'at a glance' by the improvements they had carried out to their property.[63]

Alan Peacock, liberal academic, writer and subsequently a government advisor, lays claim to introducing the idea of council house sales (and that councils should retain fixed term freeholds) in the UK in 1961.[64] Yet the idea of transferring housing away from the state and to the individual had germinated some time before this. An unlikely source of liberal inspiration was Anthony Eden, who became an advocate of a 'property owning democracy' in the 1940s and himself revived the term from the 1920s 'constructive conservatism' of Noel Skelton who feared that 'socialism has force, fire, energy indeed' but that it meant 'economic disaster and moral despair'.[65] Skelton rejected state ownership, saying 'what everybody owns, nobody owns' and came to have a profound impact on a generation of Conservative politicians.[66] Although it did not solely mean homeownership Skelton wrote in 1924 a sentiment that would infuse Conservative thinking all the way through to the 1980 Housing Act:

> Until our educated and politically minded democracy has become predominantly a property-owning democracy, neither the national equilibrium nor the balance of the life of the individual will be restored.[67]

Stanley Baldwin and Harold Macmillan both used the phrase 'property owning democracy' in the 1920s and Skelton also encouraged Anthony Eden to use it.[68] Eden aligned the term more towards homeownership with his speech to the Conservative Party Conference in 1946 while Winston Churchill later said in 1950 that this was an essential part of Conservative policy.[69]

The Bow Group published a piece aimed at increasing homeownership in its 1954 pamphlet, *Industry and the Property Owning Democracy*, authored by Russell Lewis. Three reasons for homeownership were set out. First, it was a bulwark against socialism, second it had an 'excellent effect on character' and last encouraged independence and self-confidence.[70] Lewis said that property ownership catered for the 'country's real needs'.[71] In opposition during the 1960s the idea of selling council houses to their tenants took shape for the Heath Shadow Cabinet following a local government initiative in Birmingham.[72] Subsequently Geoffrey Howe wrote to Margaret Thatcher in September 1978 that 'property-owning democracy is undoubtedly a most important theme' and this should be focused 'overwhelmingly on council house sales'.[73] In short, property ownership had long been favoured by Conservative Party politicians. They articulated a belief that homeownership was the natural order of things in British life.

Another unlikely liberal reformer, Peter Walker – subsequently considered a 'wet' in Margaret Thatcher's government – championed the idea of selling council houses to their tenants and managed to include the proposal into the October 1974 Conservative election manifesto, with agreement from Thatcher who was briefly shadow spokesperson for the environment. It said its

> proposal for extending homeownership is to give a new deal to every council tenant who has been in his home for three years or more. These tenants will have the right to purchase their homes at a price one-third below market value.[74]

Of course the manifesto pledge was unable to be implemented as Labour won the election but by 1979 the Conservatives had expanded the policy. Walker had initially floated giving away council houses to long-term tenants but Margaret Thatcher resisted this on the grounds that it would appear to punish those who had worked to buy their home. Walker pointed out that this could also be applied to those who had paid years of council rents but Thatcher was concerned on how that would look to 'our people'.[75] The 1979 manifesto said that

> discounts will range from 33 per cent after three years, rising with length of tenancy to a maximum of 50 per cent after twenty years. We shall also ensure that 100 per cent mortgages are available for the purchase of council and new town houses'.[76]

Michael Heseltine, similarly to Walker, justified the large discounts in a 1978 paper he wrote in opposition: 'The tenant in an older house has in some cases paid out more in rent than the cost of the house to the local authority.'[77]

Another influential political figure regarding council house sales was Horace Cutler, a leading member, and between 1977 and 1981 leader of, the Greater London Council (GLC). In the late 1960s Cutler advocated, and put into motion, selling council houses to tenants. Margaret Thatcher (and Hugh Rossi in the same 1978 interview) praised Cutler for transferring power from the state to the people.[78] Upon gaining power in 1979, Thatcher turned to another moderate not particularly known for his liberal leanings, Heseltine (as Secretary of State for the Environment), to implement the policy of council house sales. Therefore, compared to several other Thatcherite reforms, the Right to Buy legislation and lineage had as much to do with One Nation and traditional conservatism as economic liberals like Keith Joseph or Geoffrey Howe. The details of the scheme for the 1979 manifesto were worked through by Hugh Rossi, who had been a long-time proponent of the idea, but was also considered closer to Edward Heath than Margaret Thatcher.[79]

Neoliberal themes and council house sales

Although several of the prominent personalities involved in implementing the policy of selling council houses may have not been typical economic liberals the policy idea itself could be viewed as a barometer of the shift to liberal economic thinking under the Thatcher government. Peter Mandelson later wrote council house sales was the one Conservative policy that Labour should have admitted was worthy of reversing their position on and that opposition against it in the 1983 election was a vote loser.[80]

Council house sales satisfied broad liberal principles for several reasons. Council house provision was a state subsidy. Some saw Right to Buy as a 'cut' and a means of reducing government spending.[81] In terms of a broadly Austrian microeconomic view of the market this would distort prices and drive out producers (private landlords and construction) from the housing market.[82] Social housing was planned from central government, where resources were allocated in the way a bureaucrat saw fit and not, to the Austrian School's way of thinking, by the price mechanism in a market that would respond to demand more quickly and efficiently. A constant idea alluded to in neoliberal writing was dependency. In creating the welfare state, British governments provided numerous methods of free assistance to its citizens, from the NHS to child benefit to cheap council housing. Neoliberals believed that, once initiated, this help was difficult to withdraw. This was of course anathema to economic liberals who believed people themselves should decide how to spend their own money and that they were better at doing this than a paternalist state. Homeownership was, in part, a way of achieving this. If tenants became property owners it would widen ownership of capital, reducing state control and planning from the centre. Nigel Lawson expanded on this in his 1988 lecture, 'The New Britain, The Tide of Ideas', when he said that the 'moral' basis of capitalism was shown in homeownership and this represented a desire of the British people for 'self improvement', denied to them by previous housing policies.[83]

Housing and the role of the state cut further into liberal thinking. Friedrich Hayek's warning that bureaucracy was self-perpetuating and Keith Joseph's 'ratchet effect' of socialism could be interpreted in one respect by the increasing number of council houses built in the post-war period, and the combination of that and rent controls pushed private provision out of the market. Furthermore, according to Public Choice theory it would be in the interest of those working in government to expand their control over housing policy. Selling state assets, in this case housing stock, showed a fundamental realignment in the relation between the government and the private sector. In summary, neoliberals believed that the state should only concern itself in areas where private provision was flawed, in effect where there was either a missing market or 'market failure'. The building, buying, selling and renting of houses was not, according to them, one of these areas.[84] Therefore the policy of council house sales, or property ownership in general, had been a favourite principle of Conservative politicians. It was also a component in the party's strategy to widen its support to traditional Labour supporters. Nevertheless, as a result of the prevailing ideological climate, the policy also aligned with several neoliberal ideas.

Implementation

As seen from the differences between the 1974 and 1979 Conservative Party manifestos, the terms of council house sales became more generous. A maximum discount to tenants was proposed as 33 per cent in 1974, while by 1979 a reduction of up to 50 per cent was on offer. As Secretary of State for the Environment, Michael Heseltine decided to allocate the job of preparing the legislation to Minister of State John Stanley.[85] The Housing Act of 1980, also known as the Right to Buy legislation, included several core features. The level of discount offered on the sale of a house depended on the length of time that a person or family had lived there. This ranged from 33 per cent on a minimum of three years tenancy to 50 per cent maximum after 20 years incumbency. If a tenant wanted to sell the house within five years of buying it they would have to repay the discount. A statutory right to buy would exist for tenants who had been in either a council house or non-charitable housing association residence for at least three years.[86] These conditions were extended in 1984, such was the success of the scheme, allowing tenants that had lived in their houses the right to buy after two years and increasing the discount to 60 per cent for over 30 years incumbency.[87]

The politics and economics of council house sales

The policy of selling council houses to their tenants proved wildly popular.[88] When the Housing Act was passed in 1980 approximately 53 per cent of British homes were owner-occupied. At the end of the decade – with 1.5 million council houses sold – this figure rose to 66 per cent.[89] Cynics have said the policy was primarily an electoral winner and effectively converted many traditional Labour supporters into Conservative voters.[90] It has already been noted that architect of New Labour Peter Mandelson thought that his party in the 1980s should have accepted this was a successful and popular policy. Tony Blair, in his memoirs, went further. He described strategies such as Right to Buy as chiming with the 'aspirational' nature of the British people, something that 'old' Labour never understood or recognized.[91] As outlined previously in this chapter, Conservative politicians since the 1920s believed capital ownership would strengthen the party's support and predated its relationship with neoliberalism.

The 1976 policy document, *The Right Approach*, criticized what it believed was socialism's tendency to heighten 'class feeling' through industrial unrest and municipal housing. Homeownership was one mechanism to dilute this feeling.[92] It should also be noted that homeownership had been rising over the previous decades and in this respect favoured the Conservatives' housing policy.[93] Daniel Stedman-Jones has written that the Thatcher government simply expanded a trend backed by both major parties over several years, but that the Conservatives added 'a thick coating of ideological paint'.[94] Margaret Thatcher certainly acknowledged that homeownership favoured her government and the ethos of her domestic programme. It could, at times, even override the need to reduce inflation. In a 1979 meeting with Gordon Pepper, the monetarist admitted he was 'very worried about the money supply figures', hinting at an interest rate increase. The prime minister replied that 'it would be disastrous if the mortgage rate rose'.[95]

The prime minister came into conflict with Chancellors Geoffrey Howe and Nigel Lawson over interest relief on mortgages. Mortgage Interest Relief at Source (MIRAS) allowed homeowners to claim tax relief on their mortgage interest payments. Although MIRAS was actually introduced by the then Labour Chancellor Roy Jenkins in 1969, also to encourage homeownership, it was expanded under the Thatcher government. The prime minister said that MIRAS was a reward for 'our people'.[96] Tax relief on mortgages was considered cheaper for the state than council housing. *The Right Approach* estimated that the average annual subsidy on a newly built council house was about £1300, while the tax relief on a new mortgage was about £300.[97] Documents show Thatcher and Howe clashing over raising the mortgage relief ceiling in 1982 and 1983.[98] The prime minister consistently wanted it to rise further than the chancellor thought acceptable.

If the politics of council house sales looked like a one-way street, the economics were not as clear. The wider ownership of capital encapsulated the Thatcherite idea of 'popular capitalism' and paved the way for a programme of privatization that accelerated during the second and third Thatcher terms. Yet it did little to tackle the problem of labour mobility. By addressing homeownership and not the rental market, and also by setting the seemingly sensible five-year resale restrictions, Right to Buy may have contributed to continued inertia in regional mobility.[99] This in turn may have worsened the employment difficulties of the 1980s. The lack of new council housing stock following the 1980 Act increased demand and therefore prices, working against one of the central targets of the Thatcher government. Critics of council house sales and its implementation were to appear on both left and right.

Criticism of Right to Buy

The Right to Buy legislation satisfied some general neoliberal themes. It widened ownership of housing and capital, reduced state control and provision of housing, dependency on central government and created over a million 'capitalists' that previously may have identified more with the Labour Party. Economic liberals were less impressed, however, with the way the scheme was implemented. First, prices were subsidized and discounted, in some cases heavily. Price is a key consideration in the market process, particularly to the Austrian School. Subsidies distort this market mechanism, government intervention can lead to inflation and one criticism that stood out from the Austrian School was that subsidizing prices generated queues.[100] This tied in with a criticism of council house sales from the left. The

Thatcher government prevented local authorities from using the revenues to replenish housing stock. Social housing was then left to housing associations. This led to a shortage of new houses which in turn caused increased home-lessness (exacerbated by the 1983 Mental Health Act that meant many more patients were treated in the community). This problem was made worse by elevated rents in existing council housing.[101]

Subsidized prices and reduced housing stock did increase demand for homes in the 1980s, with some negative consequences. Going back to the question of where government should step in after a market failure, many on the left would consider the advent of increased homelessness as just that. Liberals, on the other hand, thought that state interference in the implementation of Right to Buy created new market distortions. Housing policy and the implementation of strategies such as Right to Buy were advantageous to many but disastrous for others. The liberal criticism focused on Austrian microeconomics, the market mechanism and the primacy of price. This is a pervading theme of much of Thatcherism, namely that Hayekian politics were more influential than its economics, or at least the wider school of thought Hayek encapsulated.

Right to Buy, as Skelton predicted in the 1920s, reignited (or consolidated) the British obsession with homeownership. To many it was a situation from which you could only benefit. As well as subsidizing prices of council houses the government provided further incentives with privately owned homes in general with MIRAS tax relief. Nigel Lawson, following in Howe's footsteps, wanted to limit MIRAS but met fierce opposition from Margaret Thatcher. MIRAS and price subsidies worked against the principles of economic liberalism and distorted market forces. Kenneth Clarke as Chancellor in the 1990s also complained of his similarly unsuccessful battle to remove MIRAS, believing it encouraged 'recklessness' and that the 'madness' of the housing market had been 'one of the principal causes of the continuous instability of the post-war UK economy'.[102]

The rules that governed building societies' mortgage lending also changed in the mid-1980s, which generally made it easier to buy a house.[103] Credit further fuelled an increase in owner occupation during Thatcherism and beyond. The overall critique of Margaret Thatcher's housing policy is consistent with much of the government's programme. Political strategy appeared to align with the principles of economic liberalism policy formulation. Yet a purer adherence to neoliberal models, particularly Austrian microeconomics, was jettisoned when actually implemented. In some respects this again showed that Thatcherism was closer to Fredmanite neoliberalism than the more puritan classical liberalism of Hayek. That is to say the government utilized the state to liberalize or create markets, but that the methods introduced their own contradictions. In addition, reform of the rental market, important for labour mobility and identified as such by thinkers like Hayek as well as Tory politicians like Howe and Lawson, was not attempted. Robin Harris has noted that any attempts at reform of the rental market met a 'wall of prejudice'.[104] Margaret

Thatcher compromised her free market beliefs in housing policy in the 1980s by endorsing subsidization and price distortion; encouraging more borrowing and fuelling inflation.[105] A focus on homeownership in the UK, as well as the United States is a long-term trend that has been encouraged by governments. This can, most notoriously, be seen in the subprime housing market in the US, where owner occupation was promoted aggressively and acted as a trigger for the financial crisis of 2007–8.[106] *The Economist* – nominally liberal – has talked about the British 'fetish for home-ownership' and long bemoaned 'severe shortages of supply'.[107] Murie goes further by saying that the Thatcher government's housing policy actually increased dependency on the state with its combination of subsidy, special treatment and deregulation.[108] As such, the Thatcher government went about decreasing the potency of one vested interest (state sponsored council housing) while creating another (home-owners, given their own benefits and perks, sponsored by the state). This is consistent with other case studies examined in this book.

Conclusion

The social policy examined here took inspiration from long-term Conservative thinking, the political realities of the time and to a limited extent, liberal thinkers and think-tanks. The sale of council houses has been seen as one of the most successful reforms of Thatcherism. It was a populist measure that was backed by moderate Tories from Anthony Eden to Peter Walker as well as more Thatcherite ones like Geoffrey Howe. The scheme did expand homeownership and satisfied broad neoliberal themes. The implementation (large discounts as well as other housing subsidies like MIRAS), however, proved to be problematic. In effect the government offered different types of subsidy from social housing, which favoured different interest groups (home-owners) for political reasons (making traditional Labour supporters into Conservative voters) and distorted market forces. This was to have some negative long-term consequences: increased homelessness, soaring property prices and shortage of supply. For these reasons the policy of council house sales, as well as the wider housing policy of the Thatcher government, can be viewed as a popular success but with caveats for economic liberals, particularly the focus on price of the Austrian School. Another long-term liberal project was the reform of the rental market as a means of increasing labour mobility. This was not attempted during the Thatcher years. Milton Friedman's education voucher idea – long popular with liberals in the UK – demonstrated how neoliberal models sought to incorporate state function. That education vouchers were not implemented demonstrated the limit of neoliberal policy recommendations in Britain. Nevertheless, the principle of school choice became embedded over the long term as a government objective.

Notes

1 Matthias Matthijs, *Ideas and Economic Crises in Britain from Attlee to Blair (1945–2005)* (Abingdon: Routledge, 2011), 114.
2 Virginia Noble, *Inside the Welfare State. Foundations of Policy and Practice in Post-War Britain* (London: Routledge, 2009), 3.
3 Noble, *Welfare*, 5.
4 That is to say that deficits were run to maintain employment but generally without Keynes's recommendation to run surpluses during a boom.
5 Matthew Grimley, 'Thatcherism, Morality and Religion', in *Making Thatcher's Britain*, ed. Ben Jackson and Robert Saunders (Cambridge: Cambridge University Press, 2012), 79; Marquand's idea was taken from David Marquand, 'The Paradoxes of Thatcherism', in *Thatcherism*, ed. R. Skidelsky (Oxford: Blackwell, 1988), 165.
6 Florence Sutcliffe-Braithwaite, 'Neoliberalism and Morality in the Making of Thatcherite Social Policy', *The Historical Journal* 55:2 (June 2012), 499.
7 Noble, *Welfare*, 6.
8 Werner Bonefeld, 'Adam Smith and Ordoliberalism: On the Political Form of Market Liberty', *Review of International Studies* 39:2 (July 2012), 238; Taylor Boas and Jordan Gans-Morse, 'Neoliberalism: From New Liberal Philosophy to Anti-Liberal Slogan', *Studies in Comparative International Development* 44:2 (June 2009), 146.
9 F. A. Hayek, *Social Justice, Socialism & Democracy. Three Australian Lectures by F. A. Hayek* (Turramurra, NSW: Centre for Independent Studies, 1979), 2, 39.
10 Jeffrey M. Herbener, 'Ludwig von Mises and the Austrian School of Economics', *Review of Austrian Economics* 5:2 (1991), 37; Robert Nozick, *Anarchy, State, and Utopia* (Oxford: Blackwell, 1974).
11 E. G. West, *Government Failure: E. G. West on Education* (London: IEA, 2003). On page 38 the author wrote

> on my calculations (West, 1978), in 1880, when national compulsion was enacted, over 95 per cent of fifteen-year-olds were literate. This should be compared to the fact that over a century later 40 per cent of 21-year-olds in the UK admit to difficulties with writing and spelling.
>
> (Central Statistical Office, 1995)

12 F. A. Hayek, *The Constitution of Liberty* (London: Routledge, 2006 [1960]), 329.
13 Dominic Sandbrook, *Seasons in the Sun. The Battle for Britain 1974–79* (London: Penguin, 2013), 216.
14 Milton Friedman, *Capitalism and Freedom* (Chicago, IL: Chicago University Press, 1962), 85–107, originally published as 'The Role of Government in Education', in *Economics and the Public Interest*, ed. R. A. Solo (New Brunswick, NJ: Rutgers University Press, 1955).
15 Hayek, *Constitution*, 329.
16 Milton Friedman, 'Say "No" to Intolerance', *Liberty* 4:6 (July 1991), 20, accessed 28 November 2013. http://mises.org/journals/liberty/Liberty_Magazine_July_1991.pdf.
17 Interview with Sir Alan Peacock, 26 January 2010.
18 Interview with Sir Alan Peacock, 26 January 2010.
19 Andrew Denham, *Think-Tanks of the New Right* (Aldershot: Dartmouth, 1996), 80.
20 Milton and Rose Friedman, *Free to Choose* (London: Pan Books, 1990 [1980]). Episode six of the 1980 series was 'What's wrong with our schools?'.
21 Nigel Lawson, *The New Britain. The Tide of Ideas from Attlee to Thatcher* (London: CPS, 1988), 14–15.

22 Gordon Tullock, 'No Public Choice in State Education', *Economic Affairs* 6:3 (April–May 1986), 19.

23 John Campbell, *Margaret Thatcher. Volume Two: The Iron Lady* (London: Pimlico, 2004), 351–418.

24 Kenneth Baker, *The Turbulent Years. My Life in Politics* (London: Faber and Faber, 1993), 160–168.

25 Denham, *Think-Tanks*, 81.

26 Anthony Seldon, *The Riddle of the Voucher. An Inquiry into the Obstacles to Introducing Choice and Competition in State Schools* (London: IEA, 1986), 4.

27 Margaret Thatcher Foundation (hereafter MTF), MTF 110796, Sir Keith Joseph, 'Monetarism is Not Enough'. The Stockton Lecture, 5 April 1976.

28 Andrew Denham and Mark Garnett, *Keith Joseph* (Chesham: Acumen, 2001), 140.

29 Denham and Garnett, *Joseph*, 323.

30 Interview with Lord Ryder, 23 February 2011, 'Margaret Thatcher was not as natural a thinker as Keith Joseph'.

31 Ken Clarke, *Kind of Blue: A Political Memoir* (London: Macmillan, 2016), 93.

32 Jim Prior, *A Balance of Power* (London: Hamish Hamilton, 1986), 125; MTF 117172, letter from Milton Friedman to Ralph Harris, 2 July 1981.

33 Tim Bale, *The Conservatives since 1945* (Oxford: Oxford University Press, 2012), 229.

34 Alfred Sherman, *Paradoxes of Power. Reflections on the Thatcher Interlude*, ed. M. Garnett (Exeter: Imprint Academic, 2005), 102.

35 Interview with Sir Alan Peacock, 26 January 2010.

36 Baker, *Turbulent*, 161.

37 Interview with Sir Alan Peacock, 26 January 2010.

38 Interview with Sir Alan Peacock, 26 January 2010.

39 Interview with Sir Alan Peacock, 26 January 2010.

40 Interview with Sir Alan Peacock, 26 January 2010.

41 Records created or inherited by the Civil Service College (The National Archives: Public Record Office, Kew, hereafter JY) JY 3/32; G. Cohen, *Educational Vouchers. Some Thoughts from California* (Civil Service College Working Paper no. 32, November 1982), 2.

42 Ibid., 6–9.

43 Ibid., 7.

44 Interview with Sir Alan Peacock, 26 January 2010.

45 Seldon, *Riddle*, 17.

46 Denham and Garnett, *Joseph*, 371. Quote taken from *Contemporary Record*, spring 1987, 30–31.

47 *The Economist*, 'Gaponomics', 12 March 2011, 15; Robin Harris, *Not for Turning. The Life of Margaret Thatcher* (London: Bantam Press, 2013), 245; Clarke, *Kind*, 336.

48 Margaret Thatcher, *The Path to Power* (London: HarperCollins, 1995), 117.

49 Hayek, *Constitution*, 298; Richard Vinen, *Thatcher's Britain. The Politics and Social Upheaval of the 1980s* (London: Simon and Schuster), 201.

50 Stigler and Friedman collaborated on *Roofs or Ceilings? The Current Housing Problem* in 1946.

51 Geoffrey Howe and Colin Jones, *Houses to Let. The Future of Rent Control* (London: Conservative Political Centre, 1956), 5.

52 Howe and Jones, *Houses*, 32–34.

53 Howe and Jones, *Houses*, 64.

54 Hayek, *Constitution*, 297.

55 John R. Short, *Housing in Britain. The Post-War Experience* (London: Methuen, 1982), 47.

56 Short, *Housing*, 49–58.
57 MTF 103662, Margaret Thatcher, interview for Hornsey Journal, 21 April 1978, accessed 16 March 2011. www.margaretthatcher.org/document/103662.
58 MTF 103662, Hugh Rossi, interview for Hornsey Journal, 21 April 1978, accessed 16 March 2011. www.margaretthatcher.org/document/103662.
59 Alec Nove, 'Markets? Yes, but...,' *Economic Affairs* 5:2 (January–March 1985), 47.
60 Hayek, *Constitution*, 329.
61 Ken Young and John Kramer, *Strategy and Conflict in Metropolitan Housing. Suburbia versus the Greater London Council 1965–75* (London: Heinemann, 1978), 68.
62 Margaret Thatcher, *The Downing Street Years* (London: HarperCollins, 1993), 145.
63 Charles Moore, *Margaret Thatcher. The Authorized Biography. Volume One: Not for Turning* (London: Allen Lane, 2013), 471.
64 Interview with Sir Alan Peacock, 26 January 2010.
65 Noel Skelton, *Constructive Conservatism* (London: William Blackwood and Sons, 1924), 7.
66 Skelton, *Constructive*, 19.
67 Skelton, *Constructive*, 17.
68 David Torrance, *Noel Skelton and the Property-Owning Democracy* (London: Biteback, 2010), 140.
69 Torrance, *Skelton*, 140, 211.
70 Russell Lewis, *Industry and the Property Owning Democracy* (London: The Bow Group, 1954), 3, 30.
71 Lewis, *Industry*, 30.
72 Bale, *Conservatives*, 137.
73 The Papers of Margaret Thatcher (Cambridge: Churchill Archives, hereafter THCR), 2/1/3/9; Note from Geoffrey Howe to Margaret Thatcher 7 September 1978.
74 Conservative Party Election Manifesto October 1974, accessed 16 March 2011. www.conservative-party.net/manifestos/1974/Oct/october-1974-conservative-manifesto.shtml.
75 Peter King, *Housing Policy Transformed. The Right to Buy and the Desire to Own* (Bristol: The Policy Press, 2010), 58.
76 Conservative Party Election Manifesto 1979, accessed 16 March 2011. www.conservative-party.net/manifestos/1979/1979-conservative-manifesto.shtml.
77 THCR 2/6/2/187 Paper by Michael Heseltine, 'The Sale of Council House Sales', 28 June 1978.
78 MTF 103662.
79 Michael Heseltine, *Life In The Jungle. My Autobiography* (London: Hodder and Stoughton, 2000), 181.
80 Peter Mandelson, *The Third Man. Life at the Heart of New Labour* (London: HarperPress, 2010), 77. Mandelson wrote that Labour 'could not make policy on the simple basis that everything that the Tory government did was wrong'.
81 Moore, *Volume One*, 469.
82 See Chapter 8. Using Austrian microeconomic principles this study defines a 'perfect' market as free entry, large numbers of producers and consumers and information flows that manifest in price signals. The Austrian view is that dynamic markets moving towards equilibrium through price signals act as a discovery process and a means to efficiently allocate resources.
83 Lawson, *The New Britain*, 13.
84 Friedman, *Capitalism*, 36.
85 Heseltine, *Life*, 181, 195.
86 The 1980 Housing Act, accessed 19 March 2011. www.legislation.gov.uk/ukpga/1980/51.

87 David Stafford, 'Speed Up Council House Sales', *Economic Affairs* 4:2 (January 1984), 25–26.

88 Tom Clark, 'Thatcher's flagship policies draw mixed support at her death, poll shows', *Guardian*, 9 April 2013, accessed 26 June 2013. www.guardian.co.uk/politics/2013/apr/09/thatcher-flagship-policies-guardian-icm-poll.

89 Peter Riddell, 'Ideology In Practice', in *A Conservative Revolution? The Thatcher-Reagan Decade in Perspective*, ed. A. Adonis and T. Hames (Manchester: Manchester University Press, 1994), 31.

90 Geoffrey Garrett, 'The Political Consequences of Thatcherism', *Political Behavior* 14:4 (December 1992), 377–378.

91 Tony Blair, *A Journey* (London: Hutchinson, 2010), 90–91. Blair wrote that Labour had lost touch. 'It was all about opportunity not in general but in particular: for you, as an individual. That echoed and captured something deep within human nature: the desire to be free, to be the best you can be.'

92 King, *Housing*, 53.

93 Jon Lawrence and Florence Sutcliffe-Braithwaite, 'Margaret Thatcher and the Decline of Class Politics', in *Making Thatcher's Britain*, ed. Ben Jackson and Robert Saunders (Cambridge: Cambridge University Press, 2012), 135.

94 Daniel Stedman-Jones, *Masters of the Universe. Hayek, Friedman, and the Birth of Neoliberal Politics* (Oxford: Princeton University Press, 2012), 309.

95 Records of the Prime Minister's Office: Correspondence and Papers, 1979–1997 (The National Archives: Public Record Office, Kew, hereafter PREM19), 19/183, meeting between Gordon Pepper and Margaret Thatcher on 18 July 1979.

96 Geoffrey Howe, *Conflict of Loyalty* (Basingstoke: Macmillan, 1994), 280. Then Chancellor of the Exchequer Geoffrey Howe said the prime minister had 'long wanted it (MIRAS) to be extended because it was of special value to "our people"'.

97 King, *Housing*, 56.

98 MTF 124569, No. 10 letter to the Treasury, 25 Feb 1982; MTF 131524, MT personal minute to Chancellor of the Exchequer, 28 Feb 1983.

99 Vinen, *Thatcher's Britain*, 201.

100 Norman Barry, 'Austrian Challenge to Orthodoxy', *Economic Affairs* 4:3 (April–June 1984), p. 59.

101 John Campbell, *Margaret Thatcher. Volume Two: The Iron Lady* (London: Pimlico), p. 174.

102 Clarke, *Kind*, 336.

103 Vinen, *Thatcher's Britain*, 205.

104 Harris, *Not for Turning*, 245.

105 Campbell, *Iron Lady*, 233.

106 King, *Housing*, 2.

107 *The Economist*, 'Gaponomics', 12 March 2011, 15; *The Economist*, 'Through the Roof', 24 September 2015, accessed 21 June 2017. www.economist.com/news/britain/21667973-britain-has-one-booming-market-could-do-crash-through-roof.

108 Alan Murie, 'The Housing Legacy of Thatcherism', in *The Legacy of Thatcherism. Assessing and Exploring Thatcherite Social and Economic Policies*, ed. Stephen Farrall and Colin Hay (Oxford: Oxford University Press, 2014), 143–166.

Conclusion

This book has examined the influence of liberal economic thought on the Thatcher government in a number of ways. First, by utilizing the growing literature on the subject, it has charted the rise of neoliberalism over the twentieth century. The main positions of the most significant neoliberal strands – the Ordoliberal, Austrian and Chicago Schools – have been differentiated. Second, the influence of neoliberalism on a cross section of the policies of Thatcherism has been framed. Third, the opinion of neoliberals towards the Thatcher government regarding these case studies has been outlined. Last, the extent to which some of these policies were neoliberal, and which strain of neoliberalism they best or least represented, has also been examined.

This study has not questioned whether or not Thatcherism was influenced by liberal economics but how and to what extent. There are a number of generalizations found in the literature during and since the Thatcher era. These include that Conservative governments revived laissez-faire capitalism, returned to 'Victorian values' and dogmatically applied the theories of – in particular – Friedrich Hayek and Milton Friedman.[1] The left has lambasted the Thatcher government as destroying both the working class and the post-war settlement. It has become closely aligned with the forces of neoliberalism, globalization and even – to use George Soros's formulation – market fundamentalism (often interchangeably) with these administrations, frequently in a conspiratorial tone.[2] The left also criticized New Labour as being neoliberal, and a lukewarm version of Thatcherism.[3] The pro-market right, however, has often stated that the Thatcher government was too timid in its application of liberal economic ideas. One overriding factor in the work done on this topic is the polarizing effect of both Margaret Thatcher and her government. With almost 40 years now elapsed since the Conservatives came to power in 1979, and in particular since the 2007–08 financial crisis (and its implied link to the reforms of the 1980s)[4] there is now sufficient space to reappraise the relationship between ideology and the policies of Thatcherism.

General themes

There are several key points this study has tried to make.

- The majority of the policies of the Thatcher government probably satisfied the ideas of neoliberalism, broadly conceived; examples would include ownership, monetary control, some faith in market forces, deregulation (however superficial) and the importance of private property rights.
- Many of the reforms associated with Thatcherism did not, however, satisfy the more demanding principles of Austrian microeconomics and allow markets to function at their most efficient. This was because Thatcherism was as much a political project tied to Tory 'statecraft' as an ideological crusade. Subsidies, misplaced regulation, tolerance of monopoly and neglect of competition created price and market distortions. These failed to meet the social aims of Ordoliberals and were insufficiently liberalizing for libertarians in the Austrian tradition.
- Monetary control followed some of the theoretical recommendations of Friedmanite neoliberalism and its offshoots such as the LBS. This area was an objective of every branch of neoliberalism.
- The Thatcher government made a general, if ill-defined, attempt to reduce the power of vested interests. Its most notable success – in Thatcherite terms – was the taming of trade union influence through a combination of 'step-by-step' legislation, political guile and a raft of other measures and trends, such as declining union membership and ending price and incomes policies. However, in other cases, such as privatization, financial deregulation and broadcasting policy, it reduced the influence of one set of interests but allowed another to emerge. The neoliberal think-tank IEA has suggested this may be an integral feature of liberalization in democracies.
- Many of the reforms of the Thatcher government constitute a new orthodoxy. A number of economic liberals, however, believe several Thatcherite policies did not go far enough and have shifted the debate in terms of misdirected state regulation. Their critique still invokes 'government failure', utilizing Hayekian and Public Choice tradition. This exposes the contradictions of neoliberalism – requiring the state to move towards its objectives without ever being able to fully reach them.

Limits of this study

Although Margaret Thatcher left office (at the time of writing) 27 years ago, the proximity of the period has posed some challenges with respect to sources available for this study. The 30-year rule regarding disclosure of government documents has meant the emphasis on primary archive material is skewed towards the first and second Thatcher governments. For instance, the papers concerning exchange control removal and early economic policy offer an intriguing insight into how close both individual economic liberals and neo-liberal ideas penetrated the formulation of policy. The latter case studies – for instance on electricity privatization – suffer as a result. On the other hand, the relatively short space of time since the Thatcher government was in power has meant several relevant politicians, civil servants and commentators have granted the author an interview. The wealth of material published concerning these topics by economic liberals during this period has meant this study very much looks through this lens. Neoliberals were less shy about releasing material than policymakers and government officials.

The rise of neoliberalism

The influence of the Fabian Society acted as a model for neoliberals, as well as Conservative politicians. It was one of the reasons that Friedrich Hayek established the Mont Pelerin Society in 1947 and it encouraged the formation of British think-tanks like the IEA and Bow Group.[5] Hayek believed that change and influence occurred over the long term and away from the political arena. This meant that during the 1950s and 1960s writers and think-tanks operated, by and large, outside the mainstream. The opportunity for their opinions to be taken more seriously arose during the crises of the 1970s. Hayek began his career at the Austrian School of economics, which formed in the late nineteenth century in Vienna. Along with his mentor Ludwig von Mises, Hayek has come to embody a market fundamentalist strain of neoliberalism. Hayek managed to play in part in the development of the Austrian, Ordoliberal and Chicago Schools. Although the former strand articulated a minimal state liberal 'utopia' (to use Milton Friedman's description), this ignores the historical development of neoliberalism.[6]

Writers such as Daniel Stedman-Jones, Ben Jackson, Werner Bodefeld, Rachel Turner, Taylor Boas and Jordan Gans-Morse as well as the collection by Philip Mirowski and Dieter Plehwe have shed light on the forgotten first incarnation of neoliberalism in 1930s Germany. This group, the Ordoliberals, attempted to breathe life into the discredited idea of free markets and the importance of price while accepting some role for the state in maintaining competition and attenuating what they thought were the deleterious social effects of laissez-faire. With the contextual backdrop of authoritarianism and growing collectivism of the period, both Stedman-Jones and Jackson have identified the convergence of neoliberals in the 1930s and 1940s, including the Ordoliberals, the 'first' Chicago School and to a lesser extent, Hayek. Andrew Gamble also made a link between Thatcherism and the Ordoliberals during the 1970s by invoking the latter's idea, the 'free economy–strong state'.[7]

Hayek formed the Mont Pelerin Society in 1947 and embarked upon forming a wave of liberal opinion that would turn back the fashion for central planning. He later admitted that by wanting to keep his group united he resisted criticizing other Mont Pelerin members, in particular Milton Fried-man, as well as the 'constraining liberalism' of the Freiburg School.[8] Although clearly agreeing on a great deal, this strategy may have helped disguise important distinctions and given rise to the grouping together of the various schools of thought as a homogeneous collective.

The neoliberalism of the 1930s and 1940s exerted some influence on the post-war West German state, which the Ordoliberals either worked close to or even with in government. This strain became forgotten in the English-speaking world however, as Friedman's 'second' Chicago School became the most famous proponents of economic liberalism in the 1950s. Stedman-Jones has suggested that the Chicagoans represented a more radical turn in neo-liberalism.[9] Its economic – if not philosophical – positions however, sat some-where between the Austrians and Ordoliberals. Hayek and Mises, and later Murray Rothbard, were anti-state 'libertarians' whose focus on micro-economics and price was closest to classical liberalism. Ordoliberals saw the primacy of markets but wanted to use them for social outcomes and to prevent 'proletarianization' politicizing the working class.[10] Ordoliberals were comfortable with a legally based state that would constrain monopoly and make 'market compatible' interventions in the economy.[11]

Although uneasy about government activism the Chicago School's Milton Friedman and George Stigler nevertheless were willing to utilize the state to further their goals. Neoliberal principles such as monetary control attempted to promote conditions suitable for more efficient markets. Friedman was a long-term proponent of education vouchers and Chicagoans accepted some degree of antitrust legislation, although this declined over time. This principle has been identified by writers such as Jamie Peck – that of 're-tasking' the state in favour of business or pro-market interests – and has some resonance with the policies of Thatcherism.[12] The change in role of the state has been identified by Peter A. Hall as representing a link between ideas, power pol-itics and a shift in institutional 'policy paradigms'.[13] The distinctions between the strains of neoliberalism, as well as their historical development, have not been sufficiently well-documented in much of the work on Thatcherism, hence this study.

Monetary control was the first major neoliberal policy to gain a level of acceptance with politicians, and some of the public, in Britain. This was because of the work of Milton Friedman (and Anna Schwartz) from the 1960s identifying inflation as a monetary phenomenon. The message was also con-veyed by politicians like Keith Joseph and journalists such as Peter Jay and Samuel Brittan, in newspapers like *The Times*, the *Daily Telegraph*, *The Eco-nomist* and the *Financial Times*.[14] The fault line for the establishment in this debate was 1976, when Britain had to accept the conditions of an IMF loan. James Callaghan's famous Labour Party Conference speech (written by Peter Jay) created some space for the Thatcher government to subsequently pursue the policy more dogmatically between 1979 and 1983.[15] The other area in the 1970s in which neoliberals had some impact was trade union reform. The

Winter of Discontent, in particular, created an opportunity in which politicians and the public questioned the role of the unions in British society.

Monetary control and industrial relations were direct responses to the public's concerns of the times. Wider acceptance of a pro-market programme, supply-side or microeconomic reforms made less of an impact. The work in the 1960s and 1970s of Public Choice theorists may have also had a small, if limited, effect. Rooted in the thesis of Hayek's *The Road to Serfdom*, writers like James Buchanan and Gordon Tullock launched a critique of the state. Government and its bureaucracy, according to Public Choice, were wasteful, inefficient, prone to 'rent-seeking behaviour' and inclined to inexorably expand. Politicians, accordingly, should aim to reduce the size, power and scope of the state while applying increased discipline to what remained. Public Choice theorists invoked the idea of 'government failure'. These principles may have influenced Keith Joseph (who spoke of the 'ratchet effect' of socialism and the state) and Margaret Thatcher, who recommended her civil servants read Virginia School literature.[16] Public Choice ideas appeared to infuse several Thatcherite policies, from privatization (the state should not run industry) to financial deregulation, to the internal market reforms in public services (market disciplines can constrain unproductive public sector workers and bureaucrats). Nevertheless this also aligned with longer term Conservative thinking on bringing a more managerial or business approach to bureaucracy.[17]

In rhetorical and presentational terms, Keith Joseph was the British politician who most publicly challenged the post-war settlement with neoliberal ideas. His lecture tours, the work done by his think-tank the CPS and his input into other research groups (such as the *Right Approach* and Stepping Stones), were important in questioning long-held principles.[18] He was also one of the only Conservatives to take a detailed look at Ordoliberalism, initially naming the CPS the 'Erhard Foundation' before its launch and showing interest in the work of Wilhelm Röpke.[19] In practical terms, however, Geoffrey Howe had been committed to free market ideas since the 1950s (Joseph had alternated with the orthodoxy of the times up until 1974) and applied these principles with determination once in office. Howe's commitment to policies like exchange control removal, enterprise zones and monetary control came under fire. Establishment critics, civil servants and other members of the government challenged his course, while Margaret Thatcher was often unsure. Documents from the period show Howe's policies were rooted in liberal economics and were pursued consistently despite his mild-mannered public persona. At the same time, Joseph, while Secretary of State for Trade and Industry, prevaricated over a bailout for British Leyland and whether to implement a voucher scheme while at the DES.

Economic policy

This book has attempted to show that a spectrum of liberal influence existed in the domestic policies of the Thatcher government. The monetarist phase of economic policy during the first term was one of the clearest examples of ideology in practice. Deviating from the previous orthodoxy of counter-cyclical Keynesian demand management, the government targeted the control of inflation as its primary concern. Several writers, such as Stedman-Jones and those on the left such as Andre Gunner Frank, have identified this as building on the monetary restraint of the Callaghan government, which came under pressure from the IMF.[20] The Thatcher government, however, appeared to be more committed to this approach and several Conservative politicians were aware, if not advocates, of Milton Friedman's monetarism, often through conduits such as Alan Walters, Gordon Pepper and Peter Jay. The policy had two distinct phases. From 1979 until the 1981 Budget the emphasis was control of inflation by restricting monetary aggregates. After this, deficit reduction under the influence of 'rational expectations' thinking of the kind proposed by the LBS took a more central role. Although criticized for the severity of the recession it caused, inflation had been cut back at the end of the first term, before Nigel Lawson embarked upon different monetary techniques as chancellor. Even with economic policy, apparently rooted in theory, the Thatcher government used the defeat of inflation politically. As Bulpitt pointed out, one of monetarism's key aims was to 'disentangle' the central state from 'interests'.[21] It was this dogmatic approach to reducing inflation, at the cost of soaring unemployment, that most wedded Thatcherism to an austere ideology.

The removal of exchange controls was a measure that promoted trade and therefore satisfied neoliberals of all persuasions. Milton Friedman believed this was the key initial act of Thatcherism.[22] Both exchange control abolition and the enterprise zone policy acted as important signals for the Thatcher government. The policies represented an early faith in market forces (although documents reveal Thatcher came close to reimposing inflow controls), particularly by Geoffrey Howe and the prime minister. They were stepping stones towards the set piece deregulatory reforms of privatization and Big Bang in the second term. Geoffrey Howe, Nigel Lawson and Margaret Thatcher met opposition to their economic policy from within both the Conservative Party and Whitehall. The influence of neoliberals is particularly relevant because documents appear to show liberal economic outsiders exerting more influence on policymakers than those within the government machine. A closer appraisal of enterprise zones, however, illustrates the wider programme of Thatcherism and neoliberalism. At face value, particularly with the growth of Canary Wharf, enterprise zones were a pro-market measure of deregulation and liberalization. The use of the state, however, in clearing land and providing infrastructure was also important in the London Docklands.[23] Enterprise zones were another example of how the state was 're-tasked' during Thatcherism. In addition, outside the Docklands neoliberals were less supportive of the policy.[24]

If economic policy saw a more faithful application of liberalism, social policy was more compromised. One popular success was council house sales.

Although the policy had long-standing roots in the Conservative Party, and had started several years before 1979, it aligned neatly with the liberal principles of ownership and individualism. Right to Buy, however, was only a partial success for neoliberals. It shifted the terms of ownership but the manner of implementation (subsidies, large discounts and other housing subsidies like MIRAS) caused – to liberals – market distortions. Housing policy was another example of how different interests were favoured by government. Whereas the 'post-war settlement' privileged groups like trades unions, the policies of Thatcherism accelerated the trend that solidified homeowners as 'our people'. Successive chancellors battled with the prime minister to lower the ceiling on mortgage interest relief as well as over interest rate rises. This encouraged price increases and what has been described as the British 'fetish' for homeownership.[25] In neoliberal terms these interventions distorted the market and prices, the main focus of Austrian thinking.

Last, a favourite Friedmanite idea, education vouchers, failed due to the opposition of both public opinion and vested interests. The adapted neoliberal model did find some influence in the internal market reforms of the third Thatcher government. LEAs were a political target for the Conservatives but this approach clearly did not chime with the kind of dispersion of power favoured by neoliberals such as Milton Friedman, who once said 'If government is to exercise power, better in the county than in the state'.[26] Nevertheless subsequent governments have pursued the quasi-market reforms of Thatcherism as a means to improve choice and therefore standards.

Vested interests

Economic liberals believe that vested interests have a detrimental effect on a market economy. Although not a preconceived strategy, because of the influence of both long-term Conservative thinking as well as neoliberalism, we may have expected the Thatcher government to attempt to curtail the power of special interest groups. Several of the vested interests studied here (trades unions, the 'old' City, state-controlled industries) did see their influence reduced by the Thatcher government. Trade union reform was the most – in Thatcherite terms – successful part of this strategy. Tackling industrial relations had both political and economic objectives. A more flexible labour market may have been one goal but after bringing down the Heath government, trade union power loomed large in the party's memory. To achieve trade union reform the Conservatives used a 'divide and rule' approach and when in government, an improvised 'step-by-step' approach. The slow attrition of the union movement, as well as the set piece confrontations with the NUM and printing unions, effectively reduced its influence as a vested interest and moved it to the fringes of the political process.

Financial deregulation however was a different story. The old clubby network of a hermetically sealed City was prized open by exchange control removal in 1979 and Big Bang in 1986. The resulting wealth accumulated in the new City as well as soaring trade secured London's position as an inter-national financial hub, and gave the financial service sector growing power. This allowed the City to develop into a more potent vested interest than it had been previously. For those at the Hayekian IEA, this was because of flawed or misdirected regulation.[27] The importance of the financial sector meant the British government either part-nationalized or bailed out collaps-ing banks during the 2007–08 financial crisis. 'Too big to fail' financial insti-tutions inevitably prevented new entry to the market and reduced competition. One account of the interplay between government, the Finan-cial Services Authority and representatives of the major British banks was set out in Alistair Darling's *Back from the Brink*.[28]

The Thatcher government attempted to curb the influence of the BBC by setting up the 1985–6 Peacock Committee. Despite the presence of several economic liberals on the panel it did not recommend an end to BBC funding by licence fee. The corporation had to change, adapting to both the commis-sion and its aftermath. In short though, the power of the BBC was not reduced to a great extent. The 1990 Broadcasting Act attempted to bring more commercial pressures to bear on television but managed to bolster another vested interest, that of BSkyB and the Murdoch empire. The latter has managed to exert influence over policymakers and this was in part because the Thatcher government ignored rules on monopoly and ownership in 1981 and 1990. Again this was political as Murdoch's newspapers and channels were generally more supportive of the Conservatives than the BBC. Although it is worth noting the large start-up costs of satellite broadcasting, the results of the Thatcher government's policies has been limited competition.[29]

Privatization satisfied broad neoliberal themes – withdrawal of the state, private ownership, reversal of the 'ratchet effect' – and did have benefits for the consumer. Nevertheless, the years after each large privatization saw continued monopoly (in the private sector) and regulation or legislation struggling to facil-itate competition. Electricity privatization managed to remove a vested interest but the creation of giant monopolies in the private sector risked a new group exerting influence on markets. During the electricity privatization process Cecil Parkinson and Nigel Lawson appeared to be moving to the Ordoliberal prin-ciple of enforcing competition and preventing monopoly, as a result of the crit-icism of earlier gas and telecoms sales.[30] The eventual legislation however, hastened by the electoral cycle, saw less competition than many neoliberals would have desired. Hayekians saw a 'captured' regulator, Ordoliberals presum-ably a weak legal framework.[31] The result chimed with Harvey's view that a neoliberal state attempts to create markets and then retreats from them.[32]

Thatcherism, neoliberalism and market fundamentalism

Why is it important to further examine the links between Thatcherism and neoliberalism? Look at any number of texts concerning globalization and the modern world and the term neoliberalism often looms large. The use is over-whelmingly negative and has to come to signify some malign force, either backed by sinister Western business interests or right wing politicians, or even more worryingly as a power with structural momentum in its own right.[33] The implications of this have been shown in this book to be at odds with the original architects of neoliberalism. Stedman-Jones has identified the historical development of neoliberalism from 1930s Germany to 1980s Britain and America. Peck has also described the development of neoliberalism, viewing the phenomenon as one that requires redefining, particularly in terms of how the state has to 'fix' markets, in order to survive and maintain influence among ruling elites.[34] Ben Jackson has singled out the similarities between early neoliberal thinking in comparison with its more radical 1970s version.[35] Rachel Turner sees the movement towards neoliberalism as rooted in the context of each specific country – in the US as a reaction to the Great Society of the 1960s, in Britain against union power in the 1970s and West Germany in the 1940s against the Nazis.[36]

While accepting these trends this book has attempted to set out the sepa-rate strains of thinking and core positions taken by neoliberals from its incep-tion, through Thatcherism and beyond. These differences have been made more opaque by the contemporary trend to read neoliberalism as market fundamentalism with a twist of Western imperialism. The 'Washington Con-sensus' and globalization are also terms closely associated with Thatcherism and neoliberalism. This has been documented by Boas and Gans-Morse. What we can say from all these interpretations of economic liberalism in the twentieth century is that they are more complex than many have assumed.

Although not in wide circulation, the term neoliberalism had broadly positive connotations until the 1960s, linked with Ordoliberal intellectuals like Röpke.[37] This changed in the 1970s when Augusto Pinochet's coup in Chile and its resulting economic policies were dubbed neoliberal. From this point the term took on a more sinister tone, aligned with Pinochet's author-itarian regime. Milton Friedman's support for it suggested that many neolib-erals believed markets create civil society and not vice versa. One of the reasons it is still relevant to identify the different potential policies embedded within neoliberalism is how far the modern reading has deviated from Ordo-liberalism. Several historians appear to show sympathy towards this moderate version of neoliberalism, and dismay at the way it drifted in Britain and the US towards the Chicago School's ideas.[38] This is fundamentally because Ordoliberals believed the market system was the most propitious way to organize an economy, but that it could be manipulated for social ends. The Austrian and Chicagoan interpretations see markets as able to deliver order and benefits with little or limited outside intervention. They also have an ill-defined 'freedom', sometimes articulated as 'negative liberty', as an objective.[39] It is in this respect that we see the Thatcher government more closely aligned with Friedmanite neoliberalism – to enact broadly market-friendly and often political measures – and then to step away from action that might mitigate their social implications or even that could allow the market to operate more efficiently. One example was monetary control during the first Thatcher government. For an Austrian this was too much government while for Ordoliberals monetarism was too focused on economic rather than social outcomes.

In contemporary British politics these differences still matter. When the 2010–15 coalition government went about reducing the budget deficit through cuts in 2010 they invoked the policies of the Thatcher government between 1981 and 1983. When leaders suggest they can prevent energy price rises through government fiat they are inadvertently trying to amend the perceived flaws of the privatization policies of Thatcherism, albeit the symptoms rather than the root causes.[40] Closer examination of the basic positions implicit in these policies could improve social outcomes if governments wish to remain working within a neoliberal paradigm.

Summary

This study has attempted to describe the relationship between liberal economic ideas and the policies of the Thatcher government. It has studied neoliberal literature, set out hypothetical policy models and explored where and why politicians may have implemented or deviated from these. It has examined what neoliberals thought of Thatcherism and the ideological and political legacy of the period. The actual policies implemented by the Thatcher government have had far-reaching effects. Taken as a whole they have helped create a new orthodoxy, both in Britain and internationally, in macro- and microeconomics. This has taken selective neoliberal ideas, compromised by political reality. There are several ways in which this project has tried to add to the existing literature on Thatcherism and neoliberalism.

- First, it adds to the growing work done on the development of neoliberalism, particularly by putting more emphasis on the work and lineage of the Ordoliberals.
- Second, it sets out neoliberal positions and looks at how close the Thatcher government was to these. Although invoking the philosophy of Hayek at times and having some very loose association with Ordoliberals ideas, Thatcherism was most closely linked with the Chicago School of Milton Friedman.
- Third, it reinforces the impression that while few members of the Thatcher government were ideologues (indeed, the most fervent neoliberal influence was exerted by advisors, or 'conduits' such as Alfred Sherman, Alan Walters, Gordon Pepper and journalists like Samuel Brittan), it did, however, align more closely to neoliberalism due to the prevailing or 'supporting' wind of the period.
- Fourth, it shows that some in government, such as Terry Burns, helped move the government's economic policy in a more theoretically neoliberal

direction. By implication, the state action this entailed took on a broadly Friedmanite or Chicagoan hue. Burns, as well as others such as Walters, have acknowledged the direct influence Friedman exerted on them.

- Fifth, it shows that the Thatcher government, although nominally liberal, behaved in a similar way to Hayek's reading of government, in so far as it was beholden to certain interests. During Thatcherism these included homeowners, privatized monopolies, as well as more traditional Conservative supporters in big business.

- Finally, this book emphasizes that the Thatcher government, although curbing its growth, 're-tasked' the state as opposed to reducing its size.

The contradictions neoliberalism contains can be seen in these conclusions. Ordoliberals had clear objectives and mechanisms to reach them while utilizing the benefits markets can provide. Austrians tended to outline a utopia based on principle and deduction. The latter was too much even for a prime minister whose government has been described by many as radical. Margaret Thatcher once said, 'Utopia never comes, because we know we should not like it if it did'.[41] This is why Thatcherism, with its broad alignment to neoliberal principles, was closer to Chicagoan thinking. Friedmanites believed they could move closer to a more liberal society by state-guided stepping stones. As Peck and Stedman-Jones have identified, this has meant neoliberalism has needed to consistently redefine what government can actually do. Thatcherism implemented several reforms that satisfied some liberal ideals but contradicted others.

Notes

1 Joseph Stiglitz, *Freefall. Free Markets and the Sinking of the Global Economy* (London: Penguin, 2010), 17–18; Taylor Boas and Jordan Gans-Morse, 'Neoliberalism: From New Liberal Philosophy to Anti-Liberal Slogan', *Studies in Comparative International Development* 44:2 (June 2009), 138; Nigel Lawson, 'Mrs Thatcher's Lasting Legacy', *Standpoint* (May 2009), accessed 10 May 2012. http://standpointmag.co.uk/node/1484/full.

2 Boas and Gans-Morse, 'Neoliberalism,' 137–138.

3 Ray Kiely, *The Clash of Globalisations. Neoliberalism, the Third Way and Anti-Globalisation* (Leiden: Brill, 2005), 125.

4 Charles Moore, *Margaret Thatcher The Authorized Biography, Volume Two: Everything She Wants* (London: Allen Lane, 2015), 220–221.

5 Eamonn Butler, *Hayek* (New York: Universe, 1985a), 1; interview with Lord Howe, 2009.

6 Milton Friedman, 'Say "No" to Intolerance', *Liberty* 4:6 (July 1991), 20, accessed 28 November 2013. http://mises.org/journals/liberty/Liberty_Magazine_July_1991.pdf.

7 Werner Bonefeld, 'Adam Smith and Ordoliberalism: On the Political Form of Market Liberty', *Review of International Studies* 39:2 (July 2012), 235; Andrew Gamble, *The Free Economy and the Strong State. The Politics of Thatcherism* (Basingstoke: Palgrave Macmillan, 1994b), 38–45.

8 Margaret Thatcher Foundation (hereafter MTF), 117203, Letter from Friedrich Hayek to Arthur Seldon, 13 May 1985, accessed 13 September 2012 www.margaretthatcher.org/document/117203; Manfried E. Streit and Michael Wohlgemuth 'The

Market Economy and the State. Hayekian and Ordoliberal Conceptions', in *The Theory of Capitalism in the German Economic Tradition*, ed. P. Koslowski (London: Springer, 2000), 229.

9 Daniel Stedman-Jones, *Masters of the Universe. Hayek, Friedman, and the Birth of Neoliberal Politics* (Oxford: Princeton University Press, 2012), 91.

10 Bonefeld, 'Adam Smith', 238.

11 Christian Watrin, 'Alfred Müller-Armack – Economic Policy Maker and Sociologist of Religion', in *The Theory of Capitalism in the German Economic Tradition*, ed. P. Koslowski (London: Springer, 2000), 209; Samuel Gregg, *Wilhelm Röpke's Political Economy* (Cheltenham: Edward Elgar, 2010), 89.

12 Jamie Peck, *Constructions of Neoliberal Reason* (Oxford: Oxford University Press, 2010), 4, 17.

13 Peter A. Hall, 'Policy Paradigms, Social Learning, and the State: The Case of Economic Policymaking in Britain', *Comparative Politics* 25:3 (April 1993), 279, 290.

14 Richard Cockett, *Thinking the Unthinkable. Think-Tanks and the Economic Counter Revolution 1931–1983* (London: Harper Collins, 1995), 183.

15 Ben Jackson and Robert Saunders, 'Introduction: Varieties of Thatcherism', in *Making Thatcher's Britain*, ed. Ben Jackson and Robert Saunders (Cambridge: Cambridge University Press, 2012), 19.

16 Donald J. Savoie, *Thatcher Reagan Mulroney. In Search of a New Bureaucracy* (London: University of Pittsburgh Press, 1994), 27, 106.

17 Tim Bale, *The Conservatives since 1945* (Oxford: Oxford University Press, 2012), 130–135, 138.

18 Interview with Lord Ryder, 23 February 2011.

19 Margaret Thatcher Foundation (hereafter MTF), MTF114757, 'Ralph Harris record of conversation (visit from Keith Joseph)', 14 March 1974; MTF114760, Sir Keith Joseph note ('The Erhard Foundation'), 21 March 1974.

20 Stedman-Jones, *Masters*, 5, 257; Andre Gunner Frank, 'No End to History! History to No End?', *Social Justice* 17:4 (Winter 1990), 17.

21 Jim Tomlinson, 'Thatcher, Monetarism and the Politics of Inflation', in *Making Thatcher's Britain*, ed. Ben Jackson and Robert Saunders (Cambridge: Cambridge University Press, 2012), 77; Jim Bulpitt, 'The Discipline of the New Democracy: Mrs Thatcher's Domestic Statecraft', *Political Studies* 34:1 (1986), 21.

22 Milton Friedman, *Margaret Thatcher's Revolution. How it Happened and What it Meant*, ed. S. Roy and J. Clarke (London: Continuum, 2005), 66.

23 Jack Brown, 'The London Docklands Development Corporation: 1979–1981', (London: Queen Mary University of London, unpublished MA thesis, 2012), 54.

24 Peter Stoney, 'Enterprise Zone: Incentive or Intervention?', *Economic Affairs* 8:1 (October/November 1987), 30.

25 *The Economist*, 'Gaponomics', 12 March 2011, 15.

26 Milton Friedman, *Capitalism and Freedom* (London: University of Chicago Press, 2002 [1962]), 3.

27 Philip Booth, 'More Regulation, Less Regulation or Better Regulation?', in *Verdict on the Crash. Causes and Policy Implications*, ed. P. Booth (London: IEA, 2009), 169.

28 Alistair Darling, *Back from the Brink. 1,000 Days at Number 11* (London: Atlantic Books, 2012), 61–63, 156–162.

29 Andrew Crisell, *An Introductory History of British Broadcasting* (London: Routledge, 2002), 232.

30 Cecil Parkinson, *Right at the Centre* (London: Weidenfeld and Nicolson, 1992), 260, 265, 277.

31 Colin Robinson, *Competition in Electricity? The Government's Proposals for Privatizing Electricity Supply* (London: IEA, 1988), 7, 18.

32 David Harvey, *A Brief History of Neoliberalism* (Oxford: Oxford University Press, 2005), 2.
33 Boas and Gans-Morse, 'Neoliberalism', 137–138.
34 Peck, *Constructions*, xiii, 4.
35 Ben Jackson, 'At the Origins of Neoliberalism: The Free Economy and the Strong State, 1930–1947', *The Historical Journal* 53:1 (March 2010), 132–140.
36 Rachel S. Turner, *Neoliberal Ideology. History, Concepts and Policies* (Edinburgh: Edinburgh University Press, 2008), 219.
37 A review of Röpke's book *A Humane Economy* in *The Economist* on 8 October 1960 spoke of neoliberalism in positive terms, as did an article in 1964. By 1969 *The Economist* was mentioning the term in relation to Latin American countries.
38 Stedman-Jones, *Masters*, 335; Peck, *Constructions*, 17; Patrick M. Boarman, 'Apostle of a Humane Economy: Remembering Wilhelm Röpke', *Society* 37:6 (2000), 57–65.
39 Stedman-Jones, *Masters*, 71.
40 Colin Robinson, *From Nationalization to State Control. The Return of Centralised Energy Planning*, IEA Discussion Paper No. 49 (London: IEA, 2013), 6–7, 11–14, accessed 26 December 2013. www.iea.org.uk/sites/default/files/publications/files/From%20Nationalisation%20to%20State%20Control_web.pdf; James Kirkup, 'Labour: Miliband pledges to freeze energy prices', the *Daily Telegraph*, 24 September 2013, accessed 27 December 2013. www.telegraph.co.uk/news/politics/labour/10331012/Labour-Miliband-pledges-to-freeze-energy-prices.html.
41 MTF 107332, Margaret Thatcher Speech to the College of Europe ('The Bruges Speech'), 20 September 1988.

Bibliography

Primary sources (politicians and the neoliberals)

Manuscript collections

The Papers of Baroness Thatcher (Cambridge: Churchill Archives).
The Papers of Sir John Hoskyns' (Cambridge: Churchill Archives).
The Papers of Wilhelm Röpke (Institut für Wirtschaftspolitik, Cologne).
Records of the Cabinet Office (Public Record Office (PRO): National Archives, Kew, London).
Records of the Foreign and Commonwealth Office (PRO: National Archives, Kew, London).
Records of the Prime Minister's Office: Correspondence and Papers, 1979–1997 (PRO: National Archives, Kew, London).

Online resources

Political parties

Conservative Party Manifesto (1970) *A Better Tomorrow*. [www.conservative-party.net/manifestos/1970/1970-conservative-manifesto.shtml], accessed 10 October 2010.
Conservative Party Manifesto (October 1974) [www.conservative-party.net/manifestos/1974/Oct/october-1974-conservative-manifesto.shtml], accessed 16 March 2011.
Conservative Party Manifesto (1979) [www.conservative-party.net/manifestos/1979/1979-conservative-manifesto.shtml], accessed 16 March 2011.
Conservative Party Manifesto (1983) [www.conservative.party.net/manifestos/1983], accessed 16 March 2011.
Conservative Party Manifesto (1987) [www.conservative-party.net/manifestos/1987/1987-conservative-manifesto.shtml], accessed 9 May 2011.
Conservative Research Department (1979) *Campaign Guide for Europe* (London: Conservative Central Office).
Ludwig von Mises Institute [www.mises.org], accessed 1 August 2017.
Margaret Thatcher Foundation [www.margaretthatcher.org], accessed 1 August 2017.
Parliamentary Records, Hansard. House of Commons Debates [http://hansard.millbanksystems.com/commons], accessed 1 August 2017.
The Reagan Foundation. [www.reaganfoundation.org], accessed 1 August 2017.

Interviews

Lord Burns, 12 May 2011.
Tim Congdon CBE, 24 February 2012.
Lord Howe, 13 July 2009.
Peter Lilley, 7 February 2011.
Lord Owen, 17 January 2010.
Sir Alan Peacock, 26 January 2010.
Lord Ryder, 23 February 2011.

Personal correspondence

Sir Adam Ridley, personal correspondence with the author, 2 and 15 May 2013.

Books

Baker, K. *The Turbulent Years. My Life in Politics* (London, Faber and Faber, 1993).
Becker, G. S. *The Economic Approach to Human Behavior* (London: University of Chicago Press, 1990 [1976]).
Benn, T. *The Benn Diaries* (London: Random House, 1995).
Blair, T. *A Journey* (London: Hutchinson, 2010).
Centre for Policy Studies. *Why Britain Needs a Social Market Economy* (Chichester: Barry Rose, 1975), accessed 26 May 2017. www.cps.org.uk/files/reports/original/111028103106-WhyBritainneedsaSocialMarketEconomy.pdf.
Clarke, K. *Kind of Blue: A Political Memoir* (London: Macmillan, 2016).
Darling, A. *Back from the Brink. 1,000 Days at Number 11* (London: Atlantic Books, 2012).
Donoughue, B. *Prime Minister: The Conduct of Policy under Harold Wilson and James Callaghan* (London: Jonathan Cape, 1987).
Erhard, L. *Prosperity through Competition*, translated by Edith Temple Roberts and John B. Wood (New York: Frederick A. Praeger, 1958; first published as Wohlstand für Alle in 1957).
Friedman, M. *Inflation and Unemployment: The New Dimension of Politics*, 1976 Alfred Nobel Memorial Lecture (London: IEA, Occasional Paper 51, 1977).
Friedman, M. *Why Government is the Problem* (Stanford, CA: Stanford University Press, 1993).
Friedman, M. *Capitalism and Freedom* (Chicago, IL: Chicago University Press, 2002 [1962]).
Friedman, M. *Price Theory* (London: AldineTransaction, 2007 [1962, 2nd ed. 1976]).
Friedman, M., Friedman, R. *Free to Choose* (London: Pan Books, 1990 [1980]).
Friedman, M., Friedman, R. *Two Lucky People. Memoirs* (Chicago, IL: University of Chicago Press, 1998).
Friedman, M., Schwartz, A. *A Monetary History of the United States* (Princeton, NJ: Princeton University Press, 1963).
Hayek, F. A. *Choice in Currency. A Way to Stop Inflation* (London: IEA, 1976).
Hayek, F. A. *Social Justice, Socialism & Democracy. Three Australian Lectures by F. A. Hayek* (Turramurra, NSW: Centre for Independent Studies, 1979).
Hayek, F. A. *Why I Am Not A Conservative* (University of Chicago: CIS, Occasional Paper 41, 1992 [1960]).
Hayek, F. A. *The Constitution of Liberty* (Abingdon: Routledge, 2006 [1960]).

Hayek, F. A. *Road to Serfdom* (London: Routledge, 2007 [1944]).

Heseltine, M. *Life in the Jungle. My Autobiography* (London: Hodder and Stoughton, 2000).

Hoskyns, J. *Just in Time. Inside the Thatcher Revolution* (London: Aurum Press, 2000).

Howe, G. *Enterprise Zones and the Enterprise Culture* (London: Bow Group, 1988).

Howe, G. *Conflict of Loyalty* (Basingstoke: Macmillan, 1994).

Howe, G., Jones, C. *Houses to Let. The Future of Rent Control* (London: Conservative Political Centre, 1956).

Hurd, D. *Memoirs* (London: Little Brown, 2003).

Lawson, N. *The New Britain. The Tide of Ideas from Attlee to Thatcher* (London: CPS, 1988).

Lawson, N. *The View from No. 11. Memoirs of a Tory Radical* (London: Corgi Books, 1993).

Mandelson, P. *The Third Man. Life at the Heart of New Labour* (London: HarperPress, 2010).

Moore, C. *Margaret Thatcher: The Authorized Biography, Volume One: Not for Turning* (London, Allen Lane, 2013).

Moore, C. *Margaret Thatcher: The Authorized Biography, Volume Two: Everything She Wants* (London: Allen Lane, 2015).

Nott, J. *Here Today, Gone Tomorrow: Reflections of an Errant Politician* (London: Politicos, 2002).

Owen, D. *Time to Declare* (London: Penguin, 1992).

Parkinson, C. *Right at the Centre* (London: Weidenfeld and Nicolson, 1992).

Peacock, A., Wiseman, J. *Education for Democrats. A Study of the Financing of Education in a Free Society* (London: IEA, 1964).

Prior, J. *A Balance of Power* (London: Hamish Hamilton, 1986).

Redwood, J. *Singing the Blues* (London: Politico's, 2004).

Sherman, A. *Paradoxes of Power. Reflections on the Thatcher Interlude*, edited by Mark Garnett (Exeter: Imprint Academic, 2005).

Smith, A. *The Wealth of Nations Books I–III* (London: Penguin, 1986 [1776]).

Tebbit, N. *Upwardly Mobile* (London: Weidenfeld and Nicolson, 1988).

Thatcher, M. *The Downing Street Years* (London: HarperCollins, 1993).

Thatcher, M. *The Path to Power* (London: HarperCollins, 1995).

Tullock, G. *Private Wants, Public Means. An Economic Analysis of the Desirable Scope of Government* (London: Basic Books, 1970).

Tullock, G. *The Vote Motive. An Essay in the Economics of Politics, with Applications to the British Economy* (London: IEA: Hobart Paperback No. 9, 1976).

Tullock, G. *The Politics of Bureaucracy* (London: University Press of America, 1987 [1965]).

Walters, A. *Money in Boom and Slump. An Empirical Inquiry into British Experience since the 1880s* (Tonbridge: IEA, 1971 [1969]).

Chapters

Böhm, F., Eucken, W., Grossmann-Doerth, H. 'The Ordo Manifesto of 1936'. In: *Germany's Social Market Economy: Origins and Evolution*, Alan Peacock and Hans Willgerodt, eds (first published in Ordnung der Wirtshaft, no. 2, 1936) (Basingstoke: Macmillan, 1989, pp. 15–26).

Buchanan, J. M. 'Rent Seeking and Profit Seeking'. In: *Toward a Theory of the Rent-Seeking Society*, J. M. Buchanan, R. D. Tollison and G. Tullock, eds (College Station. TX: Texas A&M University Press, 1980, pp. 3–15).

Eucken, W. 'What Kind of Economic and Social System?' In: *Germany's Social Market Economy: Origins and Evolution*, Alan Peacock and Hans Willgerodt, eds (first published in Ordo, vol. 1, 1948) (Basingstoke: Macmillan, 1989, pp. 15–26).

Friedman, M. 'The Road to Economic Freedom: The Steps from Here to There'. In: *From Galbraith to Economic Freedom* (London: IEA, 1977, pp. 43–62).

Howe, G. 'Speech to the Bow Group at The Waterman's Arms, 26 June 1978'. In: *The Right Angle. Three Studies in Conservatism*, Margaret Thatcher, Geoffrey Howe and Keith Joseph, eds (London: Bow Group, 1978).

Lawson, N. 'Foreword'. In: *Big Bang 20 Years on. New Challenges Facing the Financial Services Sector. Collected Essays* (London: CPS, 2006, pp. i–v).

Lord Howe. 'Can 364 Economists all be Wrong?' In: *The Chancellors' Tales. Managing the British Economy*, H. Davies, ed. (Cambridge: Polity, 2006, pp. 76–112).

Lord Lawson of Blaby. 'Changing the Consensus'. In: *The Chancellors' Tales. Managing the British Economy*, H. Davies, ed. (Cambridge: Polity, 2006, pp. 113–146).

Journals

Friedman, M. 'Say "No" to Intolerance', *Liberty* (4:6, July 1991, pp. 17–20) [http://mises.org/journals/liberty/Liberty_Magazine_July_1991.pdf] accessed 28 November 2013.

Hayek, F. A. 'Toward a Free Market Monetary System', *Journal of Libertarian Studies* (3:1, Spring 1979, pp. 1–8) [http://mises.org/journals/jls/3_1/3_1_1.pdf] accessed 10 February 2014.

Lawson, N. 'Mrs Thatcher's Lasting Legacy', *Standpoint* (May 2009) [http://standpointmag.co.uk/node/1484/full] accessed 10 May 2012.

Owen, D. 'Agenda for Competitiveness with Compassion', *Economic Affairs* (4:1, October 1983, pp. 26–33).

Seminars

Willetts, D. 'Inaugural John Ramsden Memorial Lecture, Liberal Conservatism', lecture given at Queen Mary University London, 10 May 2011.

Television

Friedman, M. 'Commanding Heights'. Interview on PBS, 20 January 2000. [www.pbs.org/wgbh/commandingheights/shared/minitext/int_miltonfriedman.html#10] accessed 24 April 2012.

Secondary sources

Books

Bale, T. *The Conservatives since 1945* (Oxford: Oxford University Press, 2012).

Barr, J. *The Bow Group. A History* (London: Politicos, 2001).

Barry, N. *On Classical Liberalism and Libertarianism* (Basingstoke: Macmillan, 1986).

Barry, N. *The New Right* (Beckenham: Croom Helm, 1987).

Booth, P. *Verdict on the Crash. Causes and Policy Implications* (London: IEA, 2009).

Browning, A. *Privatization 1979–1994. Everyone's a Winner* (London: Conservative Political Centre, 1994).

Burgin, A. *The Great Persuasion, Reinventing Free Markets since the Depression* (London: Harvard University Press, 2012).

Burk, K. *The First Privatization. The Politicians, the City, and the Denationalization of Steel* (London: The Historians' Press, 1988).

Burk, K., Cairncross, A. *'Goodbye Great Britain'* (London: Yale University Press, 1992).

Butler, E. *Hayek* (New York: Universe Books, 1985a).

Butler, E. *Milton Friedman* (Aldershot: Gower, 1985b).

Butler, S. *Enterprise Zones. Greenlining the Inner Cities* (London: Heinemann, 1982).

Cairncross, A. *The British Economy since 1945* (Oxford: Blackwell, 1995).

Campbell, J. *Edward Heath. A Biography* (London: Pimlico, 1993).

Campbell, J. *Margaret Thatcher. Volume Two: The Iron Lady* (London: Pimlico, 2004).

Clarke, P. *A Question of Leadership* (London: Hamish Hamilton, 1991).

Cockett, R. *Thinking the Unthinkable. Think-Tanks and the Economic Counter-Revolution, 1931–83* (London: Harper Collins, 1995).

Congdon, T. *Reflections on Monetarism. Britain's Vain Search for a Successful Economic Strategy* (Aldershot: Edward Elgar, 1992).

Congdon, T. *Money in a Free Society. Keynes, Friedman, and the New Crisis in Capitalism* (London: Encounter Books, 2011).

Conroy, H. *Callaghan* (London: Haus Publishing, 2006).

Crisell, A. *An Introductory History of British Broadcasting* (London: Routledge, 2002).

Denham, A. *Think-Tanks of the New Right* (Aldershot: Dartmouth, 1996).

Denham, A., Garnett, M. *Keith Joseph* (Chesham: Acumen, 2001).

Dick, B. *Privatization in the UK: The Free Market versus State Control* (York: Longman, 1988).

Dorey, P. *British Conservatism and Trade Unionism* (Farnham: Ashgate, 2009).

Eagleton-Pierce, M. *Neoliberalism: The Key Concepts* (Abingdon: Routledge, 2016).

Evans, E. J. *Thatcher and Thatcherism* (Abingdon: Routledge, 2004).

Faux, J. *The Global Class War. How America's Bipartisan Elite Lost Our Future – and What It Will Take To Win It Back* (Hoboken, NJ: John Wiley and Sons, 2006).

Freedman, D. *The Politics of Media Policy* (Cambridge: Polity Press, 2008).

Fry, G. *The Politics of the Thatcher Revolution. An Interpretation of British Politics, 1979–90* (Basingstoke: Palgrave Macmillan, 2008).

Funnell, W., Jupe, R., Andrew, J. *In Government We Trust. Market Failure and the Delusions of Privatization* (London: Pluto Press, 2009).

Gamble, A. *Britain in Decline* (London: Macmillan, 1994a).

Gamble, A. *The Free Economy and the Strong State. The Politics of Thatcherism* (Basingstoke, Palgrave Macmillan, 1994b).

Gamble, A. *Hayek. The Iron Cage of Liberty* (Cambridge: Polity Press, 1996).

Graeber, D. *Debt: The First 5,000 Years* (New York: Melville, 2011).

Gregg, S. *Wilhelm Röpke's Political Economy* (Cheltenham: Edward Elgar, 2010).

Hames, T., Feasey, R. *A Conservative Revolution?* (Glasgow: Bell and Bain, 1994).

Hammond, J. D., Hammond, C. H. *Making Chicago Price Theory. Friedman-Stigler Correspondence 1945–57* (Abingdon: Routledge, 2006).

Hanson, C. G. *Taming the Trade Unions. A Guide to the Thatcher Government's Employment Reforms, 1980–90* (Basingstoke: Macmillan, 1991).

Harris, R. *Not for Turning. The Life of Margaret Thatcher* (London, Bantam Press, 2013).

Hartwell, R. W. *A History of the Mont Pelerin Society* (Indianapolis, IN: Liberty Fund, 1995).

Hartwich, O. M. *Neoliberalism: The Genesis of a Political Swearword* (St Leonards: CIS occasional papers, 114, July 2009).

Harvey, D. *A Brief History of Neoliberalism* (Oxford: Oxford University Press, 2005).

Heffer, S. *Like the Roman. The Life of Enoch Powell* (London: Weidenfeld and Nicolson, 1998).

Held, D., McGrew, A. *Globalization/Anti-Globalization* (Cambridge: Polity Press, 2003).

Hennessy, P. *Whitehall* (London: Fontana, 1990).

Holland, S. *Beyond Capitalist Planning* (Oxford: Basil Blackwell, 1978).

Holland, S. *The Market Economy (from Micro to Macroeconomics)* (London: Weidenfeld and Nicolson, 1987).

Holmes, M. *The First Thatcher Government, 1979–83* (Brighton: Wheatsheaf, 1985).

Hutt, W. H. *The Theory of Collective Bargaining 1930–1975.* Hobart Paperback No. 8 (London: IEA, 1975 [1931]).

Kandiah, M. D., Seldon, A. *Ideas and Think Tanks in Contemporary Britain, Volume 2* (London: Frank Cass, 1996).

Keynes, J. M. *The General Theory of Employment, Interest, and Money.* (Basingstoke: Palgrave Macmillan, 2007 [1936]).

Kiely, R. *The Clash of Globalisations. Neo-Liberalism, the Third Way and Anti-Globalisation* (Leiden: Brill, 2005).

Kiely, R. *The New Political Economy of Development. Globalization, Imperialism, Hegemony* (Basingstoke: Palgrave Macmillan, 2007).

King, P. *Housing Policy Transformed. The Right to Buy and the Desire to Own* (Bristol: Policy Press, 2010).

Kynaston, D. *City of London, the History*, ed. D. Miller (London: Chatto & Windus, 2011).

Letwin, S. R. *The Anatomy of Thatcherism* (London: HarperCollins, 1992).

Lewis, R. *Industry and the Property Owning Democracy* (London: The Bow Group, 1954).

Marsh, D. *The New Politics of British Trade Unionism. Union Power and the Thatcher Legacy* (Basingstoke: Macmillan, 1992).

Matthijs, M. *Ideas and Economic Crises in Britain from Attlee to Blair (1945–2005)* (Abingdon: Routledge, 2011).

Middlemas, K. *Power, Competition and the State. Volume I. Britain in Search of Balance 1940–61* (Basingstoke: Macmillan, 1996).

Middleton, R. *The British Economy since 1945. Engaging with the Debate* (Basingstoke: Macmillan, 2000).

Mierzejewski, A. C. *Ludwig Erhard. A Biography* (London: University of North Carolina Press, 2004).

Milne, S. *The Enemy Within. The Secret War against the Miners* (London: Verso, 2004).

Morgan, K. *Callaghan: A Life* (Oxford: Oxford University Press, 1997).

Noble, V. *Inside the Welfare State. Foundations of Policy and Practice in Post-War Britain* (London: Routledge, 2009).

Parker, D. *The Official History of Privatization. Volume 1: The Formative Years 1970–87* (London: Routledge, 2009).

Peck, J. *Constructions of Neoliberal Reason* (Oxford: Oxford University Press, 2010).

Plickert, P. *Wandlungen des Neoliberalismus: Eine Studie zu Entwicklung und Ausstrahlung der "Mont Pelerin Society"* (Stuttgart: De Gruyter Oldenbourg, 2008).

Price Waterhouse. *Privatization. The Facts* (London: Price Waterhouse, 1987).

Pryke, R. *The Nationalised Industries. Polices and Performance since 1968* (Oxford: Martin Robertson, 1981).

Ranelagh, J. *Thatcher's People. An Insider's Account of the Politics, the Power and the Personalities* (London: Harper Collins, 1991).

Reitan, E. A. *The Thatcher Revolution. Margaret Thatcher, John Major, Tony Blair, and the Transformation of Modern Britain, 1979–2001* (Oxford: Rowman and Littlefield, 2003).

Robinson, C. *Competition in Electricity? The Government's Proposals for Privatizing Electricity Supply* (London: IEA, 1988).

Roy, S., Clarke, J., eds. *Margaret Thatcher's Revolution. How it Happened and What it Meant* (London: Continuum, 2005).

Sally, R. *Classical Liberalism and International Economic Order. Studies in Theory and Intellectual History* (London: Routledge, 1998).

Sandbrook, D. *Seasons in the Sun. The Battle for Britain 1974–79* (London: Penguin, 2013).

Savoie, D. *Thatcher Reagan Mulroney. In Search of a New Bureaucracy* (London: University of Pittsburgh Press, 1994).

Seldon, A. *The Riddle of the Voucher. An Inquiry into the Obstacles to Introducing Choice and Competition in State Schools* (London: IEA, 1986).

Seldon, A., Collings, D. *Britain under Thatcher* (London: Longman, 2000).

Shand, A. H. *The Capitalist Alternative: An Introduction to Neo-Austrian Economics* (Frome: Wheatsheaf, 1984).

Shand, A. H. *Free Market Morality. The Political Economy of the Austrian School* (London: Routledge, 1990).

Short, J. R. *Housing in Britain. The Post-War Experience* (London: Methuen, 1982).

Skelton, N. *Constructive Conservatism* (London: William Blackwood and Sons, 1924).

Skousen, M. *Vienna & Chicago. Friends or Foes? A Tale of Two Schools of Free-Market Economics* (Washington, DC: Capital Press, 2005).

Stedman-Jones, D. *Masters of the Universe. Hayek, Friedman, and the Birth of Neoliberal Politics* (Oxford: Oxford University Press, 2012).

Stiglitz, J. *Freefall. Free Markets and the Sinking of the Global Economy* (London: Penguin, 2010).

Swann, D. *Retreat of the State* (Hemel Hempstead: Wheatsheaf, 1988).

Thomsen, J. P. F. *British Politics and Trade Unions in the 1980s: Governing against Pressure* (Aldershot: Dartmouth, 1996).

Torrance, D. *Noel Skelton and the Property-Owning Democracy* (London: Biteback, 2010).

Turner, R. S. *Neo-Liberal Ideology. History, Concepts and Policies* (Edinburgh: Edinburgh University Press, 2008).

Vinen, R. *Thatcher's Britain. The Politics and Social Upheaval of the 1980s* (London: Simon and Schuster, 2009).

Webb, S., Webb, B. *The History of Trade Unionism, 1666–1920* (Edinburgh: R & R. Clark, 1920).

Wilcox, S. *UK Housing Review, 2007/08* (York: Chartered Institute of Housing/ Council for Mortgage Lenders, 2008).

Williamson, A. *Conservative Economic Policymaking and the Birth of Thatcherism, 1964–1979* (Basingstoke: Palgrave Macmillan, 2015).

Willman, P., Morris, T., Aston, B. *Unions Business: Trade Union Organization and Financial Reform in the Thatcher Years* (Cambridge: Cambridge University Press, 1993).

Young, K., Kramer, J. *Strategy and Conflict in Metropolitan Housing. Suburbia versus the Greater London Council 1965–75* (London: Heinemann, 1978).

Chapters

Booth, P. 'More Regulation, Less Regulation or Better Regulation?'. In: *Verdict on the Crash. Causes and Policy Implications*, P. Booth, ed. (London: IEA, 2009, pp. 157–170).

Brittan, S. 'The Fight for Freedom in Broadcasting'. In: *The Peacock Committee and UK Broadcasting Policy*, T. O'Malley, J. Jones, eds (Basingstoke: Palgrave Macmillan, 2009, pp. 101–120).

Butler, E. 'The Financial Crisis: Blame Governments, not Banks'. In: *Verdict on the Crash. Causes and Policy Implications*, P. Booth, ed. (London: IEA, 2009, pp. 52–56.).

Caldwell, B. 'The Chicago School, Hayek, and Neoliberalism'. In: *Building Chicago Economics. New Perspectives on the History of America's Most Powerful Economics Program*, R. Van Horn, P. Mirowski, T. A. Stapleford, eds (Cambridge: Cambridge University Press, 2011, pp. 301–334).

Catterall, P. 'Witness Seminar: The Origins of Channel 4'. In: *The Making of Channel 4*, P. Catterall, ed. (London: Frank Cass, 1999, pp. 79–115).

Falk, R. 'The Global Setting'. In: *The Iraq War and Democratic Politics*, A. Danchev, J. MacMillan, eds (London: Routledge, 2005, pp. 19–32).

Gamble, A. 'Privatization, Thatcherism and the British State'. In: *Thatcher's Law*, A. Gamble, C. Wells, eds (Oxford: Basil Blackwell, 1989, pp. 1–20).

Green, D. G. 'Introduction: A Missed Opportunity'. In: *The NHS Reforms: Whatever Happened to Consumer Choice?* D. G. Green, M. L. Burstall, J. Neuberger, M. Young, eds (London: IEA Health and Welfare Unit, 1990, pp. 1–14).

Green, E. H. H. 'The Conservatives and the City'. In: *The British Government and the City of London in the Twentieth Century*, R. Michie and P. Williamson, eds (Cambridge: Cambridge University Press, 2011, 153–173).

Grimley, M. 'Thatcherism, Morality and Religion'. In: *Making Thatcher's Britain*, B. Jackson, R. Saunders, eds (Cambridge: Cambridge University Press, 2012, pp. 78–94).

Hall, P. 'The British Enterprise Zones'. In: *Enterprise Zones. New Directions in Economic Development*, Roy Green, ed. (London: Sage, 1991, pp. 179–191).

Hyman, R. 'Trade Unions, the Left and the Communist Party in Britain'. In: *Comrades and Brothers: Communism and Trade Unions in Europe*, M. Waller, S. Courtois, M. Lazar, eds (London: Frank Cass, 1991, pp. 143–164).

Jackson, B. 'The Think-Tank Archipelago: Thatcherism and Neoliberalism'. In: *Making Thatcher's Britain*, Ben Jackson, Robert Saunders, eds (Cambridge: Cambridge University Press, 2012, pp. 43–61, 2012).

Jackson, B., Saunders, R. 'Introduction: Varieties of Thatcherism'. In: *Making Thatcher's Britain*, B. Jackson, R. Saunders, eds (Cambridge: Cambridge University Press, 2012, pp. 1–21).

Jones, J. 'PSB 2.0 – UK Broadcasting Policy after Peacock'. In: *The Peacock Committee and UK Broadcasting Policy*, T. O'Malley, J. Jones, eds (Basingstoke: Palgrave Macmillan, 2009, pp. 187–206).

Lawrence, J., Sutcliffe-Braithwaite, F. 'Margaret Thatcher and the Decline of Class Politics'. In: *Making Thatcher's Britain*, B. Jackson, R. Saunders, eds (Cambridge: Cambridge University Press, 2012, pp. 132–147).

Michie, R. 'City and Government: Changing Relationship'. In: *The British Government and the City of London in the Twentieth Century*, R. Michie, P. Williamson, eds (Cambridge: Cambridge University Press, 2011, pp. 31–56).

Minford, P. 'Inflation, Unemployment and the Pound'. In: *Margaret Thatcher's Revolution. How it Happened and What it Meant*, S. Roy, J. Clarke, eds (London: Continuum, 2005, pp. 50–66).

Mirowski, P. 'Postface: Defining Neoliberalism'. In: *The Road from Mont Pelerin. The Making of the Neoliberal Thought Collective*. P. Mirowski, D. Plehwe, eds (Harvard: Harvard University Press, 2009, pp. 417–446).

Murie, A. 'The Housing Legacy of Thatcherism'. In: *The Legacy of Thatcherism. Assessing and Exploring Thatcherite Social and Economic Policies*, Stephen Farrall and Colin Hay, eds (Oxford: Oxford University Press, 2014, pp. 143–166).

Nik-Khah, E. 'George Stigler, the Graduate School of Business, and the Pillars of the Chicago School'. In: *Building Chicago Economics: New Perspectives on the History of America's Most Powerful Economics Program*, Robert Van Horn, Philip Mirowski, Thomas A. Stapleford, eds (Cambridge: Cambridge University Press, 2011, pp. 116–147).

Nunn, H., Biressi, A. 'Shameless? Picturing the "Underclass" after Thatcherism'. In: *Thatcher and after. Margaret Thatcher and her Afterlife in Contemporary Culture*, L. Hadley, E. Ho, eds (Basingstoke: Palgrave Macmillan, 2010, pp. 137–157).

Parker, M. 'General Conclusions and Lessons'. In: *The British Electricity Experiment. Privatization: The Record, the Issues, the Lessons*, J. Surrey, ed. (London: Earthscan, 1996, pp. 295–304).

Peck, J. 'Orientation: In Search of the Chicago School'. In: *Building Chicago Economics: New Perspectives on the History of America's Most Powerful Economics Program*, Robert Van Horn, Philip Mirowski, Thomas A. Stapleford, eds (Cambridge: Cambridge University Press, 2011, pp. xxv–lii).

Plehwe, D. 'Introduction'. In: *The Road from Mont Pelerin. The Making of the Neoliberal Thought Collective*, P. Mirowski, D. Plehwe, eds (Harvard: Harvard University Press, 2009, pp. 1–44).

Plehwe, D., Walpen, B. J. A., Neunhöffer, G. 'Introduction: Reconsidering Neoliberal Hegemony'. In: *Neoliberal Hegemony: A Global Critique* (Abingdon: Routledge, 2007, pp. 1–24).

Ptak, R. 'Neoliberalism in Germany. Revisiting the Ordoliberal Foundations of the Social Market Economy'. In: *The Road from Mont Pelerin. The Making of the Neoliberal Thought Collective*. P. Mirowski, D. Plehwe, eds (Harvard: Harvard University Press, 2009, pp. 98–138).

Ranelagh, J. 'Channel 4: A View from Within'. In: *The Making of Channel 4*, P. Catterall, ed. (London: Frank Cass, 1999, pp. 53–59).

Riddell, P. 'Ideology in Practice'. In: *A Conservative Revolution? The Thatcher-Reagan Decade in Perspective*, A. Adonis, T. Hames, eds (Manchester: Manchester University Press, 1994, pp. 19–41.

Saunders, R. ' "Crisis? What Crisis?" Thatcherism and the Seventies'. In: *Making Thatcher's Britain*, B. Jackson, R. Saunders, eds (Cambridge: Cambridge University Press, 2012, pp. 25–42.).

Schofield, C. ' "A Nation or no Nation?" Enoch Powell and Thatcherism'. In: *Making Thatcher's Britain*, B. Jackson, R. Saunders, eds (Cambridge: Cambridge University Press, 2012, pp. 95–110).

Seaton, J., McNicholas, A. 'It Was the BBC Wot Won it. Winning the Peacock Report for the Corporation, or How the BBC Responded to the Peacock Committee'. In:

The Peacock Committee and UK Broadcasting Policy, T. O'Malley, J. Jones, eds (Basingstoke: Palgrave Macmillan, 2009, pp. 121–145).

Streit, M. E., Wohlgemuth, M. 'The Market Economy and the State. Hayekian and Ordoliberal Conceptions'. In: *The Theory of Capitalism in the German Economic Tradition*, P. Koslowski, ed. (London: Springer, 2000, pp. 224–260).

Surrey, J. 'Introduction'. In: *The British Electricity Experiment. Privatization: The Record, the Issues, the Lessons*, J. Surrey, ed. (London: Earthscan, 1996, pp. 3–13).

Tomlinson, J. 'Thatcher, Monetarism and the Politics of Inflation'. In: *Making Thatcher's Britain*, B. Jackson, R. Saunders, eds (Cambridge: Cambridge University Press, 2012, pp. 62–77).

Veljanovski, C. 'Privatization: Monopoly Money or Competition?' In: *Privatization and Competition. A Market Prospectus*, C. Veljanovski, ed. (London: IEA Hobart Paperback 28, 1989, pp. 26–51).

Watrin, C. 'Alfred Müller-Armack – Economic Policy Maker and Sociologist of Religion'. In: *The Theory of Capitalism in the German Economic Tradition*, P. Koslowski, ed, (London: Springer, 2000, pp. 192–220).

Williamson, P. 'The City of London and Government in Modern Britain: Debates and Politics'. In: *The British Government and the City of London in the Twentieth Century*, R. Michie, P. Williamson, eds (Cambridge: Cambridge University Press, 2011, pp. 5–30).

Wiseman, J. 'Growing without Nationalization'. In: *Privatization and Competition. A Market Prospectus*, C. Veljanovski, ed. (London: IEA Hobart Paperback 28, 1989, pp. 3–15).

Yarrow, G. 'Does Ownership Matter?' In: *Privatization and Competition. A Market Prospectus*, C. Veljanovski, ed. (London: IEA Hobart Paperback 28, 1989, pp. 52–69).

Journals

Armentano, D. T. 'Antitrust Reform: Predatory Practices and the Competitive Process', *Review of Austrian Economics* (3, 1989, pp. 61–74).

Barry, N. 'Austrian Challenge to Orthodoxy', *Economic Affairs* (4:3, April–June 1984, pp. 57–62).

Benson, B. L. 'Third Thoughts on Contracting Out', *Journal of Libertarian Studies* (11:1, Fall 1994, pp. 44–78).

Block, W. 'Hayek's Road to Serfdom', *Journal of Libertarian Studies* (12:2, Fall 1996, pp. 339–365).

Blundell, J. 'Privatization – by Political Process or Consumer Preference?', *Economic Affairs* (7:1, October–November 1986, pp. 59–62).

Boarman, P. M. 'Apostle of a Humane Economy: Remembering Wilhelm Röpke', *Society* (37:6, 2000, pp. 57–65).

Boas, T., Gans-Morse, J. 'Neoliberalism: From New Liberal Philosophy to Anti-Liberal Slogan', *Studies in Comparative International Development* (44:2, June 2009, pp. 137–161).

Bonefeld, W. 'Adam Smith and Ordoliberalism: On the Political Form of Market Liberty', *Review of International Studies* (39:2, July 2012, pp. 233–250).

Borrie, G. 'Regulating the UK', *Economic Affairs* (11:5, September 1991, pp. 12–14).

Brittan, S., Hadas, E. 'Is Capitalism Morally Bankrupt?', *Standpoint* (November 2008) [www.standpointmag.co.uk/node/573/full], accessed 5 June 2012.

Bulpitt, J. 'The Discipline of the New Democracy: Mrs Thatcher's Domestic Statecraft', *Political Studies* (34:1, 1986, pp. 19–39).

Curzon Price, V. 'Structural Aspects of the Thatcher Experiment. How to Put the Cart before the Horse and (Perhaps) Survive', *ORDO. Jahrbuch für die Ordnung von Wirtschaft und Gesellschaft* [Ordo Yearbook of Economic and Social Order] (Stuttgart: Gustav Fischer Verlag, Band 33, 1982, pp. 39–60).

Deakin, S., Pratten, S. 'The New Competition in Broadcasting: Trick or Treat?', *Economic Affairs* (20:4, December 2000, pp. 27–32).

Dilorenzo, T. J. 'The Myth of Natural Monopoly', *Review of Austrian Economics* (9:2, 1996, pp. 43–58).

Dullien, S., Guérot, U. 'The Long Shadow of Ordoliberalism', *IP Journal* (17 July 2012) [https://ip-journal.dgap.org/en/ip-journal/topics/long-shadow-ordoliberalism], accessed 20 January 2013.

Frank, A. G. 'No End to History! History to No End?', *Social Justice* (17:4 (42) Winter 1990, pp. 7–29).

Gamble, A. 'The Entrails of Thatcherism', *New Left Review* (I:198, March–April 1993, pp. 91–98).

Garrett, G. 'The Political Consequences of Thatcherism', *Political Behavior* (14:4, December 1992, pp. 361–382).

Görgens, E. 'Entwicklungshilfe als Wachstumsmotor? Zu den Erfolgsaussichten neuerer Vorschläge zur Entwicklungshilfe im Lichte empirischer Erfahrungen' [Development Aid as an Engine of Growth? Recent Propositions to Increase Development Aid, and Empirical Findings for the Past], *ORDO. Jahrbuch für die Ordnung von Wirtschaft und Gesellschaft* [Ordo Yearbook of Economic and Social Order] (Stuttgart: Gustav Fischer Verlag, Band 36, 1985, pp. 131–152).

Ha-Joon Chang, 'Breaking the Mould: An Institutionalist Political Economy Alternative to the Neoliberal Theory of the Market and the State', *Cambridge Journal of Economics* (26:5, pp. 539–559).

Hall, P. A. 'Policy Paradigms, Social Learning, and the State: The Case of Economic Policymaking in Britain', *Comparative Politics* (25:3, April 1993, pp. 275–296).

Henderson, R. 'Half Way House or Dead End?', *Economic Affairs* (6:6, August–September 1986, pp. 45–46).

Herbener, J. M. 'Ludwig von Mises and the Austrian School of Economics', *Review of Austrian Economics* (5:2, 1991, pp. 33–50).

Heuss, E. ' "Die Grundlagen der *Nationalökonomie*" vor 50 Jahren und heute' ['Die Grundlagen der *Nationalökonomie*': Fifty Years Ago and Today], *ORDO. Jahrbuch für die Ordnung von Wirtschaft und Gesellschaft* [Ordo Yearbook of Economic and Social Order] (Stuttgart: Gustav Fischer Verlag, Band 40, 1989, pp. 21–30).

Issing, O. 'Vom Primat der Währungspolitik' [The Primacy of Monetary Policy], *ORDO. Jahrbuch für die Ordnung von Wirtschaft und Gesellschaft* [Ordo Yearbook of Economic and Social Order] (Stuttgart: Gustav Fischer Verlag, Band 40, 1989, pp. 351–361).

Jackson, B. 'At the Origins of Neo-liberalism: The Free Economy and the Strong State, 1930–1947', *The Historical Journal* (53:1, March 2010, pp. 129–151).

Jackson, B. 'Freedom, the Common Good, and the Rule of Law: Lippmann and Hayek on Economic Planning', *Journal of the History of Ideas* (73:1, January 2012, pp. 47–68.).

Jackson, B. 'Currents of Neo-Liberalism: British Political Ideologies and the New Right, *c.*1955–1979', *English Historical Review* (131, 2016, pp. 823–850).

Kandiah, M. D. 'The October 1987 Stock Market Crash – Ten Years On', *Contemporary British History* (13:1, 1999a, pp. 133–140).

Kandiah, M. D. 'Witness Seminar I "Big Bang": The October 1986 Stock Market Deregulation', *Contemporary British History* (13:1, 1999b, pp. 100–132).

Lord, R. 'What's Wrong with Electricity Privatization?', *Economic Affairs* (12:3, April 1992, pp. 28–29).

Minford, P. 'The New Classical Economics', *Economic Affairs* (5:2, January–March 1985, pp. 6–11).

Molitor, B. 'Schwäche der Demokratie' [The Weakness of Democracy], *ORDO. Jahrbuch für die Ordnung von Wirtschaft und Gesellschaft* [Ordo Yearbook of Economic and Social Order] (Stuttgart: Gustav Fischer Verlag, Band 34, 1983, pp. 17–38).

Möschel, W. 'The Proper Scope of Government Viewed from an Ordoliberal Perspective: The Example of Competition Policy', *Journal of Institutional and Theoretical Economics (JITE)/Zeitschrift für die gesamte Staatswissenschaft* (157:1, 2001, pp. 3–13).

Nove, A. 'Markets? Yes, but…', *Economic Affairs* (5:2, January–March 1985, pp. 46–49).

Oberender, P. 'Der Einfluss ordnungstheoretischer Prinzipien Walter Euckens auf die deutsche Wirtschaftspolitik nach dem Zweiten Weltkrieg: Eine ordnungspolitische Analyse' [Walter Eucken's Influence on German Economic Policy after World War II], *ORDO. Jahrbuch für die Ordnung von Wirtschaft und Gesellschaft* (Stuttgart: Gustav Fischer Verlag, Band 40, 1989, pp. 321–350).

Oliver, M. J. 'The Macroeconomic Policies of Mr Lawson', *Contemporary British History* (13:1, 1999, pp. 166–182).

Parkin, M. 'Mrs. Thatcher's Monetary Policy', *ORDO. Jahrbuch für die Ordnung von Wirtschaft und Gesellschaft* [Ordo Yearbook of Economic and Social Order] (Stuttgart: Gustav Fischer Verlag, Band 33, 1982), pp. 61–80).

Preston, V. '"Big Bang": Chronology of Events', *Contemporary British History* (13:1, 1999, pp. 95–99).

Robinson, C. 'Markets, Imperfections and the Dangers of Over-Regulating Energy Markets', *Economic Affairs* (24:2, June 2004, pp. 52–55).

Robinson, R. 'Another Stick to Beat Teachers?', *Economic Affairs* (6:5, August–September 1986, pp. 46–47).

Rollings, N. 'Cracks in the Post-War Keynesian Settlement? The Role of Organized Business in Britain in the Rise of Neoliberalism before Margaret Thatcher', *Twentieth Century British History* (24:4, 2013, pp. 637–659).

Shand, A. 'Austrian Policy for the Thatcher Government', *Economic Affairs* (4:1, October 1983, pp. 13–15).

Stafford, D. 'Speed Up Council House Sales', *Economic Affairs* (4:2, Jan 1984, pp. 25–28).

Stoney, P. 'Enterprise Zone: Incentive or Intervention?', *Economic Affairs* (8:1, October/November 1987, pp. 28–30).

Sutcliffe-Braithwaite, F. 'Neo-Liberalism and Morality in the Making of Thatcherite Social Policy', *The Historical Journal* (55:2, June 2012, pp. 497–520).

Thompson, N. 'Hollowing Out of the State: Public Choice Theory and the Critique of Keynesian Social Democracy', *Contemporary British History* (22:3, September 2008, pp. 355–382).

Tullock, G. 'No Public Choice in State Education', *Economic Affairs* (6:3, April–May 1986, pp. 18–22).

West, E. G. 'Education Reform: Administrative Objections Over-ruled', *Economic Affairs* (6:3, April–May 1986, pp. 24–26).

Woll, A. 'Freiheit durch Ordnung: Die gesellschaftspolitische Leitidee im Denken von Walter Eucken und Friedrich A. von Hayek' [Freedom through Order: The Guiding Principle of Economic Policy in Walter Eucken's and Friedrich A. von

Hayek's Thought], *ORDO. Jahrbuch für die Ordnung von Wirtschaft und Gesellschaft* [Ordo Yearbook of Economic and Social Order] (Stuttgart: Gustav Fischer Verlag, Band 40, 1989, pp. 87–98).

Newspapers

Asthana, A., Vaughan, A. 'Theresa May to promise price cap on energy bills in Tory manifesto', *Guardian*, 9 May 2017, accessed 5 June 2017. www.theguardian.com/money/2017/may/08/theresa-may-to-promise-price-cap-on-energy-bills-in-tory-manifesto.

Clark, T. 'Thatcher's flagship policies draw mixed support at her death, poll shows', *Guardian*, 9 April 2013), accessed 26 June 2013. www.guardian.co.uk/politics/2013/apr/09/thatcher-flagship-policies-guardian-icm-poll.

D'Ancona, M. 'What do the Tories do now? One question, three solutions', *Guardian*, 3 July 2017, accessed 3 July 2017. www.theguardian.com/commentis free/2017/jul/03/tories-dup-deal-thatcherites-philip-hammond-ruth-davidson.

Davis, R. 'Go for growth: The International Baccalaureate is still on an upward curve', *Independent*, 18 February 2010, accessed 28 June 2012. www.independent. co.uk/news/education/schools/go-for-growth-the-international-baccalaureate-is-still-on-an-upward-curve-1903921.html.

The Economist, 13 February 1954.

The Economist, 27 July 1985.

The Economist, 8 July 1989.

The Economist, 2 June 1990.

The Economist, 15 January 1994.

The Economist, 5 March 1994.

The Economist, 'Gaponomics', 12 March 2011.

The Economist 14 April 2011.

The Economist, 'Through the roof', 24 September 2015, accessed 21 June 2017. www.economist.com/news/britain/21667973-britain-has-one-booming-market-could-do-crash-through-roof.

The Economist, 'British immigration. You're welcome', 21 December 2013, accessed 26 December 2013. www.economist.com/news/leaders/21591865-open-letter-citizens-bulgaria-and-romania-youre-welcome.

Kirkup, J. 'Labour: Miliband pledges to freeze energy prices', *Daily Telegraph*, 24 September 2013, accessed 27 December 2013. www.telegraph.co.uk/news/politics/labour/10331012/Labour-Miliband-pledges-to-freeze-energy-prices.html.

Pratley, N. 'Rupert Murdoch's Sky bid is now very likely to succeed', *Guardian*, 29 June 2017, accessed 29 June 2017. www.theguardian.com/business/nils-pratley-on-finance/2017/jun/29/rupert-murdoch-sky-bid-is-now-very-likely-to-succeed.

Preston, P. 'What the sale of *The Times* to Murdoch can teach us today', *Guardian*, 18 June 2017, accessed 18 June 2017. www.theguardian.com/media/2017/jun/18/what-sale-of-times-to-rupert-murdoch-can-teach-us.

Sandle, P., Holton, K. 'Britain says Fox bid for Sky risks giving Murdoch too much power', *Reuters*, 29 June 2017, accessed 29 June 2017. http://uk.reuters.com/article/uk-sky-m-a-fox-idUKKBN19K1D7.

The Times, 21 February 1980.

Toynbee, P. 'To condemn those who pay so little is not job snobbery', *Guardian*, 20 April 2012.

Wilson, G. 'Cameron rules out grammar schools revival', *Daily Telegraph*, 17 May 2007, accessed 28 April 2011. www.telegraph.co.uk/news/uknews/1551789/Cameron-rules-out-grammar-schools-revival.html.

Articles

BBC Website online, '1971: Workers Down Tools Over Union Rights' [http://news.bbc.co.uk/onthisday/hi/dates/stories/march/1/newsid_2514000/2514033.stm], accessed 4 October 2011.

BBC Website online, 'TUC Membership 1940–2002' [http://news.bbc.co.uk/1/hi/business/3526917.stm#membership%20graph], accessed 4 October 2011.

Coy, P. 'Will Merkel Act, or Won't She?', *Bloomberg Businessweek* magazine, 30 November 2011 [www.businessweek.com/magazine/will-angela-merkel-act-or-wont-she-11302011.html#p2], accessed 7 February 2014.

Davis, M. '"New Model" Unionism', TUC History Online, 2004 [www.union history.info/timeline/1850_1880.php], accessed 19 September 2011.

Robinson, C. 'From Nationalisation to State Control. The Return of Centralised Energy Planning', IEA Discussion Paper No. 49, (London: IEA, 2013) [www.iea.org.uk/sites/default/files/publications/files/From%20Nationalisation%20to%20State%20Control_web.pdf], accessed 26 December 2013.

Television

The Commanding Heights. The Battle for the World Economy (2002) PBS Documentary. [www.pbs.org/wgbh/commandingheights/hi/story/index.html], accessed 10 May 2012.

The Making of the Iron Lady (2008) A film by Michael Cockerell, BBC Four, 8 June 2008.

Seminars

Stedman-Jones, D. 'The Influence of Transatlantic Neoliberal Politics', seminar, Queen Mary University of London, 22 October 2013.

Websites

www.bbc.co.uk/news.
www.iea.org.uk.

Theses

Brown, J. 'The London Docklands Development Corporation: 1979–1981' (London: Queen Mary University of London, 2012, unpublished MA thesis).

Index